Dubai Red-Tape

A Complete Step-By-Step Handbook

BEST OF LUCK DEC
FROM LORRAINE

HADEF & PARTNERS

www.**live**work**explore**.com   **EXPLORER**

The Team

Publishing
Publisher Alistair MacKenzie
Associate Publisher Claire England

Editorial
Group Editor Jane Roberts
Lead Editor Tom Jordan
Online Editor Helen Spearman
Deputy Editors Jake Marsico, Pamela Afram,
Siobhan Campbell
Production Coordinator Kathryn Calderon
Senior Editorial Assistant Mimi Stankova
Editorial Assistant Ingrid Cupido

Design
Creative Director Pete Maloney
Art Director Ieyad Charaf
Account Manager Christopher Goldstraw
Layout Manager Jayde Fernandes
Junior Designer Didith Hapiz
Layout Designers Mansoor Ahmed,
Shawn Zuzarte
Cartography Manager Zainudheen Madathil
Cartographers Noushad Madathil, Sunita Lakhiani
Traffic Manager Maricar Ong
Traffic Coordinator Amapola Castillo

Photography
Photography Manager Pamela Grist
Photographer Victor Romero
Image Editor Henry Hilos

Sales & Marketing
Media Sales Area Managers Laura Zuffa,
Paul Santer, Pouneh Hafizi, Stephen Jones,
Peter Saxby
Corporate Sales Area Manager Ben Merrett
PR & Marketing Annabel Clough
Sales & Marketing Coordinator Lennie Mangalino
Marketing Assistant Shedan Ebona

Retail Sales
International Retail Sales Manager Ivan Rodrigues
Retail Sales Area Manager Mathew Samuel
Senior Retail Sales Merchandisers
Ahmed Mainodin, Firos Khan
Retail Sales Merchandisers Johny Mathew,
Shan Kumar
Retail Sales Coordinator Michelle Mascarenhas
Drivers Shabsir Madathil, Najumudeen K.I.
Warehouse Assistant Mohamed Riyas

Finance & Administration
Finance Manager Michael Samuel
Office Manager Shyrell Tamayo
Junior Accountant Cherry Enriquez
Accounts Assistant Soumyah Rajesh
Public Relations Officer Rafi Jamal
Office Assistant Shafeer Ahamed

IT & Digital Solutions
Digital Solutions Manager Derrick Pereira
Senior IT Administrator R. Ajay
Senior Software Engineer
Bahrudeen Abdul Kareem
Web Developer Anas Abdul Latheef

Contact Us

Reader Response
If you have any comments and
suggestions, fill out our online reader
response form and you could win prizes.
Log on to **www.liveworkexplore.com**

General Enquiries
We'd love to hear your thoughts and
answer any questions you have about this
book or any other Explorer product.
Contact us at
info@explorerpublishing.com

Careers
If you fancy yourself as an Explorer, send
your CV (stating the position you're
interested in) to
jobs@explorerpublishing.com

Designlab & Contract Publishing
For enquiries about Explorer's Contract
Publishing arm and design services
contact
designlab@explorerpublishing.com

PR & Marketing
For PR and marketing enquiries contact
marketing@explorerpublishing.com
pr@explorerpublishing.com

Corporate Sales
For bulk sales and customisation options,
for this book or any Explorer product,
contact
sales@explorerpublishing.com

Advertising & Sponsorship
For advertising and sponsorship, contact
media@explorerpublishing.com

Explorer Publishing & Distribution
PO Box 34275, Dubai, United Arab Emirates
www.liveworkexplore.com
www.explorerpublishing.com

Phone: +971 (0)4 340 8805
Fax: +971 (0)4 340 8806

Introduction

Table Of Contents

Explorer Products

Residents' Guides

Mini Guides

Explorer Products

Mini Maps

Photography Books

Explorer Products

Maps

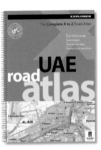

Activity Guides

Lifestyle Products & Calendars

Check out
www.liveworkexplore.com/shop

www.liveworkexplore.com

You've got the book – now log on to the website for:

- Regular newsletters on what's happening in your city
- Access to over 3,000 local listings in our directory
- Join and set up local groups
- Online maps
- Local forums and discussion boards
- Exclusive special offers
- Competitions
- E-shop

Sign up today!
Log on to www.liveworkexplore.com/signup to create your account.

E-shop
Visit www.liveworkexplore.com/shop for all our latest products and special offers.

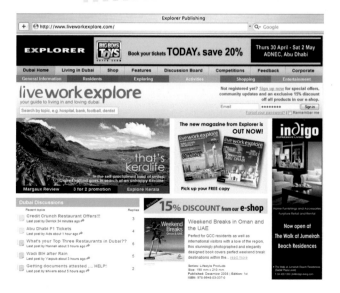

LOCAL KNOWLEDGE

Red-Tape Unravelled

How To Use Dubai Red-Tape

Like it or not, living and working in Dubai involves paperwork and bureaucracy. But help is at hand, because for every procedure you're likely to encounter, **Dubai Red-Tape** tells you – in plain and simple language – what you'll need, where you should go, what it'll cost and how long it's likely to take. From visas and licences, to housing, cars and doing business, **Dubai Red-Tape** provides step-by-step instructions and useful tips that help to make your life easier.

Each procedure is explained from beginning to end:

[1] 'Overview' tells you what the procedure will achieve, and who it's suitable for.

[2] 'Prerequisites' describes what you need to have already done beforehand, or what situation you must be in for the procedure to be relevant.

[3] 'What to Bring' is self-explanatory, listing all the documents and certificates you'll need, and what the cost is likely to be.

[4] 'Procedure' explains where you need to go (with a map reference and opening hours), describes what will happen at each stage of the process, and gives you an idea of how long things should take. Estimated charges and fees have been included, even though they are the most notoriously variable. We suggest you always take extra cash and your bank card along, and be ready to run to the nearest ATM or bank selling e-Dirhams (see p.xiii).

[5] 'Related Procedures' points you to other tasks that you may also have to deal with.

So Who Is Dubai Red-Tape For?

1– You've just arrived, you're setting up and settling in...
You'll have lots of questions, and you may not even know about all the things you're supposed to be doing. The first four chapters of the book (Visa, Housing, Communications, Driving) will come in most handy – the overview section at the beginning of each will give you the lowdown on what's involved. You should read these chapters to make sure you've got everything covered.

2 – You're already here/you're about to leave...
Dubai Red-Tape isn't just for new arrivals. It also covers everything you'll have to deal with before you leave. To find out how to disconnect services and arrange shipping, turn to the Table of Contents on p.iii, or go to the comprehensive index at the back of the book.

3 – You're in Dubai to do business...
The comprehensive Business chapter starting on p.215 has all you need to know, covering everything from immigration and labour cards to commercial agents and free zones.

Red-Tape Unravelled

Info/Law/E/Tip Boxes

In addition to the text explaining each procedure, you'll occasionally see these boxes below – 'Info' boxes are full of additional information and highlight extra services, 'E' boxes provide extra information about online services, 'Tip' boxes supply handy hints to make things go more smoothly, and 'Law' boxes explain any legal aspects you need to be aware of.

Essential Documents

Passport

You'll have to show your passport when carrying out many of the procedures listed throughout the book. You're also likely to have to provide photocopies of the pages showing your photo and residence visa, so come prepared.

Photos

For just about every licence and application, you'll need lots of colour photos with white backgrounds. Many photo shops around Dubai will take your picture and process the prints. You should ask to keep a CD or the images for when you need new copies.

NOC – No-Objection Certificate (or No-Objection Letter)

For many procedures you will require a letter from your sponsor or employer, stating that they have no objection to you renting a home, applying for a licence, buying a car, and so on. The NOC, on company headed paper, should state your name, position and passport number, and should then be signed and stamped with the company stamp.

Salary Certificate

To apply for certain services you will need to present proof of your earnings. As with a no-objection certificate, a salary certificate should be on company headed paper, and must be signed and stamped to make it 'official.'

Copies

In addition to your passport, you may also be asked for photocopies of various other documents, licences and certificates. As a security measure it's worth keeping copies of all your essential documents in a safe place anyway, should you be unfortunate enough to lose the original.

Additional Documents

Depending on the procedure, you may sometimes need additional documents such as a birth certificate, marriage certificate, driving licence (or international driving licence), education certificates, school records, professional certificates, divorce papers, or power of attorney. For more information see the table on p.6.

WHEN ASKED TO IDENTIFY THE
NUMBER ONE ATTRIBUTE CLIENTS
LOOK FOR WHEN APPOINTING
A UAE LAW FIRM, LOCAL
KNOWLEDGE COMES TOP

Hadef & Partners is a long-
established UAE law firm.
Since 1980, we have been assisting
regional and international
organisations with their UAE legal
requirements.

A trusted advisor, we are known
for our commercial acumen and
approachable manner.

www.hadefpartners.com

ABU DHABI | DUBAI

Red-Tape Unravelled

Managing Dubai's Red-Tape

Whether you've just arrived in Dubai, you've been here a while, or you're about to leave, there's always a certain amount of paperwork that needs processing. The table below gives you an overview of the red-tape you're likely to encounter and directs you to the procedure to follow to cut through it.

Getting Started

Doing Business In Dubai

While You're Here

Before You Leave

Red-Tape Unravelled

What Is eGovernment?

The eGovernment initiative aims to provide access to public services via the internet, allowing residents to apply for licences, pay bills, and carry out other procedures online, rather than having to visit a government office. Most websites do require you to register first, but it's worth persevering in order to avoid all that travelling and queuing. The instructions throughout Dubai Red-Tape tell you how to carry out procedures in person, but will also tell you if the same process can be achieved online.

What Are e-Dirhams?

Sometimes Dubai Government uses e-Dirham cards in ministries and departments, in place of cash. The same size as a credit card, the pre-paid cards can be bought at participating banks and are available in denominations of Dhs.100, Dhs.200, Dhs.300, Dhs.500, Dhs.1,000, Dhs.3,000 and Dhs.5,000. Alternatively, regular users can apply for a personalised card that can be 'topped up' at a bank whenever necessary. When it's time to pay for a service or procedure simply present your e-Dirham card, and the appropriate amount will be deducted. Some departments don't accept e-Dirhams, while others say they'll accept nothing else but, so it's best to ask as soon as you arrive.

Reader Response

If you have any suggestions or comments on this book or any Explorer product we would love to hear from you. Our reader response form on our website, www.liveworkexplore.com, is quick and easy and helps us gain essential feedback on all our books.

Tip | Typed Or Handwritten?

In general, all institutions prefer typed forms for clarity. Some departments are more lenient on this matter than others, particularly those offering personal rather than commercial services. If typed forms are necessary, you'll usually find a typing desk or office nearby where the staff will help you out for a small fee.

Tip | Arabic Or English?

Always keep in mind that any document written in Arabic is the legally binding one; the English version isn't. Therefore many institutions require that application forms are completed in Arabic. Apart from the fact that this is an Arabic speaking country, Arabic is obligatory when information accuracy is crucial, such as with immigration and labour matters, to avoid misunderstandings.

Something
for the Weekend...
From idyllic beach getaways to activity-packed city breaks, this guide is the ultimate resource for pepping up your downtime.
Weekend Breaks
Oman & UAE
EXPLORER
The Wave
Supported by:
The Wave
MUSCAT
www.liveworkexplore.com
EXPLORER

Visas

Overview

What Are The Different Types Of Visas?

All tourists, prior to entry, are issued a limited term visit or tourist visa by the Department of Naturalization and Residency Dubai (formerly the Immigration and Naturalisation Department). Those wanting to stay in Dubai for the long term need permission to do so in the form of a residence permit. Unless you're joining a spouse who is already resident and working in Dubai, you must have a job to get a residence permit.

A new employee cannot enter the country on a work visa without prior approval for a work permit by the Ministry of Labour and Social Affairs. This department is therefore closely linked with the Department of Naturalization and Residency. If you enter on a visit visa and are offered work while here, you may not work on your visit visa but your potential employer can apply for a work and residence permit for you (see Applying for an Employment Visa, p.22).

Department Of Naturalization & Residency, Dubai (DNRD)

The Department of Naturalization and Residency, located in Bur Dubai, is one of the busiest offices in Dubai. Millions of visas and permits are issued here, the department at times struggling to keep up with the ever-increasing numbers of visitors and residents. The DNRD is one of the main authorities deciding who can enter the country and they have six branches throughout Dubai. Since the introduction of eGovernment in Dubai, most visa processes can be carried out through registered typing shops. You or your company's PRO will still have to visit the DNRD for some procedures, but the new system has made things much easier.

Changes in policy occur overnight, and can be reversed just as quickly. As immigration is such an important and sensitive issue, all rule and regulation changes should be monitored continually – they can suddenly make your life easier – or more difficult.

Ministry Of Labour & Social Affairs

This federal institution is responsible for labour issues and approval of all labour-related permits (with the exception of some free zones). Only official representatives of companies deal directly with this ministry. As with the DNRD, nearly all procedures dealing with the Ministry of Labour are now processed through either the post office or authorised typing offices. Only an officially authorised person, such as the company owner, sponsor or public relations officer (PRO), may perform the labour-related procedures for each company.

Info Visa Or Permit?

There is some confusion between the term 'visa' and 'permit' and when going through your residency process you will no doubt hear both terms being used. With this book 'visa' refers to the permission given to enter the UAE while a 'permit' is the permission to reside in the country, be it for employment or as a dependent of a resident.

Visas

Overview

Entering Dubai

1 Overview

- Everyone entering Dubai needs a visa, except for citizens of GCC countries (Bahrain, Kuwait, Oman, Qatar, Saudi Arabia and the UAE).
- Certain nationalities do not need to apply in advance for a visa – the visa will be given on arrival (see p.13).
- All visit visas are for a limited term, and are issued by the Department of Naturalization and Residency (DNRD). You can apply for a visit visa at UAE embassies abroad (see Directory, p.283).
- If you plan to live in Dubai, you will initially need a work permit (if you are taking a job) and subsequently, a residence permit.
- To get a residence permit you must have a work permit, or be sponsored by your husband or father. Work permits are issued by the Ministry of Labour and Social Affairs.
- If you are accompanying a family member who has a job in Dubai (a wife accompanying her husband, elderly parents accompanying their children), you do not need a work permit before applying for your residence permit.

Sponsors

Sponsorship is an important concept for expatriates in the UAE. Rather than having financial implications, your 'sponsor' takes legal responsibility for you entering and/or living in the country. The sponsor can be a company or individual, a hotel, airline or tour operator. It is usually the sponsor who will apply for your visit visa or residence permit at the Department of Naturalization and Residency in Dubai.

If your sponsor is your future employer, the company should take care of all charges involved with the process. Families of eligible employees are not sponsored by the company, but rather by the employee himself. In most cases, he is responsible for the entire procedure and all related costs, unless the employer agrees to also cover family members.

Sponsorship plays an important role in business as well. Most types of company require a local sponsor to set up operations (see Business, p.215, and Appointing a Local Service Agent, p.249).

Visiting Dubai

All visit visas allow only one entry into Dubai. Some nationalities can extend their visas for an additional 30 days, but once the maximum length of stay has expired, you must leave the country (see Visas, p.10). There is a penalty of Dhs.100, plus another Dhs.100 for every day that you overstay your visit visa.

Becoming Residents

Once you have arrived in Dubai, your sponsor will apply for a residence permit, submitting your passport to the Ministry of Labour. This process should be initiated as soon as you enter the country, as all processing must be complete before the entry visa expires. Once the application has been approved, you will receive a residence permit in your passport. Normally the duration of the permit is three years, during which time you may leave and enter the country as often as you wish (see Residence Permit, p.21).

Your residence permit will be for the emirate in which your sponsor is registered. This should be the first consideration when applying for the visa.

Company sponsorship allows you to work only for the company that sponsored you.

| Tip | Private Vs. Public Sector Employment |

All procedures related to work visas in this chapter cover private sector employees only. Public sector or government employees and those working in free zones are subject to different employment regulations and procedures, although there may be some similarities.

| Info | 'Banning' |

'Banning' is a term that many new residents may not be familiar with, but you may unfortunately find yourself dealing with a 'ban' if your new job in Dubai doesn't work out as you expected. Previously, the banning law meant that job hopping was almost impossible for most categories of worker, but the recent relaxation in legislation has been welcomed wholeheartedly by Dubai's workforce. Even if you left your previous employer on good terms, the Ministry of Labour could put a six-month ban on you, thus preventing you from taking up any other job in Dubai for that period. Now however, as long as you leave your current job on good terms, and you get a no objection letter from your employer, you will be able to transfer your sponsorship to another employer without difficulty. Of course, your employer may refuse to give you the letter, particularly if you're leaving your current job to work for a competitor. In such cases you are likely to get a ban, although you can lodge an appeal with the ministry.

The ministry has also decided that putting a ban stamp in your passport is unnecessary and expats sanctioned with a ban will now only be registered in the ministry's database.

| Tip | Make Copies & Keep Them Within Reach |

Having copies of lost documents makes replacing them much easier. Keep copies of all important documents with you, and keep a set with someone else in case you need to access them while you are away.

Essential Documents

Essential Documents

1 Overview

There is a lot of paperwork involved in moving to a new place, and Dubai is no exception. You can save yourself some time and frustration by having all the right documents when you arrive. If you are starting a new job, note that some employers will require you to have your education certificates certified, notarised and attested. This should be done in the country where they were issued, so if you are reading this while still in your home country, get it done before you leave. If you are already in Dubai, you can use Empost or a courier service to send your documents back for attestation. (see Notarising & Attesting Documents, p.9).

Personal At some time during your setting up stage, you may need the following documents (where applicable):

Passport, birth certificate, marriage certificate, divorce papers, driving licence, international driving licence, education certificates, school records (to register children at schools), professional certificates, power of attorney.

Company You should bring the following documents from the company headquarters, home country, or country of issue, as you may need to present them when setting up an office in Dubai:

Board of Director's resolution, power of attorney, parent company's memorandum of association, main company's certificate of incorporation, and the audited accounts of the parent company.

Personal Documents

Document	Related Procedures	Notarise in Country of Issue
Passport	All procedures	No
Birth Certificate	Sponsor family members	
	Marriage	Yes
Marriage Certificate	Sponsor wife	
	Obtain a birth certificate	
	Register a new-born child	Yes
Divorce Papers	Marriage	Yes
Driving Licence	Obtain a Dubai driving licence	
	Hire a car	No
International Driving Licence	Hire a car	No
Education Certificates	Obtain a work permit	
	Set up a company	Yes
School Records	Register children at school	No
Professional Certificates	Obtain a work permit	
	Transfer sponsorship	
	Set up a company	Yes
Power of Attorney	Marriage	Yes

Essential Documents

Lost Documents

1 Overview

If an important document is lost or stolen, notify the police in person. You will be asked to return to the police station two days later, to check whether the document has been recovered. If it hasn't, the police will issue a report – you will need this before you can apply for a replacement document from your embassy or any of the ministries.

If you lose documents while here on holiday, notify the police headquarters to get a report. Your document details will be entered into their database, so that nobody can travel in or out of Dubai with your documents.

2 Prerequisites

- Document has been lost or stolen

3 What To Bring

- ☐ Photocopy of the lost document
- ☐ Letter from your sponsor, in Arabic with company stamp, verifying that you work for the company and that you have lost the document
- ☐ If sponsored by an individual, a letter from sponsor with his or signature and a photocopy of his or her passport
- ☐ Trade licence (copy)
- ☐ Establishment labour card (copy), or
- ☐ Establishment immigration card
- ☐ Two recent photos
- Fee ☐ Dhs.50

4 Procedure

- Go to the police station in the district where the document was lost, rather than to police headquarters (see Map 9-D7 or Directory, p.295)
- Pay Dhs.50 and collect a receipt from the police.
- Return two days later to check whether the police have recovered the document.
- If not, they will issue a police report addressed to the concerned department(s) (Ministry of Labour and your embassy), confirming that the documents have indeed been misplaced or stolen.
- For more information, see www.dubaipolice.gov.ae and click the link for 'Informations and Procedures' and then 'Reporting Losts'

Essential Documents

Passports

1 Overview

Validity — Passports should be valid for at least six months past the date of entry and have at least three unused pages.

Procedures — It's not a bad idea to carry your passport with you for any administrative procedure. If you are applying for or cancelling a residence permit you may need to leave your passport with the authorities.

Separate Passports — It is recommended that all family members have their own passport. Note that a child on a parent's passport may not travel unaccompanied.

Lost Passport — If you lose or damage your passport (see Lost Documents, p.7), inform the Department of Naturalisation & Immigration within three days.

Photocopies — Always bring a photocopy of your passport with you. Make sure all relevant pages with personal details are photocopied as well.

Resident Permit — If residency is required for an application, provide a copy of your residence permit together with the passport copies.

Passport Photos — Format: 4cm x 6cm, colour with white background. Always bring extra photos.

Terms & Definitions

Term	Definition	In other words...
Certified	A copy of the original document, certified by the issuing authority	The document is genuine
Notarised	A certified copy of an original document duly notarised by a Notary Public in your home country	The signature is genuine
Attested	A certified, notarised copy of an original document bearing the stamp of a UAE embassy abroad or the local Ministry of Foreign Affairs	The issuing institution is genuine

Info   Attesting Documents in the UAE

If you are unable to carry out document notarisation in your home country prior to arriving in the UAE, you can:

- Send the document to a Notary Public in your home country
- Have the notarised document attested by either your embassy or consulate in the UAE
- Have the document attested by the UAE Ministry of Foreign Affairs

You may be able to have documents notarised at a GCC embassy abroad. Check with the embassy first.

Essential Documents

Notarising & Attesting Documents in Your Home Country

1 Overview

Ensure all important documents have been notarised (and attested if applicable) before moving to Dubai. It is much quicker to do it while still in your home country.

Notarisation procedures vary from country to country and what follows is a general description of what needs to be done. It's best to contact your embassy in the UAE for precise instructions regarding authentication and costs. In all cases, a copy of the documents must be stamped by a Notary Public, then endorsed by the Ministry of Foreign Affairs and the UAE embassy in that country.

2 Prerequisites

- Documents need to be notarised

3 What To Bring

- ☐ All documents (originals) to be notarised
- ☐ All related fees (check with your notary beforehand)

4 Procedure

Notary Public
- Submit the original and one copy of the document and inform the Notary Public for which country the document is being notarised (UAE)
- If you have several documents to be notarised, ask the Notary Public to bind the documents together, list each document on a cover page and classify all as one document (this is to avoid each document being charged separately)
- The Notary Public will stamp a copy of the entire document
- Have the document authenticated by the relevant authority (for example, the Foreign & Commonwealth Office in the UK or the State Department in the US)
- Request instructions from the relevant authority for the exact procedure to follow. Typically, you have to enclose payment in the form of a cheque or postal order and a pre-paid self-addressed envelope or pre-arranged courier service for them to send the documents back to you.
- Take the notarised and authenticated documents to the UAE embassy in your home country.
- Submit the document to the Authentication Office
- If you send it by mail, provide a self-addressed return envelope
- The embassy will return the attested document to you
- Contact the embassy if there are any delays

Visas

Visas

1 Overview

The UAE Ministry of Interior specifies that all visitors to the country must have a visa ('entry visa') to enter the country. A visa allows an individual to enter the country for a short or temporary period, as opposed to a residence permit, which allows an extended stay in the UAE.

The following visas are covered in this section:

- Visit visa (on and before arrival)
- Tourist visa
- 14 day transit visa
- 96 hour transit visa

The entry visa to be applied for depends on several factors: (see tables below for details)

- Nationality
- Sponsor
- Intended period of stay
- Purpose of visit

Nationality	
Nationality	**Visa Options**
GCC nationals (Bahrain, Kuwait, Oman, Qatar, Saudi Arabia)	No visa necessary
34 nationalities (see Exempt Countries, p.13)	Visit visa upon arrival, employment or residence visa
Other nationalities	Tourist, transit, visit, employment or residence visa

Sponsor	
Sponsor	**Visa Options**
Airline, hotel or tour operator	Tourist or transit visa
UAE-based company	Transit, visit or employment visa
UAE resident	Visit visa

Intended Period of Stay		
Visa	**Maximum Permitted Stay in Dubai**	
Transit visa	96 hours	Non-renewable
Special Mission Entry Visa	14 days	Non-renewable
Tourist visa	30 days	30 days renewable
Visit visa	30 days	Non-renewable
Long-Term Visit Visa	90 days	Non-renewable
Visa on arrival	30 days	30 days renewable

Purpose Of Visit

Purpose of Visit	Visa Options
Tourist	Transit or tourist visa
Family or corporate visitor	Transit, tourist or visit visa
For future employment	Employment or visit visa
For residence without employment	Residence or visit visa

Timing
- Visitor must arrive within 60 days of date of visa issue
- Permitted length of stay includes dates of both entry and exit into/from Dubai.
- Visas valid 30 days are valid for exactly 30 days – not a calendar month.
- Visitors must leave the country before the visa's expiry date. On departure, a fine of Dhs.100 is payable to Dubai Immigration for each day overstayed, in addition to a fixed overstayed visa fine of Dhs.100.

Granting a visa does not guarantee entry. As in other countries, entry is at the ultimate discretion of the immigration authorities on arrival.

Visas must be issued for the port of arrival only; if you are flying in to Abu Dhabi, you will need an Abu Dhabi visa to enter the country.

Visitor's Costs

Visa Type	Application Fee	Renewal charge
96 hour transit visa	Dhs.100	Not applicable
Special Mission Entry Visa	Dhs.220 Dhs.10 (delivery fee)	Not applicable
Tourist	Dhs.430 Dhs.50 (maximum hotel service charge) Dhs.1000 refundable deposit Dhs.100 (urgent fee)	Dhs.620
Visit	Dhs.620 Dhs.1,000 refundable deposit Dhs.100 (urgent fee)	Dhs.500
Long-Term Visit	Dhs.1,120 Dhs.1,000 refundable deposit	Not applicable
Visa on Arrival	Free	Dhs.620

Future Resident's Costs

Visa Type	Application Fee	Renewal charge
Employment	Dhs.100	Not applicable
Residence	Dhs.100	Not applicable

Prerequisites
- Visitor holds a valid passport or a document allowing entry into Dubai and re-entry into country of residence
- Visitor's passport is valid for the maximum permitted stay in Dubai (see Intended Period of Stay table, p.10)
- If visitor needs to be sponsored (see Nationality table, p.10), the sponsor is resident in Dubai and eligible to sponsor a visitor (see Sponsor table, p.10)

- Visitor has not been deported from the UAE
- Visitor is not banned from entering the UAE
- Visitor is not an Israeli national
- Visitor will arrive and depart from Dubai International Airport

Health Requirements

- No health certificates are required for entry to the UAE, except for visitors who have been in a cholera or yellow fever area in the previous 14 days

Children Under 14

- Children travelling to the UAE on holiday must be accompanied by a parent
- Children may travel on their own or on their parent's passport (in which case they will be on the parent's visa)
- When children visit parents who are residents in Dubai, only the parents are permitted to sponsor the child (not friends or immediate relatives)

There is no refund under any circumstances once a visa application has been submitted.

Info | **Tourist Visa**

Only certified tourism agencies and hotels can apply for tourist visas. Unlike in the past, UAE residents cannot apply for tourist visas for friends or acquaintences. If you are in the country, it is possible to apply for a tourist visa extension. This extension, however, must also be processed through a tourism company or hotel.

Obtaining A Visit Visa On Arrival

1 Overview

Passport holders of the following countries will be granted a visit visa on arrival in Dubai for no charge.

List Of Exempt Countries		
Andorra	Hong Kong	Norway
Australia	Iceland	Portugal
Austria	Ireland	San Marino
Belgium	Italy	Singapore
Brunei	Japan	Spain
Canada	Liechtenstein	Sweden
Cyprus	Luxembourg	Switzerland
Denmark	Malaysia	UK
Finland	Malta	USA
France	Monaco	Vatican
Germany	Netherlands	
Greece	New Zealand	

2 Prerequisites

Validity
- 30 days from date of entry; renewable for another 30 days
- Passport is from one of the countries listed above
- Visitor has no intention to do any paid or unpaid work in Dubai during the visit

3 What To Bring

☐ Passport

4 Procedure

Location   Passport Control, Dubai International Airport   Map ref 9-B9

Hours   24 hours
- After landing at the Dubai airport, proceed directly to passport control
- A visa will be stamped into your passport

5 Related Procedure

- Renewing A Visit Visa, p.19

Visas (Tourist)

Applying For A Tourist Visa (Tourism Companies)

1 Overview

If your nationality is not listed in the table on p.13 and you intend to stay a maximum of 30 days in Dubai, your hotel, airline or travel agency may be able to apply for a tourist visa on your behalf.

2 Prerequisites

• Applicant will be sponsored by a hotel or tourism company

3 What To Bring

☐ Passport (copy)

☐ Dhs.220 – Visa fee

☐ Dhs.1,000 – refundable deposit

☐ Dhs.50 (maximum) – hotel service charge

4 Procedure

• Make the reservation with the hotel or tour company

• Send all documents and credit card details by fax or mail to the hotel or tour operator

• Up to seven days later (if you requested an urgent application, within one day), a copy of the visa will be sent to you and the original visa will be taken to the airport

• Upon arrival at Dubai International Airport, hand over your copy of the visa at the Immigration desk and collect the original visa

If sponsorship is arranged by a hotel, you must stay at that hotel. The length of stay depends on the hotel's policy.

⚠ Visitors must have a copy of the visa to be able to board the flight to Dubai. Passports must be valid for at least three months longer than the visa expiry date. This visa cannot be extended or renewed.

Info **Visa Or Permit?**

There is some confusion between the term 'visa' and 'permit', and when going through your residency process you will no doubt hear both terms being used. With this book 'visa' refers to the permission given to enter the UAE, while a 'permit' is the permission to reside in the country, be it for employment or as a dependent of a resident.

Applying For A Visit Visa (Before Arrival)

1 Overview

A visit visa can be applied for by either an individual or corporate sponsor, allowing the visitor to stay in Dubai for up to 90 days. It is issued to those who have an appointment to visit a company, or to those visiting a friend or relative who is resident in the UAE. Sometimes this visa is issued for tourism purposes as well.

Only those in certain job categories and family members are permitted to transfer a visit visa to a residence/employment permit (see Transferring A Visit Visa To An Employment Or Residence Permit, p.25).

2 Prerequisites

Validity
- One entry within two months of date of issue
- 30 days from date of entry; renewable for another 30 days
- If you remain in the UAE beyond your permitted period of stay, you will have to pay a fine of Dhs.100, plus Dhs.100 for each day you have overstayed. This fine is payable before you are permitted to leave.

Family
- Sponsor's monthly basic salary is at least Dhs.4,000 plus housing allowance, or total salary is Dhs.5,000

GCC Residents
- Visitor is a businessman, company manager or representative, or holds a professional post

Wife of GCC Residents
- The wife has a valid residence permit in her husband's GCC home country
- Her husband resides in the UAE

3 What To Bring

☐ Visitor's passport (copy)

Fees
☐ Dhs.620 – 30 day visa fee

☐ Dhs.1,120 – 90 day visa fee

☐ Dhs.100 – urgent charge (optional)

☐ Dhs.1,000 – refundable deposit fee

☐ Two application forms typed in English or Arabic (forms are available from the typing centre or can be downloaded from www.dnrd.gov.ae)

☐ A letter stating the reason and purpose of the visit. Where applicable, proof of relationship may also be required

Company Sponsor
☐ Trade licence (copy)

☐ Establishment Immigration Card (original & copy) (see Applying For An Establishment Immigration Card, p.255)

Visas

Visas (Visit)

☐ Representative card (original & copy) (see Applying For Immigration & Labour Representative Cards, p.259)

☐ The profession of the visitor as per the Immigration Department codes (found on the website, www.dnrd.gov.ae, or with a typist)

Individual Sponsor

☐ Two application forms in English and Arabic (typed)

☐ Sponsor's employment contract (original & copy)

☐ Sponsor's salary certificate (dated within the last three months)

☐ Sponsor's tenancy contract (copy), unless accommodation is provided by the employer

☐ If sponsoring wife, marriage certificate (original & copy)

4 Procedure

- Go to a typing office near the Immigration Department, where the typist will fill in the application forms for you
- Pay the application and typing fees at the typing office

Location Department of Naturalization and Residency   Map ref **7-B4**

Hours Sun – Thurs 07:30 – 19:00

- Submit all relevant documents at the visa section of the DNRD
- Collect a ticket
- Return at least two hours later to collect the visa
- Fax the visa to the visitor and make a copy of the visa
- Deposit the original at the visa counter in the airport (next to the Arrivals hall) at least two hours before the arrival of the visitor and have the copy stamped
- Pay the visa deposit fee at the bank counter
- The visitor will exchange his/her copy of the visa for the original upon arrival at the Immigration desk in the airport

5 Related Procedures

- Renewing A Visit Visa, p.19
- Transferring A Visit Visa To An Employment Or Residence Visa, p.25

Visas (Transit)

Applying For A 14 Day Transit Visa (Visa For A Mission)

1 Overview

This non-renewable visa is also known as an Entry Service Permit, as it mainly serves company visitors. It is issued to those visiting a company based in the UAE, and staying a maximum of 14 days in the country. The wife and child may accompany the applicant. GCC nationals and those from one of the 34 exempt countries (see Exempt Countries, p.13) visiting on business do not need this visa to enter the country.

Validity Urgent visas are valid 14 days from the date of issue, regular visas, seven days after collection

2 Prerequisites

- Visitor has a return ticket
- Visitor has a valid passport
- If a job title is mentioned in the passport, the visitor should belong to a professional job category

3 What To Bring

- ☐ Two application forms
- ☐ Trade licence (copy)
- ☐ Visitor's passport (copy)
- ☐ Transit visa card (original and copy)

Fees
- ☐ Dhs.320 – visa application charge
- ☐ Dhs.100 – urgent charge (optional)
- ☐ Dhs.1,000 – visa deposit fee

4 Procedure

- Purchase an e-Dirham card and request an 'urgent' slip if needed
- Go to a typing office near the DNRD, where the typist will fill in the application forms for you
- Pay the application and typing fees at the typing office
- The sponsor must sign and seal the application forms before submitting them

Location DNRD, Dubai Airport Free Zone   Map ref 9-D8

Hours Sun – Thurs 07:30 – 19:30

- Submit all relevant documents at least 48 hours before the visitor's arrival

Sponsor
- Collect the transit visa the same day (minimum two hours after submission)
- Fax the visa to the visitor and make a copy of the visa
- Deposit the original at the visa counter in the airport (next to the Arrivals hall) at least two hours before the arrival of the visitor and have the copy stamped
- Pay the visa deposit fee at the same counter
- The visitor will exchange their copy of the visa for the original upon arrival at the Immigration desk in the airport

Info **96 Hour Transit Visa**

Only airlines may issue this type of visa when flight schedules force passengers to spend an extended period of time in Dubai waiting for connecting flights. The airline will apply for the visa and it will be issued at Dubai International Airport. This visa allows transit passengers to stay for up to 96 hours in the UAE, under the sponsorship and responsibility of the airline. The Immigration Authority at the airport will stamp the traveller's passport upon arrival and state the permitted period of stay.

Info **Visa Change Flight**

When your residency application has been approved, you will have to change your visa status from 'visitor' to 'residency'. This can be done in two ways: either leave the UAE, cancelling your previous visa and re-entering on your newly issued residence entry permit, or pay Dhs.500 for the status changeover at the DNRD.

Those nationalities who qualify for a visa on arrival when entering the UAE have a cheap and convenient means to do a visa changeover. As they also qualify for a free entry visa into Oman, they can enter Oman by car at the border post just past Hatta Fort Hotel, and then re-enter the UAE immediately on their residency permit.

However, this road-travel visa change is not an option for those not on the list of nationalities who qualify for a free visa on arrival. These nationalities can either pay Dhs.500 for the visa status change at the DNRD, or leave and re-enter the country by air. See the Visa Run tip box on p.19.

Info **90 Day Mission Entry Visa**

A new visa option for doctors, engineers, lawyers and technicians is a 90 day Mission Entry visa. The visa costs Dhs.600 and can be renewed for a further 90 days for an additional fee of Dhs.1,200. The grace period for renewal or departure on this visa is seven days and visitors who qualify for this visa may bring their wives and children into the UAE as well.

Renewing A Visit Visa

1 Overview

If you are on a visit visa and you wish to stay a total of 60 days in Dubai, you will have to renew your visa within 30 days of your arrival. This one-time renewal will allow you another 30 days in Dubai before you must leave the country.

Validity Additional 30 days

2 Prerequisites

• You have stayed less than 30 days in Dubai

3 What To Bring

☐ Passport (original)
☐ Valid visit visa (original)
☐ Dhs.620 – renewal charge

4 Procedure

Location Department of Naturalization and Residency   Map ref 7-B4

Hours Sun – Thurs 07:30 – 19:30

• Up to ten days prior or at least 48 hours before expiration, go to the Visit Visa Renewal Counter
• Submit your passport and payment
• The extension will be stamped into your passport immediately

5 Related Procedure

• Transferring A Visit Visa To An Employment Or Residence Visa, p.25

Info Visa Run

For nationalities listed on p.13 there is the option of doing a visa run rather than following the above procedure. You can either fly out (Doha is a popular visa run) or drive through the Omani border at Hatta. When you re-enter Dubai you will have a new visit visa. If you choose to drive to Oman, you may incur a charge at the border of around Dhs.70. Once your paperwork has been stamped at the border you can u-turn and get your passport stamped for re-entry. For nationalities who don't get a visa on arrival it is possible to leave Dubai, usually to Kish Island, and apply for another visit visa (valid for three months) to re-enter the UAE on. While waiting on Kish Island for the new application to be processed, passengers remain in transit and therefore don't need a visa.

Residence Permit (Work)

Obtaining A Residence Permit (Employee)

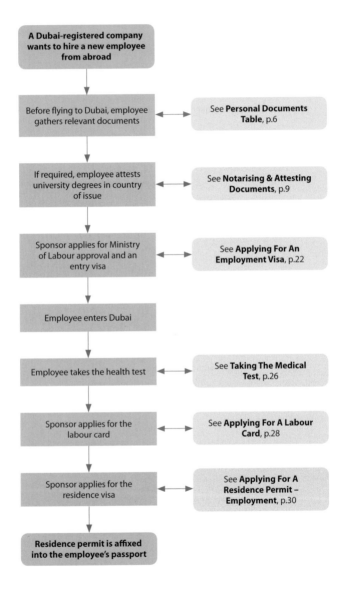

A Dubai-registered company wants to hire a new employee from abroad

↓

Before flying to Dubai, employee gathers relevant documents ⟷ See **Personal Documents Table**, p.6

↓

If required, employee attests university degrees in country of issue ⟷ See **Notarising & Attesting Documents**, p.9

↓

Sponsor applies for Ministry of Labour approval and an entry visa ⟷ See **Applying For An Employment Visa**, p.22

↓

Employee enters Dubai

↓

Employee takes the health test ⟷ See **Taking The Medical Test**, p.26

↓

Sponsor applies for the labour card ⟷ See **Applying For A Labour Card**, p.28

↓

Sponsor applies for the residence visa ⟷ See **Applying For A Residence Permit – Employment**, p.30

↓

Residence permit is affixed into the employee's passport

Residence Permit (Work)

Residence Permit

1 Overview

A residence permit allows you to live in the UAE for up to three years, entering and leaving the country freely. Note that if you are out of the country for a period longer than six months, your residence permit will expire.

Copies of EVERY document, including receipts, must be made.

If in doubt, jump the queue to ask if you are in the correct line.

There are three steps involved in obtaining a residence permit:

- Take a medical test (p.26) through the Ministry of Health. New rules make it mandatory that companies provide their employees with health care. This means you no longer need a government-issued health card to take the medical test.

- If sponsored by a company, get a labour card (p.28), issued by the Ministry of Labour

- Get a residence permit, issued by the Department of Naturalization and Residency

GCC nationals (Bahrain, Kuwait, Oman, Qatar, Saudi Arabia) do not need a residence permit to live in the UAE.

Validity General: three years

Student residence permit: one year

Domestic help residence permit: one year

Visa Types

Residence Visa	Sponsor	Maximum Validity
Employment residence visa	Employer (company)	3 years
Family residence visa	Employee (husband, father, wife, son)	3 years
Domestic help residence visa	Employee (head of household)	1 year

Info Public Sector & Free Zone Employment

Application procedures vary depending on whether the sponsor is a private or government-related company. Companies in free zones follow a different set of rules (similar to government organisations), even if they are private sector companies. The Ministry of Labour is involved in the approval of private sector applications. Employees of public and free zone companies do not need approval from the Ministry of Labour. This exemption applies to federal ministries, local departments, the Ruler's offices and representative departments, as well as public firms, companies operating in free zones, and various clubs and societies. Note that in this book all procedures relate to the non-free zone private sector.

Residence Permit (Work)

1 Overview

This procedure is handled by the hiring company prior to the arrival of the employee. More than one employee can be applied for concurrently.

In order for a company to hire an employee, the company must first get permission from the Ministry of Labour. The Visa Committee at the Ministry will assess several criteria such as the profession of the potential employee, the size of the company, the number and nationalities of current employees, and so on before issuing permission for the potential employee to be hired. Permission is issued in the form of a work permit.

Once permission has been given, an employment visa must be obtained from the DNRD. This visa will allow the employee to enter the country, then obtain a labour card (p.28) and apply for a residence visa (p.30).

Ministry of Labour Approval

A partner in a company does not need prior approval from the Ministry of Labour to obtain an entry visa. The partner may proceed directly to the Immigration application step in this procedure and apply for a partner visa.

Certain companies, depending on the type of licence and ownership, must deposit a bank guarantee for each employee they wish to hire. Currently, the guarantee for an employee is set at Dhs.3,000.

Employment Visa – Immigration

Employment Visa
If a person has a firm job offer, the employment visa will be dealt with by the future employer. This visa allows the employee to enter Dubai and follow the remaining immigration procedures to become a resident.

Partner Visa
In some cases, a partner of a company must pay a guarantee when applying for a visa, depending on the percentage of the partner's ownership in the company and the type of company.

Currently, if the company has a professional trade licence and the partner is working in the field of his degree, no guarantee is required. If it is a commercial company and the partner's share is less than Dhs.70,000, the refundable guarantee to be paid is Dhs.20,000. If the partner's share is more than Dhs.70,000, the refundable guarantee to be paid is Dhs.10,000.

Validity
One entry within two months of date of issue

Application for employment residence permit must occur within 60 days of entry

2 Prerequisites

- Employee is not over 60 or under 19 years of age

- If over 60 years of age, employee must have special qualifications, a highly ranked position, or a specialised job
- Dhs.3,000 guarantee per employee to be paid to the Labour office

3 What To Bring

Labour Approval
- ☐ Passport of applicant (copy)
- ☐ One passport photo (white background)
- ☐ Valid trade licence (copy)
- ☐ Establishment immigration card (copy) (see Applying for an Establishment Immigration Card, p.259)
- ☐ If the employee is a professional, all notarised university certificates (see Notarising & Attesting Documents, p.9)

Fees
- ☐ Dhs.200 – application fee
- ☐ Dhs.1,000-Dhs.3,000 – labour approval fee (depending on position)
- ☐ Dhs.40 – typing fee

Immigration
- ☐ Ministry of Labour work permit approval
- ☐ Valid trade licence (copy)
- ☐ Establishment immigration card (copy) (see Applying for an Establishment Immigration Card, p.259)

Fees
- ☐ Dhs.100 – application fee
- ☐ Dhs.100 – urgent receipt from bank
- ☐ Dhs.10 – visa deposit fee

- ☐ Partner's passport (copy)

Company
- ☐ A 'To whom it may concern' certificate from Department of Economic Development listing all partners' names
- ☐ Trade licence (copy)
- ☐ Company memorandum of association attested by a Notary Public
- ☐ Establishment Immigration Card (copy) (see Applying for an Establishment Immigration Card, p.259)

4 Procedure

Location Any typing office with access to 'Tas'Heel' service

Hours Sun – Thurs 07:30 – 19:30

Approval
- Go to any typing office where a typist will fill in the application form for you
- Pay the application and typing fees at the typing office
- Place all required documents into a 'labour envelope'
- Submit the envelope at any post office
- You will be given a submission receipt
- Approval or rejection is posted on the Ministry of Labour web portal within 10 days

- If the work permit is approved (your PRO can find out by logging on to the Ministry of Labour web portal), go to the post office or typing office and take a printout of the approval form
- Pay Dhs.1,000-Dhs.3,000 labour approval fee (depending on position)and attach the receipt to the approval
- If the work permit has been rejected, collect the documents from the typing office. The reason for rejection will be written on the envelope
- There may be a waiting period before a company can re-apply
- If approval is given, but a bank guarantee is required, go to your bank and deposit the required sum
- The bank will issue a letter addressed to the Labour Office
- Take a copy of the bank guarantee letter to the typing office
- Two days later, return to collect the original work permit. You will need this to apply for the entry visa
- Attach the receipt to the approval letter

Location	Department of Naturalization and Residency Map ref 7-B4
Hours	Sun – Thurs 07:30 – 19:30
Application	• Submit all documents to the Entry Permit office

 Only the company owner (sponsor) or PRO may submit the application (see Applying For Immigration & Labour Representative Cards, p.259)

- Immigration will issue an employment visa at the same time
- Send a copy of the visa to the employee/partner and make a copy of the visa
- Pay the Dhs.20 fee and deposit the original at the visa counter in the airport (next to the Arrivals hall) at least two hours before the arrival of the visitor and have the copy stamped
- Pay the visa deposit fee at the same counter
- The visitor will exchange their copy of the visa for the original upon arrival at the airport Immigration desk

5   Related Procedures

- Taking The Medical Test, p.26
- Applying For A Residence Permit – Employment, p.30
- Transferring a Visit Visa To An Employment Or Residence Visa, p.25

Info   Online Visa Services

Dubai has successfully made the switch to eGovernment. However, only companies and typing shops are allowed to use the online service and you'll still have to deliver the required documents to a post office or typing shop. All Ministry of Labour procedures must be done online through a typing office or post office. It's very rare that anybody enter the actual Ministry building

Residence Permit (Work)

Transferring A Visit Visa To An Employment Or Residence Visa

1 Overview

Family members, or certain employees (see below) are entitled to enter the country on a visit visa and change their status to an employment/residence visa without having to leave the UAE. The DNRD calls this 'Position Amendment'.

For employees, this procedure is the exception to the rule.

2 Prerequisites

Family
- The sponsor is eligible to sponsor a family member (see Sponsoring Family, p.32)

Employee
- The sponsor has approval from the Ministry of Labour to hire this person (see Applying for a Work Visa & Employment Visa, p.22)
- The employee is in one of the following job categories:

  MA/PhD holder, accountant, administrator, consultant, economist, legal expert, pharmacist, physician, bus or heavy vehicle driver, electronics or IT specialist, engineer, journalist, laboratory technician, medical technician, nurse, petroleum position, teacher

3 What To Bring

- ☐ Applicant's passport (original and copy)
- ☐ Visit visa (original and copy)

Fee
- ☐ Dhs.620 – position amendment fee
- ☐ Ministry of Labour work permit approval (see Applying for a Work Permit & Employment Visa, p.22)
- ☐ Sponsor's establishment immigration card (original and copy) (see Applying for an Establishment Immigration Card, p.259)
- ☐ Birth or marriage certificate (attested)

4 Procedure

Location Department of Naturalization and Residency   Map ref 7-B4

Hours Sun – Thurs 07:30 – 19:30
- Go to a typing office near the Immigration Department, where a typist will fill in the application form for you
- Pay the application and typing fees at the typing office
- Submit documents (including payment receipt) at the Position Amendment Counter in the DNRD

Taking The Medical Test

1 Overview

Once you have the correct visa status, i.e. you have entered the country with either a work (see p.30) or family visa (see p.32), the next step to becoming a Dubai resident is to undergo a medical examination.

The medical examination is an important part of the UAE's immigration requirements, and involves a blood test for communicable diseases, such as HIV and hepatitis, as well as a chest X-ray. The test has to be taken at one of the Dubai Ministry of Health and Medical Services' clinics. You will be assigned a test location depending on your sponsor.

Some employees require further medical tests, depending on their age or profession. You will be informed if you must undergo further examinations.

Unlike in the past, when all residents were required to obtain a government health card, employers are now required to provide health insurance for their employees. Such insurance covers most private clinics and hospitals both in the UAE and while travelling overseas (see Directory, p.279).

2 Prerequisites

- Employment visa, residence visa or Dubai residence visa
- Applicant must be at least 18 years of age (those under 18 do not need to take the test)

3 What To Bring

Medical Test
- ☐ Passport plus entry stamp (original and copy)
- ☐ Two passport photos (white background)

Fees
- ☐ Dhs.260 – health test charge
- ☐ Dhs.20 – Arabic typing charge

4 Procedure

Locations   Hospital Blood Test Section, Al Baraha Hospital   Map ref 9-B2

Hours   Sun – Thurs 07:30 – 20:30

Medical Test
- Go to any typist next to the hospital (see below) and have the blank test form filled out in Arabic
- Visit Empost counter inside hospital and fill in details for results delivery
- Submit all documents to hospital medical test counter
- You will be registered and given a ticket
- Wait for your name to be called
- A blood sample and a chest X-ray are taken
- Collect test receipt, you will need this when Empost delivers your results
- Results will be sent to you via Empost

5 Related Procedures

- Applying For A Residence Permit – Employment, p.30
- Applying For A Residence Permit – Family, p.37
- Obtaining A Labour Card When On Family Sponsorship, p.39

Visas

Residence Permit (Work)

Residence Permit (Work)

Applying For A Labour Card

1 Overview

To work in the UAE's private sector, you must have a labour card. If your employer is arranging your residency, the employer will have your labour card processed directly after your employment visa has been approved.

Regulations in free zones vary. Check with the free zone authority to determine whether labour cards are issued.

Timing | After entering Dubai on an employment visa, application must occur within 60 days.

Validity | Three years

Labour Contract | Before a labour card is issued, a labour contract must be signed. This is a standard form issued by the labour authorities detailing your employment information. This contract is printed in both Arabic and English, and as the Arabic version prevails in a court of law, it is advisable to have the Arabic contract translated prior to signing.

2 Prerequisites

- Applicant has an employment visa (p.22)
- Applicant has signed the employment contract
- Applicant has taken the medical test (p.26)

3 What To Bring

Fees | ☐ Dhs.40-Dhs.50 – Typing fee (including labour envelope and sticker)

☐ Passport (copy)

☐ Employment visa with the entry stamp (copy) (see Applying for a Work Permit & Employment Visa, p.30)

☐ Official labour contract, signed and stamped

☐ Two passport photos (white background)

☐ Medical test result (copy) (see Taking The Medical Test, p.26)

☐ If applicable, attested degree(s) (see Notarising & Attesting Documents, p.9)

☐ Establishment labour card (copy) (see Applying For An Establishment Labour Card, p.255)

☐ Trade licence (copy)

4 Procedure

Location Post Office or Typing Centre

Hours Various Timings

- Go to any registered typing office
- Have the typist fill in the official labour contract; pay the fee
- Both the employer (sponsor) and employee must sign and stamp the contract
- To save time, the employment permit application form can be completed at this stage
- Place all required documents into the labour envelope
- Submit the envelope at a post office or typing office
- You will be given a submission receipt – keep it
- The card will be mailed to the company within 30 days

5 Related Procedures

- Applying For A Work Permit & Employment Visa, p.22
- Taking The Medical Test, p.26
- Notarising & Attesting Documents, p.9

Work It Out

Working in a new country can be a little bit of a culture shock, especially when you have to get used to having Sunday lunch on a Friday and getting Monday morning blues on a Sunday.

To find out more about living and working in Dubai, finding a job, employment packages and contracts, check out the Residents chapter of the *Dubai Explorer – The Complete Residents' Guide* available in all leading bookshops and supermarkets.

Visas

Residence Permit (Work)

Residence Permit (Work)

Applying For A Residence Permit – Employment

1 Overview

The employment residence permit allows you to live and work in Dubai. In most cases, the employer will take care of this procedure for you.

Validity Three years

⚠ Once a resident, you may not stay outside of the UAE for a period longer than six months, or your residency will lapse. This is particularly relevant to children studying abroad who are on their parent's sponsorship, and wives who choose to have their baby outside of Dubai (see Temporary Entry Permit, p.42).

Validity After entering Dubai, completion of this procedure must take place within 60 days.

⚠ If you have not completed the application procedure within 60 days, you will be fined Dhs.200 for the first day overdue, and Dhs.100 each following day until the procedure has been completed.

2 Prerequisites

- Applicant has undergone the medical test (see Taking The Medical Test, p.26)
- If applicant is on company sponsorship, the labour card application has been submitted (see Applying For A Labour Card, p.28)

3 What To Bring

☐ Passport (original)

☐ Employment visa with the entry stamp (original) (see Applying for a Work Permit & Employment Visa, p.22)

☐ Two passport photos (white background)

☐ Medical test result (original)

☐ If applicable, attested degree(s) (see Notarising & Attesting Documents, p.9)

☐ Establishment Immigration Card (copy) (see Applying for an Establishment Immigration Card, p.257)

☐ Trade licence (copy)

☐ Ministry of Labour envelope submission receipt (copy) (see Applying For A Labour Card, p.28)

☐ If you are a partner in the company, a 'To whom It may concern' certificate from the Department of Economic Development containing all partners' names

Fees ☐ Dhs.370 – residence permit application fee

☐ Dhs.100 – urgent application fee (if required)

☐ Dhs.30 – typing fee

Procedure

Location Department of Naturalization and Residency   Map ref **7-B4**

Hours Sun – Thurs 07:30 – 19:30

- Go to any typing office
- Have the typist fill in the application form; pay all fees to typist
- At the DNRD office go to the Empost counter to fill out the delivery form and collect the delivery sticker
- An authorised representative of the company must submit all documents, including the Empost sticker at the Residence Section
- After submitting documents, keep the Empost receipt
- Approximately five days later, Empost will deliver the passport with residence permit to your place of work
- For urgent applications, the process can be completed on the same day. Make sure to specify that it's urgent beforehand

Related Procedures

- Applying For A Labour Card, p.28
- Taking The Medical Test, p.26
- Applying for a Work Permit & Employment Visa, p.22
- Notarising & Attesting Documents, p.9

Visas

Residence Permit (Work)

Residence Permit (Family)

Sponsoring Family And/Or A Maid

1 Overview

Family As an employee of a Dubai-based company, you can sponsor your family so that they can live here – as long as you meet certain requirements. Depending on your company and the conditions of your contract, it may be you who is responsible for taking care of family sponsorship procedures.

Sponsor The working 'head of the family' will be the sponsor for his/her spouse and children, and will have to apply for residence permits for them (although occasionally your company will do this for you). It is usually the man who will sponsor his family; only those women working in certain categories (teachers, doctors and nurses) are permitted to sponsor their husbands and children.

Work Spouses and unmarried daughters over 18 years of age, who are on a family residence permit, are allowed to work in Dubai. While no employment visa or permit is required if they work, they must have a labour card. An advantage for those working while on family sponsorship is that they can not be 'banned' if they choose to change their employment while in Dubai.

Maid Those who wish to hire a full-time maid may do so as long as the correct requirements are met. The administrative costs are higher than sponsoring family members, but the actual procedure is more-or-less the same.

Law Sharing Maids?

Unless your domestic helper is sponsored by a specialised maid service you are not allowed to hire a maid who is not on your sponsorship. In other words, 'borrowing' someone else's maid is against the law.

Info How To Find A Maid

There are numerous specialised companies in Dubai that offer services ranging from cleaning to babysitting on a regular or one-off basis, and others which offer recruitment of maids from overseas. Those bringing domestic help from abroad will assist you with the entire procedure. Word of mouth may also help you discover women on their husband's sponsorship who are providing cleaning services.

Residence Permit (Family)

Obtaining A Residence Permit For Family

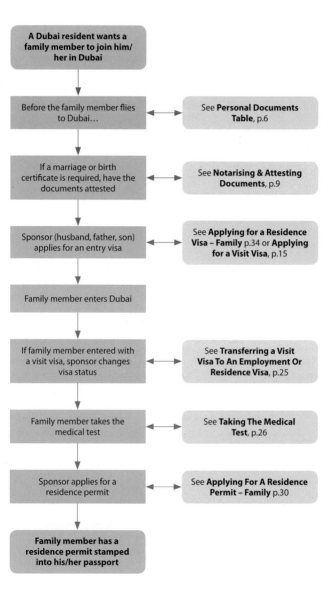

A Dubai resident wants a family member to join him/her in Dubai

Before the family member flies to Dubai…

See **Personal Documents Table**, p.6

If a marriage or birth certificate is required, have the documents attested

See **Notarising & Attesting Documents**, p.9

Sponsor (husband, father, son) applies for an entry visa

See **Applying for a Residence Visa – Family** p.34 or **Applying for a Visit Visa**, p.15

Family member enters Dubai

If family member entered with a visit visa, sponsor changes visa status

See **Transferring a Visit Visa To An Employment Or Residence Visa**, p.25

Family member takes the medical test

See **Taking The Medical Test**, p.26

Sponsor applies for a residence permit

See **Applying For A Residence Permit – Family** p.30

Family member has a residence permit stamped into his/her passport

Residence Permit (Family)

Applying For A Residence Entry Visa – Family

1 Overview

Family There are certain conditions that must be met in order to sponsor your family. The most important of these is that you meet the minimum monthly salary requirement (Dhs.4,000, or Dhs.3,500 plus housing). For further conditions, see Prerequisites (opposite).

This is a two-step process, beginning with a residence visa application. A residence visa is a one-time entry permit, allowing the family member to enter the country. A residence permit must then be applied for, allowing longer term residency (up to three years) in Dubai.

Maid The head of the family is permitted to sponsor one maid. The following must be provided to the domestic helper:

- Airfare to home country at least once every two years

- Housing, electricity and air-conditioning

- Generally, salary paid to the maid varies between Dhs.800 plus food to Dhs.1,500 per month

The steps in sponsoring a maid involve applying for a residence visa, then a residence permit, the validity of which is one year. Domestic helpers are not covered by the UAE labour law and thus do not need a labour card.

 A family is permitted to sponsor only one maid, unless the sponsor's salary and family size allow for an additional maid.

Fees In addition, the sponsor must pay a 'maid tax' of Dhs.4,800 yearly. Administration fees, a medical examination, and health card fees are also to be paid to the government, adding up to at least Dhs.6,000 annually.

Validity
- Entry must be made within two months of date of issue

- Valid for 60 days from date of entry

- Application for residence permit must occur within 60 days of entry

 Once resident, you may not stay outside of the UAE for a period longer than six months, or your residency will lapse. This is particularly relevant to children studying abroad who are on their parents' sponsorship, and wives who choose to have their baby outside of Dubai. (See Temporary Entry Permit, p.42)

Tip **Family Sponsorship From A Visit Visa**

If a family member has already entered the country on a visit visa and then wishes to become resident in Dubai, the sponsor must first apply for a residence visa. Once that has been approved, he/she can either make a visa change trip (see Visa Run, p.19) and re-enter the country with the correct visa; or pay Dhs.500 without having to leave the country.

Residence Permit (Family)

2 Prerequisites

- Sponsor is resident, working in Dubai, and earns a minimum salary according to ministry regulations

Female Sponsor
- Women who wish to sponsor a family member need special permission from the ministry. In general, this privilege is given only to doctors, nurses and teachers.

Family
- Immediate family members only (including sponsor's parents)
- Daughter is unmarried
- Son is under 18 years of age

Maid
- The sponsor's monthly salary is higher than Dhs.6,000
- The maid is not a relative
- Generally, the maid should not be of the same nationality, although in special circumstances this may be allowed – check with your embassy for additional requirements
- The maid is under 60 years of age
- The sponsor and his family both live in Dubai
- The sponsor has not sponsored another maid during the past year

3 What To Bring

- ☐ Completed application form from a typing office located near the Immigration Department
- ☐ Passport of family member or maid (copy)
- ☐ Passport of sponsor (original and copy)
- ☐ Labour contract of sponsor (original and copy)
- ☐ Two passport photos (white background)

Fees
- ☐ Dhs.100 – service charge
- ☐ Dhs.100 – urgent receipt (optional)
- ☐ Dhs.20 – visa registration fee (at airport)

Parents
- ☐ A letter from the consulate/embassy of your home country in the UAE stating that the parent is under your care and responsibility
- ☐ A one-year health insurance policy for the parent

Fees
- ☐ Dhs.5,000 security bank deposit

Maid
- ☐ Two passport photos (white background)

4 Procedure

Location Department of Naturalization and Residency   Map ref 7-B4

Hours Sun – Thurs 07:30 – 19:30

- Submit all relevant documents at the Family Entry Permit Counter (if sponsoring a maid, go to the next counter)
- You will be given the visa then and there

- Send a copy of the visa to the family member or maid
- Deposit the original at the visa counter in the airport (next to the arrivals hall) at least two hours before the arrival of the visitor and have the copy stamped
- Pay the visa registration fee (Dhs.20) at the same counter
- The visitor will exchange their copy of the visa for the original upon arrival at the Immigration desk in the airport
- The family member must now take the medical test (p.26) and apply for a residence permit (next page)

5 Related Procedures

- Applying For A Residence Permit – Family, p.37
- Taking The Medical Test, p.26
- Transferring a Visit Visa To An Employment Or Residence Visa, p.25

Info | **Sole Custody**

If you have sole custody of your child and wish to sponsor him/her, you will need some additional documentation.

In addition to the original attested birth certificate, you will need a letter from the non-custodial parent. The letter should include the following:

- Child's name (as per passport & birth certificate)
- Child's nationality
- Child's passport number
- Mention that the non-custodial parent has no objection to the child living with the custodial parent and residing in the UAE

The letter must be endorsed by the legal authority that issued the sole custody, and attested.

Residence Permit (Family)

Applying For A Residence Permit – Family

1 Overview

This is the third step (second being the medical test, p.26) in sponsoring either a family member or maid. The residence permit will allow the person to live in Dubai for a limited period of time (one to three years). The sponsor is responsible for all paperwork and costs related to this procedure.

If you need to register your newborn child, see p.43 first.

Validity One to three years, limited to length of time remaining on sponsor's residence permit

2 Prerequisites

- The family member or maid has entered the country with a residence or visit visa (see Applying for a Residence Visa – Family, p.34, or Visas, p.10)
- The family member or maid has passed the medical test (see Taking The Medical Test, p.26)

3 What To Bring

☐ Applicant's passport (original and copy)

☐ Two passport photos for each applicant and the sponsor

☐ Residence visa with the entry stamp (original) (see Applying for a Residence Visa – Family, p.34)

☐ Sponsor's passport (original and copy)

☐ Sponsor's labour contract (original and copy)

Spouse ☐ Attested marriage certificate (original and copy) (see Notarising & Attesting Documents, p.9)

Child ☐ Attested birth certificate (original and copy) (see Notarising & Attesting Documents, p.9)

Parent ☐ A letter from the consulate/embassy of the parent's home country in the UAE stating that the parent is under the sponsor's care and responsibility

Over 18 ☐ Medical test result (original) (see Taking The Medical Test, p.26)

Maid ☐ Three passport photos of the maid

Fees ☐ Dhs.370 – residence permit application fee (family)

☐ Dhs.5,080 – residence permit application fee (maid)

☐ Dhs.100 – urgent application fee (optional)

☐ Dhs.50 – typing fee

4 Procedure

Location Department of Naturalization and Residency Map ref **7-B4**

Hours Sun – Thurs 07:30 – 19:30

- At any typist's office, have the application form for your family or maid completed.
- Pay the residence permit application fee to the typist.
- If the child is on the mother's passport, add the child's name to the mother's application form and pay an additional Dhs.370 per child
- At the DNRD office go to the Empost counter to fill out the delivery form and collect the delivery sticker
- Submit all documents at the Residence Counter
- Documents will be couriered to the sponsor by Empost within five days
- The process can be completed on the same day if the application is urgent, but mention that it's a matter of urgency beforehand

5 Related Procedures

- Transferring From Father To Husband Sponsorship, p.41
- Obtaining A Labour Card When On Family Sponsorship, p.39
- Registering A Newborn Child, p.43
- Applying For A Driving Licence, p.122

Info **Sponsoring a Newborn**

If you have a child while living in Dubai, the newborn will need to be registered with both the UAE government and your home country embassy before you can process their residence permit. See p.43 for the procedure.

Info **Your Baby's Health Card**

If your child was born in a government hospital, you can apply for a health card on the premises. Just take all documents (photographs are not required) to the Information Desk, pay the fee and you'll receive a temporary health card for your child.

Residence Permit (Family)

Obtaining A Labour Card When On Family Sponsorship

1 Overview

If you are on a family residence permit (i.e. on your father's or husband's sponsorship) and you find a job in Dubai, your employer (not your sponsor) will need to apply for a labour card for you. The costs for this procedure should be paid by the employer.

Labour Contract Before a labour card is issued, a labour contract must be signed. This is a standard form issued by the labour authorities detailing your employment information. This contract is printed in both Arabic and English, and as the Arabic version prevails in a court of law, it's advisable to have the Arabic contract reviewed and translated prior to signing.

Validity One year

2 Prerequisites

- Applicant is on family sponsorship
- Applicant has signed the employment contract

3 What To Bring

Ministry of Labour Envelope
- ☐ Applicant's passport (copy)
- ☐ Residence page in passport (copy)
- ☐ Official labour contract, signed and stamped
- ☐ Two passport photos (white background)
- ☐ If applicable, attested degree(s) (see Notarising & Attesting Documents, p.9)
- ☐ Establishment labour card (copy) (see Applying For An Establishment Labour Card, p.255)
- ☐ Trade licence of employer (copy)
- ☐ Sponsor's passport (copy)

Fees
- ☐ Dhs.200 – labour contract and application fee
- ☐ Dhs.1,000-Dhs.3,000 – labour approval fee
- ☐ Dhs.40 – typing fee (including labour envelope and sticker)

4 Procedure

Location Any Typing Office

Hours Various Hours
- Go to any typing office
- Have the typist fill in the official labour contract, and pay the application fee

- Both the employer and employee must sign and stamp the contract
- Place all required documents into the labour envelope
- Submit the envelope at the typing office or any post office
- You will be given a submission receipt – keep it
- Upon approval, return to the same typing office or post office and pay the labour approval fee
- The labour card and contract will be sent to your company's PO Box

5 Related Procedure

- Transferring From Father To Husband Sponsorship, p.41

Info Freelance

Dubai Media City's 'Media Business Centre' has made it possible to work as a freelance professional in Dubai by providing the necessary sponsorship and paperwork.

You can get a freelance permit and 'hot desk' space if you fall under one of the various freelance categories, which basically include artists, editors, directors, writers, engineers, producers, photographers/camera operators and technicians in the fields of film, TV, music, radio and print media.

The permit includes a residence visa and access to 10 shared work stations. You will also get to use a shared PO Box address and fax line.

You must spend a minimum of three hours per week at the hot desk, but no more than three hours per day.

Documents required:
- Business plan
- CV
- Bank reference letter
- Portfolio/work samples
- Passport copy

Costs:
- Dhs.5,000 security deposit (refundable)
- Dhs.5,000 joining fee (one-off payment)
- Dhs.8,000 annual permit fee
- Dhs.4,000 annual membership fee
- Dhs.1,500 annual employee sponsorship fee

For more information on getting a DMC freelance permit, visit their website (www.dubaimediacity.com) or call 04 391 4555.

Residence Permit (Family)

Transferring From Father's To Husband's Sponsorship

1 Overview

A woman residing in Dubai under her father's sponsorship who marries a man resident in Dubai, must transfer her sponsorship.

2 Prerequisites

- Husband is resident in Dubai
- Husband earns a minimum monthly salary of Dhs.3,500
- At time of marriage, the woman is on her father's sponsorship

3 What To Bring

☐ Father's passport (original and copy)

☐ Husband's passport (original and copy)

☐ Wife's passport (original and copy)

☐ Attested marriage certificate (original and copy) (see p.9)

☐ Original medical test results (see p.26)

☐ Four passport photos of wife (white background)

☐ Labour contract (original and copy)

☐ If husband is an employee, his employment contract (copy)

☐ If husband is a partner in a company, trade licence (copy) and a 'To whom it may concern' certificate issued by the DED

Fees ☐ Dhs.530 – transfer fee

☐ Dhs.100 – urgent fee (optional)

4 Procedure

Location Department of Naturalization and Residency   Map ref 7-B4

Hours Sun – Thurs 07:30 – 19:30

- Go to a typing office, submit all relevant documents and have the typist fill in the sponsorship transfer application form
- Enter the DNRD and go to the Empost counter to fill out the delivery form. Collect the delivery stickers
- Submit all typing documents and Empost sticker to the Visa Transfer Counter
- The approved application will then be sent via Empost
- Once the sponsorship has been transferred, the wife must apply for a residence permit (see p.37)

5 Related Procedures

- Taking The Medical Test, p.26
- Applying For A Residence Permit – Family, p.37
- Obtaining A Labour Card When On Family Sponsorship, p.39

Info **Temporary Entry Permit**

If a family member has been out of the country for a period longer than six months, the residence permit is officially cancelled. The sponsor may, however, apply for a temporary entry permit that will waive the cancellation and allow the 'absconded' person to enter Dubai.

This situation may occur, for example, when a wife delivers a child in her home country. In this case, the husband must go to the Incoming/Outgoing Department on the first floor of the Department of Naturalization and Residency. He will submit a 'green card', which is a Dhs.100 receipt from an 'e-Dirham' bank (see p.217), his original passport and a copy of it and his wife's passport copy. He must fax her a copy of the visa, but there is no need to deposit the visa at the airport. Entry into Dubai must occur within 14 days from the date of issue.

Residence Permit (Family)

Registering A Newborn Child

1 Overview

If you wish to get a residence permit for your child, you must first register the child with the concerned authorities. If the child was born in Dubai, the child must be registered with the embassy/consulate and have a passport (or be entered in the mother's passport). If the child was born outside Dubai, the foreign birth certificate must first be attested by the UAE Ministry of Foreign Affairs.

In general, it is the father who will attend to all the paperwork, as he will be the sponsor and will need to sign all related documents.

If a child born in Dubai has neither a visa nor a residence permit, the child may not leave the country under any circumstances.

Timing Arrangements for a residence permit for a baby born in the UAE must occur within four months (120 days) of the baby's date of birth.

If you fail to register the baby on time, the legal guardian must pay a fine of Dhs.100 per day until registration is complete.

2 Prerequisites

- Father is resident in Dubai
- Father is eligible to sponsor a child (minimum total monthly salary of Dhs.4,000)
- Child will live in Dubai

3 What To Bring

- ☐ Attested birth certificate (see Obtaining a Birth Certificate, p.183, and Notarising & Attesting Documents, p.9)
- ☐ At least three passport photos of the child with the eyes open
- ☐ Both parents' passports (original and copy)
- ☐ If father's name is not indicated in the mother's passport, attested marriage certificate (original and copy)

Fees
- ☐ Dhs.10 – Ministry of Health attestation charge (exact change)
- ☐ Dhs.150 per document (1 English, 1 Arabic) – Ministry of Foreign Affairs attestation charge (exact change)

4 Procedure

Location Embassy/Consulate (see Directory, p.283)   Map ref **Various**

Hours Normally 08:00 - 13:00

- Contact your embassy or consulate to determine specific requirements regarding registration of the child and application for a passport

- With all required documents, go to your embassy or consulate to register the birth in your home country and apply for the child's passport

Location Ministry of Foreign Affairs   Map ref **8-F4**

Hours Sun – Thurs 08:30 – 12:00

- Submit all documents at the counter in the room you are directed to, and have them stamped
- Pay the attestation charge at the cashier (same room, counter 3)
- Give the documents (Arabic and English birth certificates) to the person at counter 5, room 5
- He will then sign the documents
- Double check to ensure you have been given the correct documents
- This office is very small. Expect long queues.

Location Department of Naturalization and Residency   Map ref **7-B4**

Hours Sun – Thurs 07:30 – 19:30

- Upon receipt of the child's passport and within four months of birth, start immigration procedures for your child (see Applying for a Residence Visa – Family, p.37)

5 Related Procedure

- Applying For A Residence Visa – Family, p.37

Work It Out

Working in a new country can bring on a little bit of a culture shock, especially when you have to get used to having Sunday lunch on a Friday and getting Monday morning blues on a Sunday.

To find out more about living and working in Dubai, finding a job, employment packages and contracts, check out the Residents chapter of the *Dubai Explorer – The Complete Residents' Guide* available in all leading bookshops and supermarkets.

Residence Permit (Family)

Tip | **Getting Help With Those Visa Issues**

Dubai's Ministry of Interior, Naturalisation and Residency Administration, has entered into a partnership with DNATA Agencies to provide assistance with visas. The DNATA Travel outlet near Clock Tower in Deira offers speedy issuance and renewal of residence visas, as well as issuance and cancellation of visit visas.

Info | **Cancelling Your Visa**

Your visa and how you cancel it will depend on the type of document you have. If you're here working, you're more than likely to be on a residence visa that has been sponsored by your employer. In such cases, as soon as your employment ends, so does your privilege to a work visa. Just as your employer would have been responsible for sorting out your paperwork, it is their responsibility to cancel it.

There's not much paper work involved, you'll have to submit your passport and sometimes sign a waiver or a memorandum of understanding clarifying that you have received all monies owed to you and so on.

If you are in Dubai on a spousal visa, and have – for example – separated or just need to leave, you will need the help of your husband or wife to cancel your status. Again your spouse's company will have completed the paperwork, and they will accordingly get their employee (your husband or wife) to sign off on the cancellation papers.

The whole process takes about five days – whichever visa you happen to be on – and is reasonably smooth sailing.

UAE ID Card

Applying For A National Identity Card

1 Overview

In 2006, the UAE Federal Government announced plans to implement a national identity card that would combine a resident's driving licence, labour card, health card and e-gate card into a single ID card. By the end of 2010, all residents will have to register for the Emirates ID programme. The National ID will eventually act as the only acceptable form of identification in many situations, including all bank and government procedures.

2 Prerequisites

- Applicant is a UAE resident and at least 15 years old

3 What To Bring

- ☐ Completed pre-registration form
- ☐ Passport with residence permit (original)
- ☐ Dhs.100-Dhs.300 – Emirates ID fee, Dhs.100, plus another Dhs.100 for each additional full year left on your residence permit

4 Procedure

Emirates Identity Authority Service Center   Map ref **Various**

Sun – Thurs 07:30 – 20:30, Sat 08:00 – 14:00

- Log on to www.emiratesid.ae and download the pre-registration application or go to any post office and pick up an application form for Dhs.40
- Fill out the form completely and print two copies, one of which you will keep
- Book an appointment by calling 800 52 3432, or by logging on to www.emiratesid.ae and using the online booking system
- On the day of your appointment, head to the assigned EIDA Service Center with the completed pre-registration form, your original passport and the required fee. Even if you have an appointment, expect very long queues
- Submit your documents and have your fingerprints recorded and photo taken
- Your ID card will be sent to you via Empost within 14 days

5 Related Procedure

- Applying For A Work Permit & Employment Visa, p.22

UAE ID Registration Centres		
Area	Location	Phone
Al Barsha	Next to Jebel Ali Horse Racing Arena	04 383 2223
Al Karama	Inside the Karama Central Post Building	04 334 2055
Al Rashidiya	Behind Al Rashidiya Council Building	04 284 5252

Web Update

While Dubai's government is committed to cutting back on the red-tape involved in setting up in Dubai, both for individuals and businesses, changes in rules and regulations are inevitable. Therefore, if there have been any changes or additions to the procedures included in this book they will appear on the Explorer website. Just log on to **www.liveworkexplore.com** and click on the Red-Tape link. This page will tell you if there have been any changes to specific procedures – giving you the heads up before you head off to plough through Dubai's administrative maze.

Moving?

Contact us at: enquiry@relogulf.com
Or call the team on: 04 5015748

Housing

Overview

How Do I Get Settled Into A New Home In Dubai?

Tip **Home Sweet Home**

There are number of popular residential areas in Dubai, all with their own set of pros and cons, be they price, space or amenities. If you are trying to decide where to lay your hat then check out the Residential Areas section within the Residents chapter of the *Dubai Explorer – The Complete Residents' Guide* available in all leading bookshops and supermarkets.

Overview

Housing

Since the opening of the property market to foreigners in 2002, the city has witnessed both an incredible boom and a crushing correction. From 2002 to 2008, property prices skyrocketed and new freehold developments were constantly being announced. By the end of 2008, however, most of those inflated prices fell dramatically. The future of property in Dubai is uncertain and the correction of 2008 serves as a stark reminder that investments of any kind must be carefully thought out. In this chapter, you'll find some basic guidelines to purchasing freehold property in Dubai and obtaining a mortgage.

Should you decide that buying property is not right for you, this chapter also has a section on renting a home in Dubai – from finding a suitable property to signing the lease.

Water & Electricity

Once you've secured a place to live, utilities need to be hooked up. All procedures relating to water and electricity are listed, from connecting a service and reconnecting it if you've forgotten to pay your bills, to disconnecting services if you're leaving Dubai.

The Dubai Electricity & Water Authority, known as DEWA, provides electricity, water supply and sewerage services. This government department provides excellent service, and shortages or stoppages are rare. The head office is modern and service is swift and efficient. DEWA has been awarded numerous prizes for customer service and its drive for greater efficiency. Following the e-government initiative, DEWA's website (www.dewa.gov.ae) offers various services to consumers, provided you have the correct encryption software.

Gas

As there is no real procedure involved with obtaining gas for your stove, this chapter includes a quick overview of the subject, including costs and a list of the main gas suppliers in Dubai. Make the call and you'll have gas hooked up in your home within an hour.

Tip — Moving Tips

- Book moving dates well in advance
- Don't forget insurance – purchase additional insurance for irreplaceable items
- Make an inventory of the items you want moved (and keep your own copy)
- Ensure everything is packed extremely well and in a way that can be checked by customs and repacked with the least possible damage; check and sign the packing list
- Keep a camera handy to take pictures at each stage of the move (valuable in case of a dispute)
- Do not pack restricted goods of any kind
- Ensure videos, DVDs and books are not offensive to Muslim sensibilities

Info — Expert Help

Removal Companies

Unless you send your personal belongings with the airline you are flying on, you will need a removal company. A company with a wide international network is usually the best and safest option. Most offer free consultations, advice, and samples of packing materials.

Relocation Experts

Relocation experts help you settle into your new life overseas as quickly and painlessly as possible. Assistance includes finding accommodation and a school for your children. They may also offer advice on the way of life in the city, and put you in touch with social networks.

Info — Customs

It is normal for customs to search your shipment. You will be asked to remain present while the authorities open your boxes to ensure nothing illegal or inappropriate is brought into the country.

Moving

Shipping Your Personal Belongings

1 Overview

The two main options when moving your belongings to or from Dubai are air and sea freight. Air freight is best for moving small amounts, whereas sea freight is better (and cheaper) for larger consignments. Booking an entire container reduces the amount of handling your goods are subjected to, but obviously some destinations are not easily accessible by sea.

2 Prerequisites

- You are moving to Dubai from overseas, or leaving Dubai for another country, and wish to ship your belongings.

3 What To Bring

If collecting goods shipped to Dubai:

☐ Airway bill/tracking number

☐ Passport (and copy)

If you are picking goods up for someone else:

☐ An authorisation letter written and signed by the owner

☐ Copy of their passport and your own

4 Procedure

If collecting goods shipped by air:

Location Dubai Cargo Village (04 211 1111)   Map ref 9-A7

Hours 24hrs

- Call ahead, quoting the airway bill or tracking number, to confirm that your shipment has arrived
- Take the airway bill or tracking number to the desk to locate your shipment
- Pay fees:

Delivery cost	Dhs.100
Handling cost	Dhs.20 (for 200kg and less); Dhs.0.10 for every kilogram over 200kg

- Take your invoice to the customs desk (04 282 8888) with your airway bill number or tracking number
- Your shipment will be searched by customs officers
- Depending on the agreement you have with the removal company, either their representative in Dubai will help you transport the boxes, or you can make arrangements locally

moving?

relax.
we carry the load. _{SM}

Door to door moving with Allied Pickfords

Allied Pickfords is one of the largest and most respected providers of moving services in the world, handling over 50,000 international moves every year.

We believe that nothing reduces stress more than trust, and each year thousands of families trust Allied Pickfords to move them. With over 800 offices in more than 40 countries, we're the specialists in international moving and have the ability to relocate you anywhere anytime. Move with Allied to Allied worldwide.

Call us now on +971 4 408 9555
www.alliedpickfords.com
general@alliedpickfords.ae

Renting

Renting A Home

1 Overview

Renting a property is a popular option for expat residents in Dubai. Rent is often paid on an annual or biannual basis with postdated cheques, although more and more landlords are accepting more cheques in return for a higher leasing price. For new residents, this advance payment can create difficulties, but some companies pay the landlord directly and deduct the rent from your salary on a monthly basis. Alternatively, banks are usually willing to offer loans (although there are many variables and you will need to show your local salary transfer going into your account for three months). As cheques must be local, a bank account is a prerequisite to renting a home. 'Bouncing' cheques is a criminal offence here, and can result in a jail term, so make sure you have enough money in your account when your cheques are due. Be aware that rentals are now regulated by the Real Estate Regulatory Agency (RERA). As a result, all tenancy agreements need to be processed through the Land Department. If using a real estate broker, he or she will do this for you. If you are renting directly from the landlord, be sure the contract you sign is official. Otherwise, it will be difficult to file any official claim if there is a dispute.

Additional Rental Costs

- Refundable water and electricity deposit (see p.71)
- Real estate commission (5% of annual rent in a one-off payment)
- Maintenance charge (depends on location, often paid by landlord)
- Municipality tax (now called a housing fee and added to your monthly DEWA bill) (5% of annual rent)
- Refundable rental security deposit (Dhs.2,000 – Dhs.5,000)
- In some cases, a damage deposit is also required (usually a fully refundable, one-off payment)

RERA Law

- Landlords cannot raise the yearly rent more than 5% of the rent amount for the first two years of occupancy
- Tenancy contracts must be completed on the standard 'Form G' provided by the land department (www.rpdubai.ae)

2 Prerequisites

- Dubai bank account
- Residence permit (and copy)

3 What To Bring

Individual
- ☐ Passport (and copy)
- ☐ No objection letter (NOC) from employer
- ☐ Salary certificate (copy)

☐ Rent cheque (or agreed-upon number of post-dated cheques covering the remaining period of the lease)

☐ Deposit

☐ Real estate commission

☐ Valid trade licence (copy)

☐ Passport of the person signing the rent cheque (copy)

4 Procedure

- Find a home you like
- Try to negotiate the rent and terms
- Read the lease agreement thoroughly to be aware of termination, damage, subletting, liability clauses and other factors, that may affect you
- Sign the RERA-certified lease
- Hand over the rent cheque(s), deposit and commission

5 Related Procedures

- Connecting Water And Electricity, p.64
- Purchasing Gas, p.73
- Applying For A Telephone Line, p.78

Housing

Renting

Info Lease Termination

Security Deposit
Before returning your security deposit, the landlord may ask you to submit final utilities bills and/or clearance certificates (see p.70 and p.72).

Damage Deposit
When vacating the premises, return the villa or apartment in the same condition as you received it. Likewise, the villa or apartment should be both clean and freshly painted before you move in.

Home Improvements
If you have made 'improvements' to your home, do not expect the landlord to compensate you for your investments; on the contrary, you may be asked to compensate the landlord to return the home to its original condition.

Info Expert Help

For advice on rent disputes, you can approach the Rent Committee which is located in the Dubai Land Department building opposite the Sheraton Hotel in Deira. Opening hours are from 07:30 – 14:30. Take your passport copy, tenancy contract and any correspondence regarding the lease with you. Visit www.rpdubai.com for more information.

Buying

Buying A Home

1 | Overview

Currently, non-GCC Nationals are permitted to own land only in certain property developments, but the number of 'freehold' developments has increased dramatically in the past few years. The past few years has also seen an increase in government regulation in the real estate market. New laws have made the market safer for individual investors and more difficult for fraudulent agents and developers. The Land Department offshoot that has been put in place to oversee these laws is the Real Estate Regulatory Agency, or RERA (www.rpdubai.ae).

Where to buy property and who to buy from depends on your reason for buying. If your purchase is purely for investment reasons, you may choose to buy an unfinished property 'off-plan' directly from a developer. If you're looking for a home to live in, you might instead choose to purchase a finished property from the secondary market. In that case, you'll be dealing directly with a real estate agency. All property transactions must be registered with RERA and must involve a RERA-registered real estate agent.

After deciding where and with whom to invest, you must decide whether you need to apply for a mortgage (p.60). Most banks offer mortgage services, so shop around for the best deal. Keep in mind that some developments can only be financed by certain mortgage providers, so be sure to ask the developer or real estate agent which banks you can use.

If you're in the position to pay for a property without a mortgage, you can often use that as a bargaining chip, especially for secondary sales.

What Is Freehold?

As the owner of a freehold property, you are the absolute owner of the property and the land it is on for the duration of your life. You have the right to sell the property to another owner, or to pass it on to somebody in your will, after your death.

In Dubai, many developers include a clause in the agreement that requires a property owner to get the developer's consent before selling the property to a third party.

Even though the owner of a freehold property is the absolute owner of the buildings and the land, he or she must still follow any laws and regulations controlling the property. For example, there may be regulations preventing you from painting the exterior of your house a different colour, and you may have to use approved service companies.

For New Or Uncompleted Property (If You're Buying Off Plan):

• Register your interest by contacting the relevant developer

• Visit the developer's office, and decide on a suitable payment plan.

• Pay deposit and claim contract

For Property Already Built:

- Find a reliable real estate agent to help you negotiate the contract – be sure the agent is RERA registered
- Once a property and price is decided on, have your agent write up a letter of intent, outlining the terms of the deal
- At the time of signing the letter of intent, put a deposit on the property. This deposit will be held by the real estate agent until the final transfer is made
- All final contracts must be made at the Land Department

Other Costs Involved In Buying a Home

- Brokerage fees, usually 2% of the total sale price
- Transfer fees paid to RERA, currently 2% of the total sale price
- Mortgage fees (p.60)
- Mandatory maintenance fees to be paid to developer

To avoid any nasty surprises, always ask about these costs before you sign anything, and clarify what they cover.

Homeowner's Visa

The laws concerning homeowner's residence visas have recently changed. For a homeowner to be eligible for the renewable six month multiple-entry visa, the property must be worth at least a million dirhams and the homeowner must prove an income of at least Dhs.10,000 per month. This visa is not an employment permit, but family members can be included.

Housing

Buying

Info **Secondary Market**

It makes sense to use a well-known agency if you are buying a resale property. As the seller, you are (usually) required to get permission from the developers to sell your house. Developers can no longer charge a transfer fee, but they often charge a service fee (on top of the 2% transfer fee) to transfer the property through the land department.

Law **Legal Advice**

Despite laws that clarify the meaning of 'freehold', restrictions on properties remain and most developments require payments of annual service charges and significant transfer fees when you sell. Disagreements often arise between parties so it is important to seek legal advice from a firm specialising in real estate law. Hadef & Partners (www.hadefpartners.com) has a dedicated Real Estate department.

Buying

Obtaining A Mortgage

1 Overview

Since the property market saw a major correction at the end of 2008, mortgage lending regulations have been changing. Each bank maintains different requirements for mortgages, so be sure to find a bank that works for your situation. Also remember that some developments can only be financed by certain banks – check with the developer to see which banks are compatible. Currently, few banks are willing to lend more than 70% of the value of the property.

2 Prerequisites

- Applicant is between the ages of 21 and 65 years
- Applicant has had fulltime employment for a minimum of three years
- Applicant's sponsoring company has been in operation for at least three years
- Insurance policy covering the property and the life of the person responsible for mortgage payment
- Confirmation from the developers or management company that your property has been reserved

3 What To Bring

- ☐ Passport (original and copy)
- ☐ Labour card (original and copy)
- ☐ Salary certificate
- ☐ Bank statements for the last year
- ☐ Letter from your bank confirming you have no outstanding loans
- ☐ Registration form with the reserved plot

4 Procedure

- Contact the financing office linked with the property
- Agree on the financing details
- Obtain pre-approval document, stating how much the bank is willing to lend
- Sign a letter of intent with the seller, pay the deposit
- Bring the signed letter of intent back to the bank
- Submit all documents and sign the relevant paperwork
- Once a holding deposit has been paid, your mortgage will be processed

Nearly all developers ask for a 10% deposit to reserve a property. The balance of the purchase price should then be paid in instalments during the construction of the property (unless it is not a new property). The final instalment is due when you take possession of the property. If you change your mind and wish to withdraw from the purchase, you may stand to lose most or all of the money that you have already paid during the construction phase. At the very least, you will have to pay a penalty of 1% of the purchase price.

Tip	Keep Up To Date

Being relatively new, the area of property ownership for non-Nationals is constantly changing and evolving. Be sure to check with the developers you are dealing with that you have all the latest information. Other good resources are the property pages in the local papers, magazines like *Property Weekly*, and the RERA website (www.rpdubai.ae).

Housing

Buying

Buying

Registering A Property

1 Overview

In order for the 'full' transfer of ownership of the property to the investor to take place, the transfer needs to be completed through the Dubai Land Department (www.rpdubai.ae). Most developers will complete this procedure for you, regardless of whether you're buying off-plan or a completed property. If you find that you have to register your property on your own, be sure to double check with the Land Department before your appointment as procedures often change.

2 Prerequisites

- An agreement of sale will have been reached
- The developer has acknowledged full payment of property

3 What To Bring

☐ Passport (original and copy)

☐ NOC letter from developer stating that full payment has been made

☐ Contract (original and one copy)

☐ The seller will present the certificate of property ownership (which includes the map location of the property)

☐ Service fee – (up to 2% of sale price)

4 Procedure

Location Dubai Land Department   Map ref 8-H4

Hours Sun – Thurs 07:30-14:30

- The buyer and seller, or their appointed representatives, go to one of the service windows at the Land Department and tell the member of staff that they want to register a sale of property
- The buyer presents his passport copy and full contact details
- The buyer and seller proceed to the registration room where the seller will receive payment from the buyer for the amount of the sale in the presence of a Land Department official
- The details of the sale are entered into an electronic form which is printed and signed by both parties. This will register the sale with the department
- Pay the service fee to the cashier
- The new title is issued in the buyer's name, along with a map location of the property

Housing

Buying

Water & Electricity

Connecting Water & Electricity

1 Overview

DEWA (Dubai Electricity & Water Authority) is the only supplier of water and electricity in Dubai.

Before moving into a property, you will have to connect the water and electricity supply. Most premises are registered and connected by the landlord upon completion of construction, and then disconnected until the tenant moves in. Therefore, DEWA considers the procedure outlined below a 'reconnection' of the service.

The person named on the tenancy agreement will be regarded as the consumer by DEWA.

Accounts cannot be transferred from one tenant to another without prior settlement of the final bill.

Accounts cannot be transferred between premises.

2 Prerequisites

- Premises have been connected before and there is a consumer account number (see opposite)

3 What To Bring

- ☐ Passport (original and copy)
- ☐ Consumer account number
- ☐ Tenancy agreement (copy)

Security Deposit
- ☐ Apartment – Dhs.1,000
- ☐ Villa – Dhs.2,000

Reconnection Fees
- ☐ Small meter – Dhs.30
- ☐ Large meter – Dhs.100

4 Procedure

Location DEWA Head Office or branches   (Map ref 7-D8)

Hours Sun – Thurs 07:30 – 20:30

- Pick up the Security Deposit/Change of Address application form from the frontline service counter at the DEWA office
- Complete the form in English or Arabic
- Submit all documents at the frontline service counter to determine the required security deposit
- Submit the application form and pay both the determined security deposit and reconnection charge at the cashier

Ensure that the name on the security deposit receipt is that of the person authorised to collect the security deposit refund. Keep this receipt for future reference and to claim the security deposit when you move out of the premises.

5 Related Procedures

- Paying For Water & Electricity, p.66
- Reconnecting Service (When Service Is Cut Off), p.68
- Disconnecting Service & Settling Accounts, p.70

Info Consumer Account Number

The consumer account number is a unique nine digit reference number that is assigned permanently to each premises. You will need this number for every transaction made with DEWA. The account number can be found:

- With the landlord or the real estate agent
- On the tenancy agreement
- On the DEWA number plate next to the front door or near the meter

Info Online Utilities Connection

Connection ('reconnection') can be arranged online at http://e-services.dewa.gov.ae. You will need access to a high-speed connection (ADSL) as well as a fax machine or scanner.

Follow the prompts, pay with your credit card, and you will receive a security deposit receipt number. Write this number on your tenancy agreement, then either fax it to 324 9345 or scan and upload it to the same site. Your utilities will be connected the same day.

Info Contact DEWA

You can call the 24 hour DEWA Customer Care Centre on 04 601 9999 or email customercare@dewa.gov.ae. In an emergency call 991.

Water & Electricity

Paying For Water & Electricity

1 Overview

To avoid being disconnected, DEWA bills must be paid before the due date. Bills are sent monthly to your postal address.

DEWA also offers an email and SMS service notifying you of unpaid bills. Apply for this at any DEWA office or on www.dewa.gov.ae.

2 Prerequisites

- Existing DEWA account

3 What To Bring

☐ Bill or consumer account number (see DEWA Overview, p.64)

☐ Depending on chosen method of payment (see below), either cash, cheque or credit card

4 Procedure

Payment	Location	Comments
In Person		
Deposit Box	Any DEWA office	Insert bill and crossed cheque in an envelope and deposit in the box
Various Banks	Check the back of your DEWA bill to see which banks offer the service.	Note: some banks offer payment services to their customers, while others offer the service to all DEWA customers. Some charge a Dhs.10 fee
ENOC/EPPCO	Any ENOC or EPPCO petrol station	Service is available 24 hours a day, every day
Empost or Emirates Post	Any Emirates Post Office	Service is available during Empost working hours
By Post		
Mail to	DEWA, PO Box 564, Dubai	Enclose bill and crossed cheque
Online		
Log on to	www.dewa.gov.ae	View and pay bills online with a credit card or bank account. The last 13 months' bills and adjustments can be viewed

5 Related Procedure

- Consolidating Bill Statements, p.69

Info Utilities Charges

- Electricity: 20 fils per kWh (if under 2,000 kWh)
- Water: 3 fils per gallon (if under 6,000 gallons)
- Sewerage: 0.05 fils per gallon of water consumed

Info Change Of Mailing Address

Either collect and complete a 'Security Deposit/Change of Address' application form at the frontline service counter at any DEWA office, or make a change of address request by letter, fax or email. A service charge of Dhs.10 for each change of address will be debited from your account. Remember to include your consumer account number and the name of the account holder.

E Online Registration

To use DEWA's online services, you must first register. Log on to www.dewa.gov.ae and follow the prompts. You will be asked to enter at least one consumer account number or the statement account number (consolidated bills), your telephone number, email address, plus a username and password. The service will usually be activated within 24 hours. A DEWA employee may contact you to validate your information.

Once the registration has been approved, you can view and pay your DEWA bills online. Whenever a new bill has been issued, you will be informed via email. For further information about online services or for registration enquiries, contact DEWA by phone (04 601 9999) or by email (customercare@dewa.gov.ae).

Housing

Water & Electricity

Water & Electricity

Reconnecting Service (When Service Is Cut Off)

1 Overview

If you fail to pay the bill within 14 days of the due date, you will receive a reminder, then your water and electricity service will be cut off by DEWA. Once your services have been cut, you will have to go to DEWA in person to request reconnection, and pay all outstanding amounts plus a reconnection charge.

2 Prerequisites

• Services have been cut off

3 What To Bring

☐ Bill or consumer account number

☐ Outstanding amount to be paid (cash or cheque)

Fee ☐ Dhs.30 – reconnection charge (small meter)

☐ Dhs.100 – reconnection charge (large meter)

4 Procedure

Location DEWA Head Office   (Map ref 7-D8)

Hours Sun – Thurs 07:30 – 20:30

• Pay the amount outstanding plus the reconnection charge to the cashier at any DEWA office

• Keep your receipt

• A technician will come to the premises and reconnect services on the same day

5 Related Procedure

• Disconnecting Service & Settling Accounts, p.70

Tip **24 Hour Reconnection Service**

If you need to be reconnected after normal working hours (07:30 – 20:30) or on a holiday, contact DEWA by calling 991 or 04 601 9999.

Consolidating Bill Statements

1 Overview

As an additional service, DEWA allows individual or commercial consumers with more than 20 DEWA consumer account numbers to consolidate all accounts into one bill statement with an independent statement code number.

If any deletions or changes in the statement account are required, follow the same procedure as detailed below.

2 Prerequisites

- The company or individual has more than 20 consumer account numbers in the same name

3 What To Bring

- ☐ All consumer account numbers
- ☐ A written request addressed to the Senior Manager Billing Services indicating the consumer account numbers and asking that they be grouped together ('consolidated')

4 Procedure

Location DEWA Head Office Billing Services   Map ref 7-D8

Hours Sun – Thurs 07:30 – 20:30

- Submit the request to Billing Services in person or
  - Mail to: PO Box 564, Dubai
  - Fax to: 324 9345
  - Email to: cbd@dewa.gov.ae
- You will receive an independent statement code with your next bill

5 Related Procedures

- Paying for Water & Electricity, p.66
- Disconnecting Service & Settling Accounts, p.70

Housing

Water & Electricity

Water & Electricity

Disconnecting Service & Settling Accounts

1 Overview

Disconnecting DEWA services consists of two steps: paying the final bill and having the security deposit refunded. You need to notify DEWA in advance that you will be vacating the premises and the final bill can only be paid in cash. You need to settle the final bill in order to have your security deposit refunded.

2 Prerequisites

- The premises will be vacated in a minimum of two days

3 What To Bring

- ☐ Consumer account number
- ☐ Date you will be vacating the premises
- ☐ A contact telephone number
- ☐ Original security deposit receipt (see Connecting Water & Electricity, p.64)
- ☐ If you have lost the original receipt, a completed indemnity form from the security deposit counter
- ☐ If the security deposit is in a company name, a stamped letter from the company requesting that the deposit be refunded. The name of the person who will receive the money or cheque should be mentioned in the letter
- ☐ Recipient's passport (copy) or labour card (copy) to verify identity
- ☐ Final bill payment receipt

4 Procedure

Location DEWA Head Office   (Map ref 7-D8)

Hours Sun – Thurs 07:30 – 20:30

Disconnection
- At least two days before you plan to vacate the premises, notify DEWA either in person or by email, or fax
- Supply your customer account number
- Indicate the date the premises will be vacated
- Leave a contact telephone number
- On receipt of your notification, DEWA will send a technician to take a final meter reading and to disconnect the supply

Notification
- You will be notified when the final bill is ready (if you have a mobile phone, you will receive notification by SMS)
- You will receive the final bill by post, or you can collect it personally from the frontline service counter

Bill Payment

Two options exist for settling final bills:

Option 1

Pay Final Bill

- Pay the final bill at the cash counter at any DEWA office
- Collect the final receipt
- Ensure the bill is stamped 'final bill' by the cashier

Refund Security Deposit

- Submit the relevant documents and the final bill receipt at the security deposit counter at the DEWA head office and request a refund
- Sign the refund voucher and submit it to the cashier
- Collect the security deposit from the cashier (if you are closing a commercial account, you will receive a cheque)

Option 2

Settle Final Bill With Security Deposit

- Submit the relevant documents and the final bill at the Security Deposit Counter at a DEWA office and request a refund
- Go to the frontline service counter where a staff member will adjust the final bill by deducting the amount from the security deposit
- If there is a credit, you will receive the remaining amount in the form of cash or a cheque at the cash counter
- If there is a debit, pay the remaining amount (cash only)

Housing

5 Related Procedure

- Obtaining A Clearance Certificate, p.72

Water & Electricity

Water & Electricity

Obtaining A Clearance Certificate

1 Overview

In general, the final bill payment receipt is considered a final settlement when you move out of the premises. However, some landlords request a clearance certificate as additional proof that all outstanding amounts have been paid to DEWA, before they will return your rental security deposit.

2 Prerequisites

- The water and electricity supply has been disconnected
- The final bill has been paid

3 What To Bring

☐ Final bill/receipt (paid)

☐ Passport copy (if consumer not registered with DEWA)

Fee ☐ Dhs.10 service charge

4 Procedure

Location DEWA Head Office   Map ref 7-D8

Hours Sun – Thurs 07:30 – 20:30

- Submit the final bill/receipt (paid)
- If consumer is not registered with DEWA (if they live in another emirate but work in Dubai), submit copy of passport
- Collect service charge slip for payment
- Pay the service charge
- Present the service charge receipt and collect the clearance certificate

Overview

There is no mains gas supply in Dubai. Individual gas cylinders can be purchased from numerous gas companies around town. The supplier will deliver and connect the cylinders for you. Customers are no longer required to pay a security deposit for gas cylinders.

Charges **New Connection:** (includes price of regulator, pipe, clips & cylinder)

- Large cylinder (44kgs/100lbs) – Dhs.675
- Medium cylinder (22kgs/50lbs) – Dhs.500
- Small cylinder (11kgs/25lbs) – Dhs.400

Gas Refill:

- Large cylinder (44kgs/100lbs) – Dhs.187
- Medium cylinder (22kgs/50lbs) – Dhs.86
- Small cylinder (11kgs/25lbs) – Dhs.53

Housing

Gas

Info — Gas Providers

• Al Fahidi Gas Tech	04 351 6452
• Al Shafaq Gas Distribution	04 334 7441
• Ali Abdulla Ali Gas	04 271 1527
• Alsalam Gas Distributors	04 271 4022
• Oasis Gas Suppliers	04 396 1812
• Union Gas Company	04 266 1479

Check the commercial telephone directories for other suppliers in Dubai.

Tip — Setting Up Home

From getting your phone connected to working out how your sewerage works, there's a whole host of things to get your head round when moving into your new abode. For more information on setting up home in Dubai check out the Residents section of the *Dubai Explorer – The Complete Residents' Guide* available in all leading bookshops and supermarkets.

The ultimate boating guide

Communications

Overview

Tip Don't Forget The 050, 055 Or 056

Don't forget to dial the correct prefix when calling mobile phones. Etisalat lines begin with either 050 or 056 and du lines begin with 055. You'll need to use these prefixes whether you're calling from a landline or a mobile number.

Overview

Telecommunications

The bulk of this chapter is about getting connected, be it by telephone, mobile phone or internet. Thanks to the well-established telecommunications sector in Dubai, you won't feel isolated; staying in touch with friends, family and colleagues around the world is no problem.

Depending on where you live, your home services will be provided by either Etisalat or du. Most new developments are serviced by du, whereas apartments and villas in non-freehold parts of the city are almost all serviced by Etisalat. Both companies provide similar home services and pricing. Residents who wish to use the landline services of a company other than the one specified for their area can choose to sign up for either 'Call Select' by du, or 'Etisalat Select' by Etisalat, which allow customers to use whichever service provider they wish, regardless of who provides the line.

Etisalat

Etisalat's head offices can be easily recognised by the massive golf ball on the top of their buildings in Deira and by the Trade Centre roundabout. There is also a low-rise office on the Sheikh Zayed Road behind the Dusit Thani Hotel, sans golf ball. Inside, the counters are all clearly marked and well-organised. Etisalat's website (www.etisalat.ae) allows customers to follow many procedures online.

du

Du's head office is located in Media City, but the company maintains kiosks in Dragonmart, Mall of the Emirates, Ibn Battuta Mall, Jumeira Centre and Deira City Centre, where customers can pay bills and sign up for new services. Du's website (www.du.ae) allows customers to pay bills online and register for additional services. Since du packages their communications services, the procedure for signing up with du is the same, regardless of the service being provided. For information on all du services, turn to p.110.

Emirates Post & Empost

In Dubai, you will not find a postman knocking at your door unless you subscribe to a special service. Here, all mail is sent to post boxes rather than to the address of your home or office. This chapter covers how to rent a PO Box – a must for most people and all companies setting up in Dubai.

Emirates Post, formerly the 'General Post Authority', is the government authority responsible for all postal services for individuals and companies. Check out their website, www.emiratespostuae.com.

Communications

Overview

Telephone

Applying For A Telephone Line (Etisalat)

1 Overview

Etisalat will install up to five telephone lines at a residence. A business may install more lines, depending on its size.

Telephone Costs

Charges   Calls made to a landline within an emirate are free. Calls elsewhere in the UAE cost Dhs.0.18 per minute at peak hours and Dhs0.06 at off-peak times. Calls to mobiles cost Dhs.0.30 per minute, regardless of time.

Dhs.45 – current quarterly rental charges for a telephone line

2 Prerequisites

Private Line • Subscriber must be resident in Dubai

Commercial Line • Company must be registered in Dubai

3 What To Bring

Private Line
- ☐ Tenancy agreement or proof of premises ownership (copy)
- ☐ Passport (copy)
- ☐ Residence permit (copy)

Commercial Line
- ☐ Completed application form in English or Arabic (typed or handwritten) signed by the National partner, sponsor or authorised nominee, with the company stamp
- ☐ Passport of National partner, sponsor or authorised nominee (copy)
- ☐ Passport of non-GCC owner/partner (copy)
- ☐ Residence permit of non-GCC owner/partner (copy)
- ☐ Valid trade licence (copy)
- ☐ If the trade licence does not mention the location, a no objection letter from the Economic Department (original)
- ☐ If the premises are an office: an office site plan (copy)
- ☐ If the premises are a warehouse: a tenancy contract (copy) mentioning whether it is a warehouse, shed or store

    If the above details are not mentioned in the tenancy contract: a letter (original typed and stamped) from the company confirming that the premises will be used either as a warehouse, shed or store

Fee
- ☐ Dhs.225 – registration fee including first quarter rental
- ☐ Additional cash for supplementary services (for further services, see p.92)

4 Procedure

Location Etisalat, Various (see p.300)

Hours Sun-Thurs 08:00-20:00; Sat 08:00-13:00

- Collect the application form from any Etisalat office (not kiosk)
- Complete the form in English or Arabic (typed or hand-written) and select any supplementary services needed (call waiting, call barring, etc)
- Take a ticket and wait for your number to be displayed
- Submit all documents
- Pay the fees (cash or credit card) at the same counter
- The salesperson will assign you a telephone number
- Ensure you are able to provide access to your residence or business so that a technician can install the connection

Activation
- One to four working days
- International dialling activation: one day after the local line is connected

5 Related Procedures

- Paying Bills, p.81
- Transferring A Line To Another Subscriber, p.87
- Applying For Supplementary Services, p.92

Tip Subscription Through 182,101 Or www.etisalat.ae

There is no subscription fee if supplementary services are applied for on 182, 101 or via the e-shop (online). For a list of subscription fees when applying in person, see p.80.

Additional Sockets
If you want more than one socket in your home or office, request extra sockets when applying for the line to avoid having the technician return at a later date. The first additional socket is Dhs.50, and sockets thereafter are Dhs.15, with no rental charge.

Communications

Telephone

Telephone

Charges (in Dhs.)			
Service	Subscription through e-shop, 182 or 101	Subscription at Etisalat Offices	Rental Charges per Quarter
Call waiting	Free	50	15
Call forwarding –			
• Unconditional	Free	50	15
• On busy	Free	50	15
• On no reply	Free	50	15
• On switched off	Free	50	15
Conference calling	Free	50	15
STAR package	Free	50	30
Caller ID	Free	50	15
Code control barring-STD	Free	50	25
Code control barring-ISD	Free	50	25
Do not Disturb	Free	50	15
Follow Me	Free	50	5
Hot Line with Time Out	Free	50	45
Hot Line without Time Out	Free	50	120
Automatic Alarm Service	Not possible	30 fils per usage	Free
Al Mersal Messaging Service	50	50	15

Activation And Deactivation Codes**		
Service	Activation Codes	Deactivation Codes
Call Waiting	*43#	#43#
Call Forwarding –		
• Unconditional	*21* (desired no.) #	#21#
• On Busy	*67* (desired no.) #	#67#
• On No reply	*61* (desired no.) #	#61#
• On switched off	*62* (desired no.) #	#62#
Conference Calling	* *	Not applicable
STAR Package	Not applicable	Not applicable
Caller ID Service	Not applicable	Not applicable
Code Control barring – SD &STD	*33* (personal code) #	#33(personal code) #
Do not Disturb	*26#	#26#
Follow Me	146	Not applicable
Hot Line with or without Time Out	*53* (desired no.) #	#53#
Al Mersal Messaging Service	Dial 125 for subscription then dial 123 for set up	

**See Service Descriptions Table on p.93

Paying Bills

1 Overview

Etisalat bills are itemised for international and mobile telephone calls (inter-emirate calls can be itemised on request for a fee of Dhs.200 per month) and must be paid within 30 days. All service charges are clearly noted, with descriptions on the back of the bill. Bills are mailed monthly, and computer generated recorded reminders are sent to both post-paid mobile (GSM) phones and landlines. An SMS reminder is also sent to mobile users who have missed their payment due date, noting the amount that must be paid and the due date.

Internet Charges

See Residential Service Overview, p.104

See Commercial Service Overview, p.106

Telephone Charges

Local Calls

Calls made within an emirate on and to a landline are free.

Calls made between mobile phones or from a mobile phone to a landline and vice versa are charged at a rate of 30 fils/minute at peak hours.

International Calls

For a listing of international telephone call charges, visit Etisalat's www.etisalat.ae site, call 101, or look in the front of Etisalat's annual telephone book (available free of charge at any Etisalat office). Off-peak hours for international calls are from 21:00 – 01:00 and 14:00 – 16:00 daily and all-day on Fridays, as well as some public holidays. Super off-peak timings are from 01:00 – 07:00 daily.

SMS

Short Message Service charges do not change according to peak or off peak timing and are charged at a rate of:

- 30 fils for a local SMS
- 90 fils for an international SMS

Tip	Bill Inquiry

Call 142, go to any of Etisalat's public payment machines (often near large supermarkets) or check online at www.etisalat.ae.

Communications

Telephone

Telephone

Payment Options	Location	Comments
In Person		
Counter	Any Etisalat office or kiosk	• Present bill, telephone number, or user name • Cash and credit card accepted
Payment Machine	Any Etisalat office and most shopping malls	• 24 hour payment using a touch-screen machine
Cheque Deposit Box	Any Etisalat office	• Insert bill counterfoil and crossed cheque in an envelope • Receipt will be mailed to you
By Post		
Mail to:	The Chief Cashier Etisalat Accounts Department PO Box 400, Dubai	• Mail bill counterfoil and crossed cheque • Receipt will be mailed to you
Online		
Log on to:	www.etisalat.ae	• View and pay bills online • Both current and past bills, adjustments and payments can be viewed • **See Applying For Online Services**, p.90, to learn how to access this service
At A Bank		
Bank Counters, Telebanking & ATMs	Banks listed on p.276	If your bank is not listed in this table, check with your bank to determine if it offers this service. Several banks also allow you to pay your Etisalat bills online

Info Maysour

This is a prepaid telephone service for landlines. It's ideal for residential or business telephone lines as it gives you the convenience of receiving incoming calls for a full year, while making outgoing calls on a prepaid basis to match your budget needs.

The package is available for Dhs.170. A standard telephone set is provided along with an initial credit of Dhs.10 worth of outgoing calls. Subsequent annual renewal is available for Dhs.120 only.

For further information, assistance or subscription to Etisalat's Maysour Prepaid Telephone Service please contact your nearest Etisalat office or business centre.

- Take a ticket and wait for your number to be displayed
- Submit the form and receipt

Reactivation   2-3 days

 It is not always possible to obtain the same telephone number again.

5   Related Procedures

- Paying Bills, p.81
- Closing Accounts & Settling Final Bills, p.88

| Info | Obtaining A Surveyor Number |

When applying for a new telephone line, or when transferring a line to new premises, a working telephone number near the new premises must be supplied. If neither you nor the Etisalat salesperson can supply a number, a surveyor number (the Etisalat identification for your building location) must be obtained. To get the surveyor number you need to know the exact location of the new premises (use the *Dubai Street Atlas*) and if possible go to the Etisalat office in the district of your new premises (if there is one). You will need to take a copy of the tenancy agreement or proof of premises ownership, a passport copy and residence permit copy. At the Etisalat office you need to complete the required form and take it to the Surveyor Counter and show the tenancy agreement with the land plot number on it.

Communications

Telephone

Transferring A Line (Account) To A New Location

1 Overview

When moving to new premises, the telephone line(s) (accounts) may be transferred. If the new location is in the same exchange area, it may be possible that the telephone number is transferred along with the line.

2 Prerequisites

- Existing telephone line

3 What To Bring

☐ Tenancy agreement or proof of premises ownership of the new location (copy)

☐ Telephone number of any working telephone at the new premises, or the nearest premises, or the surveyor number (see Obtaining a Surveyor Number, p.84)

☐ Last paid bill (copy)

Private Line ☐ Passport (copy)

☐ Residence permit (copy)

☐ No objection letter from sponsor in either English or Arabic

Commercial Line ☐ Completed application form in English or Arabic (typed or handwritten) signed by the National partner, sponsor or authorised nominee, with the company stamp, or

☐ A written request signed by the National partner, sponsor or authorised nominee

☐ Passport of National partner, sponsor or authorised nominee (copy)

☐ Valid trade licence with the location where the service is required (copy)

☐ If the trade licence is not updated with the new location: a no objection letter from the Economic Department (original)

☐ If the new premises are offices: an office site plan (copy)

☐ If the new premises are a warehouse: a tenancy contract (copy) mentioning whether it is a warehouse, shed or store

If the above details are not mentioned in the tenancy contract: a letter (original typed and stamped) from the company confirming that the premises will be used either as a warehouse, shed or store

Fee ☐ Dhs.100 service charge

Communications

Telephone

4 Procedures

Location   Etisalat, Various (see p.300)

Hours   Sun-Thurs 08:00-20:00; Sat 08:00-13:00

- Collect the application form from any Etisalat office
- Complete the form in English or Arabic (typed or hand-written)
- Pay the final bill (cash or credit card) at the cashier by providing either the bill or the telephone number; collect the receipt
- Take a ticket and wait for your number to be displayed
- Submit all documents (including receipt)
- You will be given a new telephone number (if the previous number is not being transferred)

The service charge will be included in your next bill.

Activation   3 working days

5 Related Procedure

- Obtaining A Surveyor Number, p.84

Tip Recorded Message

A recording can be installed on the old number to inform callers of your new telephone number.

Simply fill in the application form and request interactive voice recording (IVR) service. Subscription costs Dhs.150 for the first month, and Dhs.100 for the following months – however long you want to run it for – and will be included in your next bill.

Note that this service can only be ordered once and cannot be re-ordered. Hence, order the recording for a longer rather than a shorter period, just in case.

Tip Setting Up Home

From getting your phone connected to working out how your sewerage works, there's a whole host of things to get your head round when moving into your new abode. For more information on setting up home in Dubai check out the Residents section of the *Dubai Explorer (The Complete Residents' Guide)* available in all leading bookshops and supermarkets.

Transferring A Line To Another Subscriber

1 Overview

It is possible to transfer a telephone line to another person or company ('subscriber') rather than cancelling the current line and activating a new one.

Mobile, Wasel (pay-as-you-go) and landlines can be transferred.

2 Prerequisites

- Existing telephone, mobile or Wasel line
- New subscriber must be resident in Dubai

3 What To Bring

☐ For a Wasel transfer, just one form of ID.

For telephone or post-paid mobile transfers:

Private Line
☐ Tenancy agreement or proof of premises ownership (copy)
☐ Last paid bill (copy)
☐ Passport of the party releasing the line (copy)
☐ Residence permit of the party releasing the line (copy)
☐ Passport of the new subscriber (copy).
☐ Residence permit of the new subscriber (copy)

Commercial Line
☐ Completed application form in English or Arabic signed by the National partner, sponsor or authorised nominee, with the company stamp
☐ Passport of National partner, sponsor or authorised nominee (for both parties) (copy)
☐ Valid trade licence (copy)

Fee
☐ Dhs.100 – service charge

4 Procedure

Location Etisalat, Various (see p.300)

Hours Sun-Thurs 08:00-20:00; Sat 08:00-13:00

- The final bill must first be paid by the original telephone line subscriber
- Collect and complete the application form in English or Arabic (typed or hand-written)

Both parties must sign the 'Transfer' section on the back of the form

- Take a ticket and wait for your number to be displayed
- Submit all documents (including final receipt)
- Pay the fee (cash or credit card) at the same counter

Activation Same day

Communications

Telephone

Telephone

Closing Accounts & Settling Final Bills

1 Overview

A telephone line may be cancelled at any time, but it must be done in person at any Etisalat office.

2 Prerequisites

- Existing Etisalat telephone line

3 What To Bring

☐ Passport (copy)
☐ The last telephone bill or telephone number or subscriber name

4 Procedure

Location   Etisalat, Various (see p.300)

Hours   Sun-Thurs 08:00-20:00; Sat 08:00-13:00

- Collect the application form from any Etisalat office
- Complete the form in English or Arabic (typed or hand-written)
- Tick 'Disconnect the Line (Permanent) From: (enter date)'
- Attach your passport copy to the form
- Proceed to the cashier and request a final bill
- Pay the bill and obtain a receipt

Disconnection   Immediate.
Timings

5 Related Procedure

- Transferring A Line To A New Location, p.85

Info   Getting A Clearance Certificate

In general, the final bill is considered proof of final settlement when you move out of your premises. However, some landlords may request a clearance certificate as additional proof before returning the rental security deposit to the tenant. In order to get a clearance certificate you will first have to pay the final bill and have the telephone line disconnected. You need to submit the final bill receipt to the cashier at any Etisalat office and request a clearance certificate. The certificate will be issued immediately and the service charge is Dhs.20.

Applying For An Etisalat Calling Card (ECC)

1 Overview

An Etisalat Calling Card (ECC) is available free of charge to every telephone line subscriber. This PIN–protected card is not pre-paid and all calls made using this card are charged to your monthly bill. With this card, both local and international calls can be made from any telephone in the UAE. Calls from international destinations can also be made to the UAE.

Rates are the same as dialling from a regular telephone when calling within and from the UAE. When dialling from overseas, standard international rates apply.

2 Prerequisites

- An existing Etisalat telephone or GSM account

3 What To Bring

- ☐ Telephone or GSM application form, depending on which account you wish to use
- ☐ One form of valid ID

4 Procedure

Location Etisalat, Various (see p.300)

Hours Sun-Thurs 08:00-20:00; Sat 08:00-13:00

- Collect the application form from any Etisalat office
- Complete the form in English or Arabic (typed or hand-written)
- Tick 'Etisalat Calling Card Service' on the form
- Take a ticket and wait for your number to be displayed
- Submit all documents to the salesperson
- The salesperson will give you an Etisalat Calling Card

You may request a personalised card, though this will take up to three days to process.

Within the UAE
- Dial 800 8080 (toll-free) and follow the voice prompts

In Abroad
- Dial the HCD (Home Country Direct Telephone Service) telephone number of the country you are visiting

To find this number, see the instructions on the reverse of your Etisalat Calling Card.

- HCD numbers are also listed on www.etisalat.ae on the Business Solutions page

Activation Up to four working days

Communications

Telephone

General Telecom Services

1 Overview

Etisalat customers may access personal billing information and make payments or changes to the services they subscribe to by logging on to www.e4me.ae.

The first step to being able to access this information is to register online at the above website.

2 Prerequisites

- Any Etisalat account in your name

3 What To Bring

- Your Etisalat mobile number or landline number

4 Procedure

Location   Any computer with internet

Hours   Anytime

Log on
- Log on to www.e4me.ae
- Fill in the registration form following the prompts

Registration Number
Option 1
- Enter your mobile phone number
- You will instantly receive an SMS message with a number
- Enter this number onto the site within 15 minutes
- If registration is successful, you will instantly receive a registration number, customer number and username on the screen

Option 2
- Enter your internet address or landline number
- Call 800 888 3463
- The customer service agent will verify your identity by asking for some personal details
- If you answer the questions correctly, the agent will give you a registration number, customer number and username

With the above steps, you may access general billing information online. If you wish to have access to specific call details, you will have to obtain a password from Etisalat first. Go to the E4Me Counter at any Etisalat Business Centre and present your registration number and username (see facing page). The salesperson will give you a password to access your personal information online.

Activation Immediate

5 Related Procedure

• Paying Bills, p.81

Tip **Application Assistance**

If you do not feel comfortable with the online application procedure, go to any Etisalat Business Centre and a salesperson will gladly guide you through the process.

Tip **Helpful Numbers**

Directory Enquiries (landline/mobile – Dhs.1 for the first minute; 50 fils for every 30 seconds after)	181
Fault Reporting (free of charge)	171
Customer Service Helpline (landline – 30 fils per enquiry; mobile – 30 fils per minute	101

Tip **Eastenders, Desperate Housewives, 24 & Lost**

Just because you've left your home country it doesn't mean you have to say goodbye to all your home comforts, especially not your favourite TV shows. There are a number of satellite television providers in Dubai showcasing popular shows and movies from around the world. For more information see the Residents section of the *Dubai Explorer – The Complete Residents' Guide* available in all leading bookshops and supermarkets.

Communications

General Telecom Services

General Telecom Services

Applying For Supplementary Services

1 Overview

Etisalat offers its clients a variety of additional services from call forwarding to call waiting to code controlled barring. All of these can be applied for in person at the Etisalat office for a charge. For a comprehensive list of services and the corresponding charges, see p.80. If you activate supplementary services through 182, 101 or online there are no charges – see the table on p.93 for further details.

2 Prerequisites

• Existing telephone or mobile phone line

3 What To Bring

Private Line
☐ By SMS: a mobile account registered in your name
☐ Passport (copy)
☐ Residence permit (copy)

Commercial Line
☐ Completed application form in English or Arabic (typed or handwritten) signed by the National partner, sponsor or authorised nominee, with the company stamp, or
☐ A written request signed by the National partner, sponsor or authorised nominee
☐ Passport of National partner, sponsor or authorised nominee (copy)
☐ Valid trade licence (copy)

4 Procedure

Location Etisalat, Various (see p.300)

Hours Sun-Thurs 08:00-20:00; Sat 08:00-13:00

• Collect the application form from any Etisalat office
• Complete the form in English or Arabic (typed or hand-written)
• Take a ticket and wait for your number to be called
• Submit all documents at the counter
• In order to activate the services requested, specific codes must be entered into the phone (for a listing of these codes, see p.80)
• Service charges will be included in the next bill

Activation Immediate

5 Related Procedure

• Paying Bills, p.81

Supplementary Service Definitions & Availability

Service	Description	Tel.	Mob.	Wasel
Call waiting	Allows receipt of a call while you are on another call	Yes	Yes	Yes
Call forwarding -	Diverts all incoming calls to any telephone, GSM or voice mail	Yes	Yes	Yes
• Unconditional	All calls			
• On busy	When your line is busy			
• On no reply	When you don't answer			
• On switched off	When your phone is switched off	No	Yes	Yes
Conference calling	Allows up to a 5-party conference call	Yes	Yes	No
STAR package	Combination of 3 services: call forwarding (unconditional), call waiting and add-on conference	Yes	Yes	Yes
Caller ID service	Enables you to see the number of the person calling you.	Yes	No	No
Code control barring -STD	Bars UAE and international calls (0+00)	Yes	Yes	No
Code control barring -ISD	Bars international calls (00)	Yes	Yes	No
Do not disturb	Diverts all calls to a pre-recorded announcement	Yes	No	No
Follow me	Allows you to forward calls remotely from any telephone to any other telephone within the UAE by dialling 146	Yes	No	No
Hot Line with Time Out	Calls a frequently dialled number automatically each time you lift the handset (within 5 seconds)	Yes	No	No
Hot Line without Time Out	Immediately calls a frequently dialled number each time you lift the handset	Yes	No	No
Automatic alarm service	Allows you to set an alarm	Yes	No	No
Messaging Service (Al Mersal)	Automatic answering service greets callers with your personal greetings, inviting them to leave a message and which you can listen to from any phone in the UAE	Yes	Yes	Yes
EWAP	Access to internet on mobile	No	Yes	Yes

Communications

General Telecom Services

Tip   Free!

To avoid paying application charges for supplementary services, either call 182, 101 or use www.etisalat.ae. Register your details with Etisalat's 'e-shop' to access a number of services, including adding supplementary services to your telephone line. For a list of available services and their charges for walk-in customers, see p.80.

Mobile Phone

Overview

Mobile phones are practically a must in the UAE and can be purchased from either Etisalat or du, specialised telecommunications shops, electronics shops, or large supermarkets.

In order to use a mobile phone with a Dubai telephone number, you will first have to obtain a SIM card from Etisalat of du, which is inserted into the back of the phone. There are two mobile phone service options, and your choice depends on your needs and requirements.

Post-paid plans allow you to make an unlimited number of calls, as long as the monthly bills are paid. Pre-paid plans work on a credit basis, which must be recharged in order to continue making calls. This is a popular choice for new arrivals to Dubai, as no residence permit is required for registration. For a detailed comparison of the services, see the table on the facing page.

Unlike in many other countries, there are no free calling times or mobile package options offering unlimited evening and weekend calls.

Info — Mobile Broadband

Etisalat offers EWAP Service to customers with WAP (Wireless Application Protocol) enabled handsets.

3.5G is also available and provides customers access to information with their 3G and GPRS enabled mobile phones.

Info — Najm

Najm is perfect for people who spend a lot of time on their mobile phone. You can pay a set monthly amount for 500, 1,000 or 2,000 minute packages (that include free texts), which works out cheaper than your normal call rate. A variety of other services are included, but international calls are not part of the package and will be billed separately.

Tip — Temporary Mobile Stop-Gap

Pick up an Ahlan Visitor package from Etisalat Outlets and Dubai Duty Free for Dhs.90 and you instantly get your own mobile line and number for 90 days, including 90 minutes. All you need is your passport. Unfortunately, it's not renewable once the three months are up.

Mobile Phone Services (Etisalat) – Options

Service	GSM (Post-paid)	Wasel
Product	Standard mobile service	Prepaid mobile service
Residence permit required	Yes	No
Subscription duration	Unlimited	1 year of incoming calls
Target group	Residents without limitations on calls	Residents with control of call expenses & frequent visitors
Minimum salary	Dhs.5,000	No
Payment	Monthly bill	Phonecards
SMS (Short Message Service)	Yes	Yes
Roaming	Yes (Dhs.2,000 deposit) (see p.97)	Yes (limited)
Cost: peak/min	24 fils	24 fils
Cost: off-peak/min	18 fils	18 fils
Subscription charge (1 time only)	Dhs.185	Dhs.165
Renewal ('Rental')	Dhs.60 every 3 months after first 3 months	Dhs.100 per year after first year
SMS Message Centre Number	+971 50 606 0000	+971 50 606 0000
Help	101	101 (120 and the prepaid card number to recharge)

Communications

Mobile Phone

Info   **Need Two SIM Cards?**

Taw'am allows you to have two SIM cards with the same number (standard mobile or GSM and Wasel).

There is a one-off charge of Dhs.100, with no additional rental charges for Taw'am. Call 101 or log on to www.etisalat.ae for further details or to sign up.

Note: In case a card is lost, blocked or damaged, both SIM cards will be replaced. A new dual SIM card will be issued at a price of Dhs.100

Tip   **Subscription In Stores**

It is possible to subscribe to the du or Etisalat pre-paid services at several electronics stores around Dubai. Bring a passport copy with a valid residence permit, or entry permit, pay, and you will be given a telephone number on the spot. Keep an eye open for special offers including free Wasel subscription with mobile purchase. You may also order Wasel4me by logging on to www.e4me.ae or call 7000 11 111 and your card will be delivered to you anywhere in the UAE within 24 hrs through a new partnership deal between Etisalat, the Corporation's Contact Centre, and Empost.

Mobile Phone

Applying For A Post-Paid Line

1 Overview

Standard mobile phone service allows both local and international dialling and call receipt. But unless roaming is added as a supplementary service (see the Info box, p.97), it cannot be used outside the UAE. For an overview of the two mobile line options offered by Etisalat, see the Mobile Phone Services – Options table on p.95. Standard mobile accounts are billed monthly and the bills include a quarterly rental charge. Check www.du.ae for updates on all the du mobile services, unavailable at time of print.

Validity Unlimited

Charges **Etisalat**

- Dhs.165 – subscription fee (one time only)
- Dhs.100 – annual renewal fee
- 30fils for the first minute, 15fils for each additional minute – cost: peak/min (07:00 – 14:00; 16:00 – 24:00)
- 15fils – cost: off-peak/min (14:00 – 16:00; 00:00 – 07:00)

du

- Dhs.124 (with Dhs.62 free credit) – subscription fee (one time only)
- Dhs.30 – monthly fee
- 0.5fils/second – calls to all national mobiles and landlines

2 Prerequisites

- Subscriber must be resident in Dubai and over 21 years of age
- Minimum monthly salary of approximately Dhs.5,000

3 What To Bring

- ☐ Passport (copy)
- ☐ Residence permit (copy)
- ☐ Salary certificate from employer demonstrating monthly salary
- ☐ Relevant subscription fee

4 Procedure

Location Etisalat, Various (see p.300) or du, Various (see p.300)

Hours Sun-Thurs 08:00-20:00; Sat 08:00-13:00

- Collect the application form from any Etisalat or du office
- Complete the form in English or Arabic (typed or hand-written) and select any supplementary services needed
- Submit all documents

- Pay the fee (cash or credit card) at the same counter

 Supplementary service charges are included in your next bill

- The salesperson will give you a SIM card

5 Related Procedures

- Paying Bills, p.81
- Replacing A SIM Card, p.100

Info Roaming

If you wish to receive and/or make calls while outside the UAE with a post-paid plan, roaming capabilities must be applied for. Both Etisalat and du require a refundable deposit of Dhs.2,000 for roaming capabilities. This deposit is not applicable to UAE Nationals and locally-owned companies.

Info Reporting A Lost Or Stolen Mobile

If your mobile is lost or stolen, report the loss immediately by calling 101 for Etisalat or 04 369 9155 for du. You will be asked for your name, telephone number and your passport number. The operator will then deactivate the SIM card.

Note: You are liable for all calls made from your phone until it is reported lost or stolen to Etisalat or du.

Communications

Mobile Phone

Mobile Phone

Applying For Pre-Paid Services

⌐1 Overview

Pre-Paid services allow you to receive unlimited incoming calls and make pre-paid (pay-as-you-go) outgoing calls via purchased phone cards (available from shops, petrol stations and supermarkets). This service includes connection, one year's rental, and SIM card charges. You can receive calls while outside the UAE, provided you have enough credit in your card, but international rates apply. As this is a prepaid service, there are no monthly telephone bills.

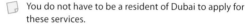

You do not have to be a resident of Dubai to apply for these services.

Validity One year, renewable

Charges **Etisalat**

- Dhs.165 – one year's subscription
- Dhs.100 – annual renewal
- 24fils – cost: peak/min (07:00 – 14:00; 16:00 – 24:00)
- 18fils – cost: off-peak/min (14:00 – 16:00; 00:00 – 07:00)

du
- Dhs.55 – one year's subscription
- Dhs.55 – annual renewal
- 0.5fils – cost/second to local mobiles and landlines

⌐2 Prerequisites

- Subscriber must be over 21 years of age

⌐3 What To Bring

- ☐ Passport (copy)
- ☐ Residence permit (copy), or
- ☐ Entry stamp in passport (copy)
- ☐ Relevant subscription fee

⌐4 Procedure

Location Most electronics shops

- Collect the application form from any Etisalat or du office or authorised vendor
- Complete the form in English or Arabic (typed or hand-written)
- Submit all documents
- Pay the fee (cash or credit card) at the same counter
- The salesperson will give you a SIM card

Activation Immediate

5 Related Procedure

- Replacing a SIM Card p.100

Info **Pre-Paid Instructions**

Even if you have no credit on your phone, SMS messages can be received while in the UAE. In order to send messages though, you must have credit.

Recharging/Adding Credit
Options to recharge the card for outgoing calls:

- Use a prepaid Etisalat or du phone card (available at petrol stations, corner shops and supermarkets)
- Log on to www.etisalat.ae or www.du.ae and pay by credit card (minimum Dhs.50)
- Use an Etisalat payment machine (for Etisalat only) but note that credit is payable in Dhs.50 units only
- Some banks allow customers to add credit via online banking
- Emirates Post outlets in the UAE have machines that accept cash to credit an Etisalat connection

Subscription Renewal
Etisalat

- Etisalat will notify you via SMS when it is close to renewal time.
- On the day of renewal, be sure to have a credit balance of at least Dhs.100 on your mobile account.
- Etisalat will automatically deduct the Dhs.100 renewal fee from your balance.

du
- When it is time to renew, make sure you have a credit balance of at least Dhs.55.
- Call 1355 and follow the instructions

Balance Inquiry
To determine the balance amount, dial *121# for Etisalat or *135# for du, then press the 'send' key

Roaming
Both Etisalat and du pre-paid customers can receive calls and messages when overseas. While roaming charges apply for incoming calls, incoming messages are free. Around 70 countries support Etisalat and du customers wishing to make outgoing calls and send messages too, as long as they have enough credit.

Communications

Mobile Phone

Mobile Services

Replacing A SIM Card

1 Overview

If the SIM card is lost or damaged, Etisalat will replace it with a new SIM card and the same telephone number for a Dhs.50 fee.

You are liable for all calls made from your phone, even if it has been stolen, until the loss has been reported to Etisalat. To avoid abuse, report losses immediately. See p.97 for more information.

2 Prerequisites

• Existing mobile line

3 What To Bring

☐ Passport (copy)

Fee ☐ Dhs.50 – replacement fee

4 Procedure

Location Etisalat, Various (see p.300) or du, Various (see p.300)

Hours Sun-Thurs 08:00-20:00; Sat 08:00-13:00

• Collect the application form from any Etisalat office or du shop
• Complete the form in English or Arabic (typed or hand-written)
• Submit all documents
• Pay the replacement fee (cash or credit card) at the same counter
• The salesperson will give you a replacement SIM card with the same telephone number

Activation Within 15 minutes

Info Tarjim

The service offers Etisalat mobile users the ability to translate Arabic text into English and vice versa.

• Send a text message that contains words/sentence to be translated to 1001.
• Arabic messages should be up to 70 characters.
• English messages should be up to 160 characters.
• Pricing – each SMS will cost 60 fils. For assistance please call 101

Internet Overview

1 Overview

Etisalat and du are the sole providers of internet services in the UAE. Despite du's recent growth in the sector, Emirates Internet & Multimedia is still the sole provider of domain names in the Emirates.

For a detailed comparison of services, commercial and residential, see the tables on p.103.

Both du and Etisalat operate through their own proxy server, which means certain sites are restricted. If you find a blocked site that you believe should be unblocked, report it to Etisalat or du by clicking the link in the 'blocked' page.

Since du's internet service is usually packaged with their landline and television services, the procedure for du internet activation is described on p.110.

Etisalat Internet Help   800 6100

Related procedures

- Residential Service Overview, p.104
- Commercial Service Overview, p.106
- Internet Roaming, p.109
- Applying for a UAE Domain Name, p.108
- Paying Bills, p.81

| Tip | **du In Your Home** |

All of du's home services are wired through the same sockets in your home. As a result, the sign-up and set-up is very streamlined. Most du customers opt for service packages that include cable television, landline and internet services. For information on all du home services, see p.110.

| Tip | **Dial 'n' Surf** |

This facility allows you to surf the internet without subscribing to Etisalat internet. You will need a computer with a modem and a regular phone line; no account number or password is required. The Dial 'N' Surf service is nominally priced and you have to pay 12 fils/minute which is charged directly to the telephone you are connecting from. Simply dial 500 5555 to gain access.

| Tip | **Installation Assistance** |

If you are not comfortable with computers, request a paid installation service (Dhs.100) when applying for residential internet service. A technician will come to your residence to install the package for you.

Communications

Internet Services

Etisalat Personal Internet

	Dial-Plus	ISDN LAN (local area network)	Al Shamil
Description	PSTN (telephone line)	ISDN (digital line)	ADSL line
Maximum Speed	Up to 56kb/s	64 or 128 kb/s	Up to 4Mb/s (downstream)
Connection Type	Dial-up	Dial-up	Continuous connection
Services Included	Email address	Email address	Email address
Registration Fee	Dhs.100	Dhs.200	Dhs.200
Monthly Charges	Dhs.20	Dhs.20 (Dhs.100/quarter)	Dhs.149 – 256K
			Dhs.189 – 512K
			Dhs.249 – 1M
			Dhs.349 – 2M
			Dhs.449 – 4MB
Cost – Peak (06:00-01:00)	Dhs.1.80/hour	64 kbps: Dhs.1.80/hour 128 kbps: Dhs.3.60/hour	Not applicable
Cost – Off Peak	Dhs.1/hour 128 kbps: Dhs.2/hour	64 kbps: Dhs.1/hour	Not applicable
Dial-Up Number	400 4444	400 4444	Not applicable

Etisalat Commercial Internet

	Dial-Plus	ISDN LAN (local area network)	Business One
Technology Description	PSTN & ISDN	ISDN	ADSL
Target Company	Small to medium	Medium to large	Medium to large information on the Web
Maximum Speed	PSTN: up to modem speed ISDN: 64kb/s to 128kb/s	64 kb/s	Up to 1 Mb/s (upstream) Up to 8 Mb/s (downstream)
Connection Type	Dial-up	Unlimited: continuous Limited: click connected	Continuous connection
Services Included		• Domain name registration • 10MB Web hosting space • Static IP address	• Domain name registration • Up to 4 GB Web hosting space • Up to 60 GB/month data transfer • upto 60 email accounts
Installation/Modem Fee	Dhs.100	Dhs.1,000	Dhs.200/Dhs.300
Monthly Charges	Dhs.20 Limited Access: Dhs.500	Unlimited Connection: Dhs.3,000	Dhs.295-2,795 (depending on speed)
Cost – Peak (06:00-01:00)	64kb/s: Dhs.1.80/hour 128kb/s: Dhs.3.60/hour Limited Access: Dhs.6/hour	Unlimited connection: Not applicable	Not applicable
Cost – Off Peak (01:00-06:00)	64kb/s: Dhs.1/hour 128kb/s: Dhs.2/hour	Not applicable	Not applicable
Dial-Up Number	400 4444	Not applicable	Not applicable

Internet **Communications**

Internet

Applying For Residential Service (Etisalat)

1 Overview

Etisalat Internet offers various internet access options for residential users, from a basic dial-up connection to a high-speed ADSL connection. See Residential Service Table, p.102, for a listing of speeds, charges and services. Note that this service cannot be used for commercial or business purposes. For a listing of commercial internet services, see p.102.

Charges • See Residential Service Table, p.102

2 Prerequisites

- Subscriber must be resident in Dubai
- Standard telephone line

ISDN • Modem with a minimum speed of 56K

- Digital line

ADSL • An appropriate telephone line (call 800 6100 or log on to www.
(Al Shamil) alshamil.net.ae to determine whether your area has telephone lines which can provide this service)

- An Etisalat-approved modem (recommended)

  📋 An Etisalat technician may need to check the capacity of the line and location before accepting the application.

  📋 If you purchase a modem on the market, check for the Etisalat approval stamp to ensure system compatibility.

3 What To Bring

☐ Passport (copy)

☐ Residence permit (copy)

Fee ☐ Subscription fee (see Residential Service Table, p.102)

ADSL ☐ Dhs.108 – 240 external; Dhs.600 internal (ADSL modem purchase)

4 Procedure

Location Etisalat, Various (see p.300)

Hours Sun-Thurs 08:00-20:00; Sat 08:00-13:00

- Collect the internet services application form from any Etisalat office
- Complete the form in English or Arabic (typed or hand-written)
- Take a ticket and wait for your number to be called
- Submit all documents
- Pay the subscription fee (cash or credit card) at the same counter

- The salesperson will give you your internet package and email address
- Billing commences with the first log-in or 21 days from the date of application, whichever is first

ctivation   Same day if there is no technician visit

Info   Prepaid Internet

Prepaid internet cards that allow you to access the internet without having an account are available. From the computer's modem you can dial 128 plus the 14 digit number on the card and you will be given immediate access to the internet. This means you can access the internet from any phone line in the UAE. Credit on prepaid scratch cards is 12 fils per minute. Etisalat prepaid scratchcards are available in denominations of Dhs.25, 50, 100, 200 and 500.

Info   VoIP

At the moment, voice over internet protocol (such as Skype) is not allowed by Etisalat or du. If you already have a VoIP program installed on your computer, you may be able to use it in computer to computer calls. Computer to telephone calls are blocked, however.

Info   ADSL Service

Etisalat's ADSL service (also known as 'Al Shamil') does not provide you with an email address. If you wish to have an Emirates email address, you will have to register for the basic dial-up connection as well. This will provide you with a username and password, which allows you to check your mail from any computer, both in the UAE and when you are overseas. Note that if you subscribe to ADSL and basic dial-up at the same time, the basic dial-up subscription fee will be waived, though you will have to pay both monthly charges. For more information about ADSL service, log on to www.alshamil.net.ae.

Info   du

If you live in an area serviced by du, turn to p.110. Since most du-serviced areas are relatively new, the wiring for landlines, internet and television are streamlined into the same socket. The process for signing up for services is also streamlined.

Internet

Applying For Commercial Service (Etisalat)

1 Overview

Etisalat offers various internet access options for business users, from a basic dial-up connection to dedicated access, depending on the size and needs of the company. See Commercial Service Table on p.103 for a list of speeds, charges and services.

Charges See Commercial Service Table, p.103

2 Prerequisites

- Company is registered in Dubai or in one of Dubai's free zones

3 What To Bring

- ☐ Completed application for internet services form in English or Arabic (typed) signed by the National partner, sponsor or authorised nominee, with the company stamp
- ☐ Passport of National partner, sponsor or authorised nominee (copy)
- ☐ Passport of non GCC owner/partner (copy)
- ☐ Residence permit of non GCC owner/partner (copy)
- ☐ Valid trade licence (copy)
- ☐ Power of attorney to sign on behalf of the company
- ☐ If a free zone company: a letter from the free zone authority verifying registration with the free zone

Fee ☐ See Commercial Service Table, p.103

Business One ☐ Modem purchase – Dhs.775 external; Dhs.600 internal

4 Procedure

Location Etisalat, Various (see p.300)

Hours Sun – Thurs 08:00 – 20:00; Sat 08:00 – 13:00

- Go to any Etisalat office, take a ticket and wait for your number to be called
- Submit all documents
- Pay the subscription fee (cash or credit card) at the same counter
- The salesperson will give you your internet package and email address
- Billing commences after installation

Activation Depends upon service applied for

Internet   Communications

5 Related Procedure

- Applying For A UAE Domain Name, p.108

Tip Installation Assistance

Companies receive automatic installation assistance on sign-up for business services. A technician will install the commercial internet package and hardware (if applicable) on your computer for you. Contact Etisalat for installation fees, which depend on the services applied for.

Info Obtaining An Email Address

In order to obtain an Emirates email address in the UAE, you must subscribe to an Etisalat internet service. A commercial user name is limited to eight characters and the address depends on the nature and status of the company (co.ae = company, org.ae = non-profit organisation, sch.ae = school, mil.ae = military, gov.ae = government, ac.ae = academy or university). A typical commercial email address will be: user@company.co.ae.

Communications

Internet

Internet

Applying For A UAE Domain Name

1 Overview

Domain names are now available to all customers. As predominantly commercial customers will use this service, *Red-Tape* focuses on commercial application. UAE domain names for the internet may be registered and reserved for future use without signing up for internet services. For more information, visit www.uaenic.ae.

2 Prerequisites

- Residential or commercial internet customer

3 What To Bring

☐ Completed and signed Domain Name Registration application form in English or Arabic

☐ Passport copy with valid residency page of sponsor

☐ Valid trade licence copy

☐ Power of attorney to sign on behalf of the company

☐ If a free zone company: a letter from the free zone authority verifying registration with the free zone

4 Procedure

Location   Etisalat, Various (see p.300)

Hours   Sun – Thurs 08:00 – 20:00; Sat 08:00 – 13:00

- Visit www.uaenic.ae to determine availability of the domain name you would like to reserve
- Go to any Etisalat sales office, take a ticket and wait for your number to be called
- Submit all documents and pay the subscription fee (cash or credit card) at the same counter
- The salesperson will give you confirmation of the registered domain name

Activation   Immediate

> **Tip**   **UAEnic & Domain Name Rules**
>
> Applicants for a domain name can also apply directly through UAEnic via fax. Go to www.nic.ae for more information. There is also a distinct set of rules for UAE-hosted web domains. The detailed list can be found on the same website.

Internet   Communications

Internet Roaming

1 Overview

Internet roaming allows Emirates Internet customers to go online from almost anywhere in the world, at the price of a local call. Emirates Internet is member of iPass, a global roaming internet centre, allowing access from over 500 internet service providers (ISPs) world-wide. For a list of the 150 countries in which this service can be used, log on to www.ipass.com.

Charges
- 30 fils per minute (Dhs.18 per hour)
- A one-off service charge of Dhs.10 per month, during the month in which the roaming service is used

2 Prerequisites

- An Emirates Internet account
- Computer with a modem and access to a telephone line

3 What To Bring

☐ Your Emirates Internet username (email address) and password

4 Procedure

- Log on to www.ipass.com and go to the Access Points page to determine whether there is an iPass Internet Service Provider in the country to which you are travelling
- If yes, download a free software package called 'iPass Offline Hotspot Finder' onto the computer you will use while travelling

iPass Offline Hotspot Finder has an updateable phonebook containing dial up numbers of every ISP in its world-wide network.

iPass Offline Hotspot Finder also frees you from having to configure network settings while travelling.

- When travelling, to locate the nearest ISP in the iPass network, check in the iPass phonebook on your computer
- Dial that ISP number
- Log on with your Emirates Internet username (e.g. username@eim.ae)
- All international access will be billed to your Emirates Internet account

International users dial 400 3535 to access the internet while in the UAE.

| Tip | Help! |

For assistance or further information on any of the listed internet services, call 101 or log on to www.etisalat.ae.

Communications

Internet

Applying For du Services

1 Overview

Most new developments are serviced by du. Since du signed contracts to service these developments in the planning stages, most of the buildings within the developments are pre-wired for du services. This means that all three du services – television, landline and internet – are wired through the same sockets. As a result, service sign-up and installation is streamlined.

2 Prerequisites

Customers must own or reside in an area serviced by du – residential or business.

3 What To Bring

☐ Application form (obtained from any du office, or downloaded from www.du.ae)

Individual Application
☐ Owners: passport and proof of ownership copies

☐ Tenants: passport and tenancy agreement copies

Company Application
☐ If company pays: copy of valid trade licence, tenancy agreement, proof of ownership and a stamped application form

☐ If company employee pays: copy of passport, tenancy agreement, proof of ownership and a authorisation letter from the company stating employee's name

☐ A one-off installation payment of Dhs.200, regardless of how many services are being installed

4 Procedure

Location du, Various (see p.300)

Hours Hours vary depending on location

- Choose the services you would like (telephone, internet, broadband, choice cable TV company) and complete the application form
- Submit the form along with the correct documents to the office above (only one visit to the office is required)

Fee
- Pay the installation fee

A basic telephone line rental will cost an additional Dhs.15 a month, and one month's payment is required in advance depending on your overall chosen package (this is usually added to your first bill).

Activation 4-5 days to get connected. Be aware that if a building is very new, it may take time before du services can be installed. Contact du before applying to see if your building is ready for activation or not.

Paying your Bills

If you wish to pay your bill by credit card, you can fill out a credit card standing order form available from the office, or download it from www.du.ae and return it to the office or fax it back on 04 390 5554.

Many local banks also allow users to pay their du home bills through their internet banking services. Check with your bank for further information.

If you would prefer to pay cash, you will need to pay a Dhs.200 deposit and pay your bill in person at any du shop at the end of each month.

du Internet Service Options			
Speed	Cost	Installation	Do I need a modem
256 Kbps	Included in basic service package	200	No
512 Kbps	Additional Dhs.40/month	200	No
1 Mbps	Additional Dhs.100/month	200	No
2 Mbps	Additional Dhs.200/month	200	No
4 Mbps	Additional Dhs.300/month	200	No
8 Mbps	Additional Dhs.450/month	200	No
12 Mbps	Additional Dhs.600/month	200	No
*Installation is waived if internet is ordered at the same time as other services			

TV Fees Through du	
	Basic Package
Installation Charge	Dhs.199
Deposit for Set-Top Box (STB)	Dhs.150
Monthly Decoder Fee	Dhs.30
Monthly Service Fee	See p.113

Tip **Freedom & Choice**

Customers that choose to receive cable television service through du can choose from several channel providers, including Showtime, Orbit, and ART. The packages available through du are nearly identical to the satellite counterparts, but come directly through the installed du outlets so there is no need for external hardware like a satellite dish.

du Communications

Cable Television Options – Etisalat

	E-Vision Basic	Orbit	Showtime	ART Basic
Installation Charge	Dhs.250 plus Dhs.200 deposit for each decoder and three months paid up front*	Dhs.250 plus Dhs.200 deposit for each decoder and three months paid up front*	Dhs.250 plus Dhs.200 deposit for each decoder and three months paid up front*	Dhs.250 plus Dhs.200 deposit for each decoder and three months paid up front*
Monthly Subscription Charge	Dhs.58	Mega, Prime, Pinoy Dhs.99 – 189	Premier, Movies or Family Dhs.205 – 245	Dhs.59
Features	MBC, Dubai One, Al Jazeera Melody, Rotana, BBC, CNN, Fox Movies.	Basic Package, plus Discovery Channel, 7 movie channels, Pinoy channels, 7 kids' channels as well as news, sports, and music	Basic Package plus Documentary, 8 movie channels, 4 kids' channels, music, sports, news and lifestyle channels	99 channels, including some sports channels

*Decoder deposit waived if paying with credit card. Additional outlets Dhs.25 each. Minimum contract period is 6 months.

Cable Television Options – du

	Basic Package	Orbit	Showtime	ART
Installation Charge	Dhs.200 plus 150 deposit for each decoder	Dhs.200 plus Dhs.150 deposit for each decoder	Dhs.200 plus Dhs.150 deposit for each decoder	Dhs.200 plus Dhs.150 deposit each decoder
Cost of Set-Top Box (STB)	Dhs.799 if not returned	Dhs.799 if not returned	Dhs.799 if not returned	Dhs.799 if not returned
Monthly Subscription Charge	From Dhs.29	Mega, Prime, Pinoy Plus or combo – Dhs.89 – 239	Premier, Movies or Family Dhs.195 – 235	Entertainment, Sports or World Dhs.85 – 195
Features	MBC, Dubai One, Al Jazeera Melody, Rotana, BBC, CNN, Fox Movies.	Basic Package, plus Discovery Channel, 7 movie channels, Pinoy channels, 7 kids' channels as well as news, sports, and music	Basic Package plus Documentary, 8 movie channels, 4 kids' channels, music, sports, news and lifestyle channels	3 movie channels, 13 sports channels, as well as several Arabic channels

*other fees: Dhs.30/month for decoder, Dhs.199 for service package downgrade, Dhs.500 early contract termination

Communications **Television**

Postal Services

Applying For A PO Box

1 Overview

There is no home postal delivery system in the UAE; all mail is delivered to the Central Post Office and subsequently distributed to post boxes in one of 22 post office branches. For post office locations, see p.297.

While many residents direct mail to a company mailbox, it is also possible to rent a personal post office box.

Validity The rental period runs from January 1st – December 31st. You can rent it for one year or a portion of a year and it can be renewed for up to three years.

2 Prerequisites

- Applicant must be resident in Dubai

3 What To Bring

Private Box
- ☐ Passport (two copies)
- ☐ Valid residence permit (two copies)
- ☐ Two passport photographs
- ☐ Completed application form (available from post office or downloaded from www.emiratespost.co.ae)

Fees
- ☐ Dhs.50 – initial registration fee
- ☐ Dhs.200 – annual rental fee
- ☐ Dhs.10 for each key
- ☐ Dhs.200 – annual renewal

Company Box
- ☐ Completed and signed application form with a company stamp
- ☐ Valid trade licence (copy)
- ☐ If trade licence is not ready yet, a letter from the Dubai Department of Economic Development confirming that the company has applied for a trade licence and that the department has no objection to the applicant opening a post box

Fee
- ☐ Dhs.50 – initial registration fee
- ☐ Dhs.500 – annual rental fee
- ☐ Dhs.500 – annual renewal
- ☐ Dhs.10 – rental for each key

4 Procedure

Location Post Office, Various (see p.297)

Hours Sun – Thurs 08:00 – 20:00

- Select a post office where you would like to rent a post box
- Go to that post office, submit all documents and pay the rental fee

Additional Services

- You will be assigned a box number
- Renew rental yearly by paying the annual rental fee

Validity Rental is for one calendar year.

Info You've Got Mail!

Rather than popping by your PO box to check if you have mail, you can track your deliveries online at www.emiratespost.co.ae (where you can also apply for or renew a PO box online). Customers can pay an annual fee of Dhs.50 to be informed by email when postal items that require a signature or company stamp have been delivered. In addition, EziMail offers the personal collection of customers' mail from their PO box, delivered in a sealed satchel to an office or residence at a convenient time.

Info EMPOST Service

To save time and effort, Emirates Commercial Services Corporation, Empost, has introduced a brand new service to Emirates Post's customers who wish to rent private post boxes. Empost facilitates the renting process by delivering the post box key to the subscriber as well as collecting forms required, for only Dhs.9.

Info Business Mail

If an individual or company receives mail in such large volumes that their post box simply cannot accommodate it all, they can rent a bag to hold the mail. The Private Mail Bag Service is not available to commercial building post box subscribers though. Pricing: Dhs.475 per month (for volumes up to 75kgs) to Dhs.1375 per month (for volumes up to 750kgs). Other business services from Empost include Mandoub, a PRO service, Direct Mail and tailor-made logistical services for mailroom management.

Communications

Postal Services

The No. 1 off-road guide to the UAE

The ultimate accessory for any 4WD, *UAE Off-Road Explorer* helps drivers to discover this region's 'outback'. Just remember your 4WD was made for more than just the school run.

Supported by:

Includes Dhs.200 voucher for Off-Road Zone

UAE Off-Road Explorer
What your 4WD was made for

Driving

Overview

Overview

Driving

This chapter deals with everything to do with getting around Dubai by car. For ease of reference, the chapter has been divided into three sections: Driving Licence, Vehicle, and Traffic Accidents & Fines.

Driving Licence

It's essential that you have the correct documents when driving in Dubai. If not, the insurance on the vehicle may become invalid, and you will find yourself in trouble with the police. If you currently have a foreign licence, you may be permitted to transfer it to a Dubai licence. The flowchart on p.121 will guide you through the steps involved in obtaining a licence.

Vehicle

Once you're licensed to drive a private vehicle in Dubai, the next step is often to buy a car. A car dealership will help you through the various procedures, but if you're buying – or selling – privately, you'll need to know which steps to follow. You will also need to purchase a Salik tag, which will allow you to pay for Dubai's road tolls.

Traffic Accidents & Fines

Sadly, serious traffic accidents are a daily occurrence on Dubai's busy roads. Repair shops are forbidden to repair any car (even if the damage is only minor) without a police report, so the procedure for getting police reports is covered in some detail.

Dubai Traffic Police

Dubai Traffic Police deals with all traffic offences and fines and, unlike traffic police in other emirates, they are usually very friendly, relaxed and calm. For a list of police stations, including external police desks, see p.296.

EPPCO Tasjeel & Emarat Shamil Centres

EPPCO Tasjeel and Emarat Shamil Centres will test your vehicle prior to registration. Between them they have several testing stations around Dubai and both centres have done an impressive job in creating a pleasant atmosphere and in streamlining the procedure. For a list of locations, see p.299. A number of external police desks are located at testing stations, which means that you can get the whole registration process completed in one place (see the list of external polices desks on p.295).

Road & Transport Authority

Dubai's traffic and licensing laws are subject to seemingly constant changes. The RTA was launched by the government in November 2005 and it has taken over responsibility for most procedures described in this chapter. Among other things, it is responsible for all transport and traffic projects in Dubai, and preparing transport legislation. The RTA is a good source of information on Dubai driving and licensing laws. Call 800 9090 or visit www.rta.ae.

Overview

1 Overview

This section covers procedures for both new and experienced drivers. Everything from transferring your current driving licence, to registering with a driving school and taking all tests is listed in detail.

To drive a private vehicle (non-rental or leased vehicle) in Dubai you must have a permanent Dubai driving licence or your car insurance will be invalid. You may be able to drive a vehicle with an international or foreign driving licence if you first obtain confirmation from the insurance company. Note that as soon as you receive your residence permit, you must apply for a Dubai driving licence.

Info Road Control Committee

Plainclothes policemen in unmarked cars regularly patrol the streets for traffic offenders. They are even more active since the introduction of more severe traffic laws in November 2006 to counter the rapidly rising number of traffic accidents and violations. Be warned that if a driver disregards the law, a full report will be made and a fine or ban imposed, but the driver will not necessarily be stopped at the time.

If you see a dangerous driver on the road, call 800 4353 to lodge a complaint.

Info Eye Tests

To apply for a Dubai driving licence, you must first take an eye test. You can do so at any authorised optician around Dubai, and at most hospitals and clinics. Let them know it's for a driving licence. You will need two passport photos, and will be charged a small fee. You'll receive a certificate that you will need to present when applying for your licence.

Obtaining A Dubai Driving Licence

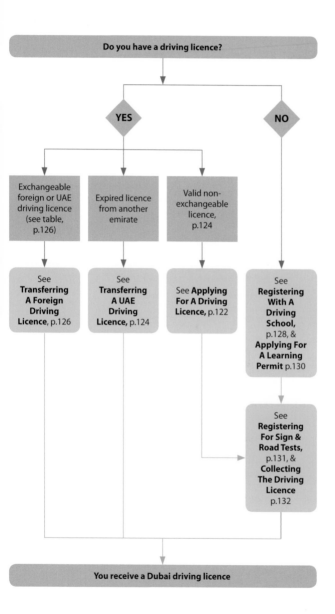

Do you have a driving licence?

YES   **NO**

Exchangeable foreign or UAE driving licence (see table, p.126)

Expired licence from another emirate

Valid non-exchangeable licence, p.124

See **Transferring A Foreign Driving Licence**, p.126

See **Transferring A UAE Driving Licence**, p.124

See **Applying For A Driving Licence**, p.122

See **Registering With A Driving School**, p.128, & **Applying For A Learning Permit** p.130

See **Registering For Sign & Road Tests**, p.131, & **Collecting The Driving Licence** p.132

Overview

Driving

You receive a Dubai driving licence

Driving Licence

Applying For A Driving Licence

1 Overview

Once you have obtained a Dubai residence permit and you wish to drive a private car (non-rental or leased) in the UAE, you must apply for a Dubai driving licence.

International and foreign driving licences are valid for use only up to the date on which the residence permit is issued.

If you have a valid exchangeable licence from another country, see Transferring a Foreign Driving Licence on p.126. You may transfer it to a Dubai licence the same day and you do not need to follow the procedure below.

In all other cases, you will need to go to one of the five driving institutes authorised to issue licences (see p.129). You can complete the full application process at these institutes as they have RTA officers on site (see Registering With A Driving School, p.128).

Validity 10 years

2 Prerequisites

- Applicant must be resident in Dubai
- Applicant must be at least 18 years of age

3 What To Bring

☐ Passport (original and copy)
☐ Residence permit (copy)
☐ One passport photograph (6cm x 4cm)
☐ Eye test certificate (see p.120)

Fees ☐ Dhs.100 – application fee
☐ Dhs.20 – typing fee

4 Procedure

Location Approved driving institutes, Various (see p.280)

Hours Sun – Thurs 07:30 – 14:30

Registration • Collect the driving licence application form from any

- Have the form typed in Arabic at the typing office
- Submit all documents at the customer service counter
- The officer will process the paperwork and return the documents to you
- Take the documents to the cashier and pay the required application fee

- The officer will inform you which step to follow next
- If you have an invalid or non-exchangeable driving licence, you will either have to take a road test or attend a driving school (see Registering For Sign & Road Tests p.131, or Registering with a Driving School p.128)
- If you do not have a driving licence, you will have to attend driving school (see Registering With A Driving School p.128)

Tip Driving School Assistance

If you are learning to drive with an approved driving school, then the school should be able to help with your licence application.

Law Probationary Driving Licence

Drivers between the ages of 18 and 21 receive annual renewable probationary driving licences. Strict regulations apply with probationary licences. If the driver is found guilty of a dangerous offence, causing a serious accident, running a red light, or accumulates more than 12 black points (see p.162) in one year, the licence is withdrawn and the application procedure must be started again from the beginning (this includes sitting all tests).

Be Prepared

Before you get behind the wheel make sure you have your wits about you. The driving in Dubai leaves rather a lot to be desired and the number of traffic accidents is quite shocking. For more information on driving habits refer to the Driving section of the Residents chapter in the *Dubai Explorer – The Complete Residents' Guide*, available in all leading bookshops and supermarkets.

Driving Licence

Transferring A UAE Driving Licence To Dubai

1 Overview

If you are moving to Dubai from another emirate and you already have a driving licence issued in that emirate, you can continue to drive with your current licence. Once it expires you can renew it in the original emirate, but below is the procedure for having it changed to a Dubai licence.

Validity 10 years

2 Prerequisites

- Applicant must be resident in Dubai
- Driving licence is from another emirate

3 What To Bring

- ☐ Passport (original and copy)
- ☐ Residence permit (copy)
- ☐ Driving licence (original and copy)
- ☐ NOC from the RTA (see below)
- ☐ Traffic Police file from current emirate (see below)
- ☐ Driving licence application form typed/hand-written in Arabic (see below)
- ☐ One passport photograph (6cm x 4cm)
- ☐ Eye test certificate (see p.120)

Fees
- ☐ Dhs.110 – application fee
- ☐ Dhs.20 – typing fee

4 Procedure

Location RTA licensing offices, Various (see p.298)

Hours Sun – Thurs 07:30 – 14:30

- Go to the transfer licence counter
- Request a no objection certificate from the RTA addressed to the Traffic Police of the emirate that issued your current driving licence

Other Emirates
- Present the letter to the Traffic Police of the emirate that issued your current licence
- They will give you a stamped and sealed copy of your Traffic Police file
- Collect the driving licence application form from an RTA office
- Have the form typed in Arabic at the typing office
- Submit all documents at the customer services counter

Reactivating A Disconnected Line

1 Overview

If the telephone bill is not paid within a specified period, the line will be disconnected in two stages. The first stage allows only receipt of calls; the second stage involves complete deactivation of the line.

Landline Telephone

- Outgoing calls will be cut 2 days after bill payment due date
- Incoming calls can still be received (non-payment penalty already applies) for 15 days after the payment was due
- The line will be disconnected 45 days after the payment was due.
- The number will be cancelled 3 months later

Mobile Telephone

- Outgoing calls will be cut two days after bill payment due date
- Incoming calls can still be received (non-payment penalty does not yet apply) for 15 days after the payment was due
- The line will be disconnected 45 days later
- The number will be cancelled 3 months later

2 Prerequisites

- Existing telephone or mobile phone line – unpaid, bill overdue

3 What To Bring

- ☐ Bill or subscriber name or telephone number
- ☐ Amount due
- ☐ Dhs.50 – landline penalty charge if bill exceeds Dhs.500
- ☐ Dhs.25 – mobile phone penalty charge

4 Procedure

Location Etisalat, Various (see p.300)

Hours Sun-Thurs 08:00-20:00; Sat 08:00-13:00

Incoming Calls Only
- Pay the outstanding amount (plus penalty) through any of the payment options outlined on p.82
- Outgoing call service will be reconnected within one day

Disconnected Line
- Pay the outstanding amount plus the penalty at the cashier at any Etisalat office
- The telephone line will be reactivated the same day

Cancelled Line
- Once the line has been cancelled, arrears must be settled at any Etisalat office before a new line can be applied for
- Collect and complete the application form in English or Arabic (typed or hand-written)

- The officer will process the paperwork
- Take the documents to the cashier and pay the required application fee
- Submit all documents and the receipt at the data entry counter
- Wait for your name to be called and your documents will be given back to you
- Queue for your photograph to be taken
- Your licence will be ready within 5 – 10 minutes

5 Related Procedures

- Renewing A Driving Licence, p.134
- Importing A Vehicle Into The UAE, p.154

Info **Car Rental**

Until you acquire full residency you may drive a rental car with an international licence, or with a valid exchangeable foreign licence (see Exchangeable Foreign Driving Licences table, p.126).

Passport? Deposit?
Note that car rental firms are not permitted to retain customer passports; give them a photocopy of your passport and if they insist on having the original, contact the police. It's also illegal for them to request a deposit from you (although they will request your credit card details in order to collect future payments).

Info **mParking Service**

Existing parking meters are gradually being phased out and replaced by high-tech ones with advanced specifications. There is also a new system called the mParking Service which allows you to purchase a parking permit by sending an SMS to 7275 (PARK). The required amount will be deducted from your mobile phone credit or added to your bill. You will also be sent a reminder via SMS if your permit is about to expire. You can register for this service at www.mpark.rta.ae or by calling 800 9090.

Driving Licence

Driving

Driving Licence

Transferring A Foreign Driving Licence To Dubai

1 Overview

The RTA allows licence holders of certain countries to transfer (or exchange) their valid licence to a Dubai licence without having to take a driving test.

Validity 10 years

Exchangeable Driving Licences			
Australia	France	Norway	South Korea
Austria	Germany	Oman	Spain
Bahrain	Greece	Poland	Sweden
Belgium	Ireland	Portugal	Switzerland
Canada	Italy	Qatar	The Netherlands
Czech Republic	Japan	Romania	Turkey
Denmark	Kuwait	Saudi Arabia	United Kingdom
Finland	New Zealand	South Africa	United States

Iranian Nationals Some Iranian government employees may exchange their licence for a Dubai driving licence. Others must take the sign and road tests with the RTA (see Registering For Sign & Road Tests, p.131).

Canadian Nationals Holders of Canadian driving licences must obtain an affidavit (in English) from the Canadian Consulate in Dubai verifying that the licence is genuine, before applying for a licence transfer.

Other Nationals Licences from Greece, Canada, Turkey, Japan and South Korea must be translated at the relevant consulate before a licence transfer can be applied for. If in doubt, check with your consulate first.

2 Prerequisites

- Applicant must be resident in Dubai
- Applicant must be 18 or older (if under 21, proof of parent's permission)
- Driving licence from one of the countries listed above must be valid, or within one year of the date of expiry
- The applicant must be a citizen of the country the licence was registered in

3 What To Bring

- ☐ Passport (original and copy)
- ☐ Residence permit (copy)
- ☐ Current driving licence (original and copy)
- ☐ Two passport photographs (6cm x 4cm)
- ☐ Eye test certificate (see p.120)

- ☐ Driving Licence Application form in Arabic (typed or hand-written)
- ☐ Letter from your consulate verifying the driving licence (if applicable, eg Canada)
- ☐ No objection letter from your sponsor
- ☐ Translation of driving licence (if applicable – see list opposite)

Fee ☐ Dhs.110 application fee

4 Procedure

Location RTA licensing offices, Various (see p.298)

Hours Sun – Thurs 07:30 – 14:30

- Collect the driving licence application form from any RTA office
- Have the form typed in Arabic at the typing office
- Submit all documents at the control counter
- The officer will process the paperwork
- Take the documents to the cashier and pay the required application fee
- Submit all documents and the receipt at the data entry counter
- Wait for your name to be called for your photograph to be taken
- Your licence will be ready within 5 – 10 minutes

5 Related Procedures

- Renewing A Driving Licence, p.134
- Replacing A Driving Licence, p.136
- Buying A Vehicle, p.140

Tip Licence Consistency

You may not be able to exchange your driving licence – even if your driving licence was issued in a country on the exchangeable driving licence list - if your passport was issued in a country that is not on the list. You will then have to follow the same procedure as non-exchangeable licences (see p.126). It is best to check your eligibility with the RTA (800 9090).

Tip Expired Licence?

If your licence expired more than one year ago, you will have to take all driving tests prior to receiving your Dubai driving licence.

Driving Licence

Driving

Driving Licence

Registering With A Driving School

Driving Licence

Driving

1 Overview

If you have never owned a driving licence, or if you cannot transfer your licence issued in your previous country of residence, you will have to attend a driving school and take driving tests.

Many driving schools will take care of the full application process for their students. Five driving institutes (see p.129) have been authorised by the RTA to open a Traffic Police file and issue driving licences. Driving tests are conducted at these institutes' premises by officers from the RTA. You can take lessons through a smaller driving school (which can often offer more flexibility) and then do your tests at one of the five institutes, or you can complete the entire process through one of the authorised institutes.

Depending on the competency of the driver, the process of learning to drive and passing the tests could take between two and five months. Learners can apply for a licence for manual or automatic vehicles.

Testing   The testing process consists of four components:

- Internal parking test, overseen by the driving school
- Signal (highway code) test, overseen by the driving school
- Assessment test, overseen by RTA officers
- Road test, overseen by RTA officers

2 Prerequisites

- Applicant must be at least 18 years of age
- Motorbike: applicant must be at least 17 years of age

3 What To Bring

- ☐ Passport (original and two copies)
- ☐ No objection letter from your sponsor
- ☐ Residence permit (copy)
- ☐ Eight passport photographs
- ☐ Eye test certificate, p.120

Fee   ☐ Dhs.3,000 (approx) – basic fee for 40 lessons (cost varies according to school and number of lessons – this does not include tests and other charges that will need to be paid)

4 Procedure

- Choose a reputable driving school
- Sign up and submit all documents
- The school will process the paperwork with the RTA

Driving Licence

- You will receive a learning permit immediately or, if you're using one of the school's smaller branches, after about two days

- Attend 40 classes and a varying amount of lectures

- When your instructor feels you are prepared, you will take the first internal test with the driving school (parking test)

- Once you've passed that test, your instructor will set a date for the second (signal test). The third and fourth test must be carried out at one of the five authorised driving institutes. The third test is for the RTA to assess whether you are ready to take the fourth (and final) practical road test

5 Related Procedures

- Applying For A Driving Licence, p.122
- Registering For Sign & Road Tests, p.131

Applying For A Driving Licence, p.122 — Registering For Sign & Road Tests, p.131

Info Female Or Male Instructor?

Women are required to take lessons with a female instructor. If a woman wishes to take lessons with a male instructor, she must obtain a no-objection letter from her sponsor and the RTA. This letter must indicate the name of the instructor and the institute. The institute will organise matters with the RTA.

Tip Pre-Booked Driving Lessons

Some driving schools insist that you pay for a set of pre-booked lessons. In some cases the package extends to 40 lessons and can cost up to Dhs.3,000. These lessons must be taken on consecutive days and usually last 30 minutes. You can also take classes on Fridays – but this is also charged at a higher rate.

On the other hand, some companies offer lessons on an hourly basis, as and when you like, at a cost of around Dhs.50 per hour. Choose according to your needs and the school's reputation.

Info Driving Institutes

The five driving institutes authorised by the RTA to instruct and test learner drivers and to process the paperwork are:

Al Ahli Driving School	04 341 1500
Belhasa Driving School	04 324 3535
Dubai Driving Centre	04 345 5855
Emirates Driving Institute	04 263 1100
Galadari Driving School	04 267 6166

Driving Licence

Driving

Driving Licence

Applying For A Learning Permit

1 Overview

A learning permit allows a new driver to practise in the company of a driving instructor. Normally the driving school applies for the permit on the student's behalf, but you might have to apply on your own.

2 Prerequisites

- Applicant must be resident in Dubai
- Applicant has applied for a permanent driving licence (see Applying For A Driving Licence, p.122)

3 What To Bring

- ☐ Passport (original and copy)
- ☐ Residence permit (copy)
- ☐ Two passport photographs (6cm x 4cm)
- ☐ Eye test certificate (see p.120)
- ☐ Driving licence application form
- Fee ☐ Dhs.40 – application fee

4 Procedure

Location Approved driving institute, Various (see p.280)

Hours Sun – Thurs 07:30 – 14:30

- Collect the driving licence application form
- Have the form typed in Arabic at the typing office
- Submit all documents at the customer service counter
- The officer will process the paperwork and return the documents to you
- Take the documents to the cashier and pay the application fee
- The application will be approved the same day – but you may have to wait up to two months to start your lessons

5 Related Procedures

- Registering With A Driving School, p.128
- Registering For Sign & Road Tests, p.131

Driving Licence

Registering For Sign & Road Tests

1 Overview

After passing the internal test (parking) with the driving school, you must register for the sign and road tests. You may also have to attend some lectures. You will sit three tests, each on a different date.

2 Prerequisites

- Applicant has applied for a Dubai driving licence (see p.122)
- If attending a driving school, applicant has passed the internal test

3 What To Bring

- ☐ Passport (original and copy)
- ☐ Residence permit (copy)
- ☐ Eight passport photographs (6cm x 4cm)
- ☐ Eye test certificate (see p.120)
- ☐ Application form
- Fee ☐ Dhs.80 sign test fee + Dhs.80 assessment test fee + Dhs.80 road test fee + Dhs.100 service charge

4 Procedure

Location Approved driving Institute, Various (see p.280)

Hours Various

- Complete the driving licence application form
- Submit all documents
- Pay the test fee
- You will be given a time and date for the sign test
- Once you have passed the sign test, return to the same counter with the pass certificate
- You will be given a time and date for the assessment test
- Once you have passed the assessment test, return to the same counter with the pass certificate
- You will be given a time and date for the final road test. There is a waiting period for the road test (average one month)
- If you fail, you will need to take four to six lessons before retaking the test, then return to the counter, pay for your lessons and the test fee, and you will be given a new test time and date
- After passing all tests, collect your licence (see Collecting The Driving Licence, p.132). You may have to attend a final lecture on road safety

5 Related Procedure

- Applying For A Driving Licence, p.122

Driving Licence

Collecting The Driving Licence

1 Overview

This is the final step in obtaining your Dubai driving licence after you have passed all the tests.

2 Prerequisites

- Applicant has passed the internal, sign, assessment and road tests (see Registering For Sign & Road Tests, p.131)

3 What To Bring

☐ Pass receipt

☐ One form of ID (passport or labour card)

Fee ☐ Dhs.110 – service charge

4 Procedure

Location Approved driving institute, Various (see p.280)

Hours Sun – Thurs 07:30 – 14:30

- After passing all tests, submit the pass receipt to the driving school
- You may have to attend a final lecture on road safety and car maintenance while the school processes your paperwork and opens your file for the Traffic Police
- Pay the required fee
- Have your photograph taken
- Your licence will be ready within 5 – 10 minutes

5 Related Procedures

- Renewing A Driving Licence, p.134
- Replacing A Driving Licence, p.136

Law Carry Your Driving Licence

If you fail to produce your driving licence during a police spot check not only will you be fined, but you also risk having the car impounded and having to appear in court. If you take your licence to the police within 24 hours, your fine will be reduced.

Driving Licence

Applying For An International Driving Licence

1 Overview

Residents of Dubai who are travelling overseas and who wish to drive in another country can apply for an international driving licence at Emirates Post outlets, and the Automobile & Touring Club or its 20 sub-agents. Note that the Dubai Traffic Police do not handle this procedure.

⚠ If you wish to use your Dubai driving licence as a form of identification while travelling, note that your date of birth is not shown on it.

Validity   One year

2 Prerequisites

- Applicant has a valid Dubai driving licence

3 What To Bring

- ☐ Valid Dubai driving licence (original and copy)
- ☐ Completed application form
- ☐ Passport and residence permit (copy)
- ☐ Two passport photos (6cm x 4cm)

Fee ☐ Dhs.150 – licence fee

4 Procedure

- Go to an Emirates Post Office or one of the outlets listed below
- Submit all documents
- Pay the licence fee
- The licence will be prepared for you while you wait

📄 Before purchasing an international licence, check the requirements of the country you are visiting; some countries allow visitors to drive with a UAE-issued driving licence.

5 Related Procedure

- Applying For A Tourism Certificate, p.150

Info ATCUAE's Licence Outlets In The UAE

The Automobile & Touring Club's licensed outlets include: Dnata, Eppco, International Motoring Club, Belhasa Driving Centre, Belhasa Travel & Tourism, Emirates Driving Centre, DCA Social & Sports Club, Arabian Automobile Association and Shakiba Travel.

Driving Licence

Driving

Driving Licence

Renewing A Driving Licence

1 Overview

Dubai driving licences must be renewed every 10 years, and probationary licences yearly. The procedure for renewal is similar to licence registration. Before the licence is renewed, all outstanding traffic fines must be cleared (see Paying Fines, p.160).

2 Prerequisites

- Applicant holds a Dubai driving licence (valid or expired)

3 What To Bring

- ☐ Passport (original and copy)
- ☐ Driving licence (original)
- ☐ Eye test certificate (see p.120)

Fee
- ☐ Dhs.110 – renewal charge for full or probationary driving licences
- ☐ Money for outstanding traffic fines (if applicable)

4 Procedure

Location RTA licensing offices/approved driving institutes, Various (see p.298)

Hours Sun – Thurs 07:30 – 14:30

- Submit all documents at the customer service counter
- The officer will process the paperwork and return the documents to you
- Take the documents to the cashier and pay the required fee and any outstanding fines
- Submit all documents and the receipt at data entry counter
- Wait for your name to be called for your new photograph to be taken
- Your licence will be ready within 5 – 10 minutes

Tip **Licence Renewal Outside Dubai**

No matter where you are, you can renew your Dubai driving licence online at www.rta.ae. While you will be charged a credit card commission and courier service charge, you will not have to undergo the prerequisite eye test.

Provide the personal details requested; the police will validate the information and send you a username and password by email. Log on and follow the prompts. The Traffic Police will courier your new driving licence to you. Note that when renewing this way, your previous photo will be used for your new licence.

Law **Zero Tolerance**

The Dubai Police exercise a strict zero tolerance policy when it comes to drinking and driving. If you're involved in an accident, regardless of whose fault it is, and you have consumed any alcohol, your insurance is automatically void and you are likely to end up in jail. Be smart – don't drink and drive.

Driving Licence

Driving

Driving Licence

Replacing A Driving Licence

1 Overview

If you lose your Dubai driving licence, you must first report the loss with Dubai Police, you can then have it replaced at any RTA licensing office. Damaged licences can also be replaced at an RTA licensing office.

2 Prerequisites

- Current driving licence has been lost or damaged

3 What To Bring

- ☐ Passport (original and copy)
- ☐ Damaged driving licence (if applicable)
- ☐ One passport photo (6cm x 4cm)
- ☐ If replacing a lost licence you will need an eye test certificate

Fee ☐ Dhs.110 – replacement fee (lost or damaged)

4 Procedure

Location RTA licensing offices, Various (see p.298)

Hours Sun – Thurs 07:30 – 14:30

- Collect the driving licence application form from an RTA driving licence office
- Submit all documents at the control counter
- The officer will process the paperwork and return the documents to you
- Take the documents to the cashier and pay the replacement fee
- Submit all documents and the receipt at the data entry counter
- Wait for your name to be called for your photograph to be taken
- Your licence will be ready within 5 – 10 minutes

Info **The End Of Temporary Licences**

The RTA has abolished temporary driving licences. Those with driving licences from their own country that are on the exchangeable licence list may drive rental vehicles while on a visit visa. Those without an exchangeable licence, or who have a licence issued from a different country than their passport may not drive in Dubai until they have a residence permit and can apply for a Dubai driving licence (which involves taking 40 classes).

Info **Obnoxious Driver Hassling You?**

Dubai Police would like motorists to assist with keeping errant drivers under tabs. Call 800 4353 or log on to www.dubaipolice.gov.ae to report lawbreakers and maniacs on the road.

Driving Licence

Driving

Buying A Vehicle Overview

1 Overview

- Remember that car dealers, shipping companies and various other service companies will assist you with many of the following procedures, for a fee.

- All application forms listed can be filled out in either English or Arabic and can be either hand-written or typed.

Law Blood Money

If you cause someone's death while driving, even accidentally, you are liable to pay a sum of money known as 'blood money' to the family of the deceased. The amount per victim is decided by the court. Make sure that your insurance policy covers this cost, and check the terms and conditions very carefully. Insurance companies will only pay if they cannot find a way of claiming that the insurance was invalid (for instance, if the driver was speeding, driving without a licence, under the influence of alcohol etc). You will be locked up until you or the insurance company comes up with the amount, or the family of the deceased waives the right to blood money.

Info Oman Insurance & Tolls

It's wise to check whether your insurance covers you for the Sultanate of Oman, as even if you're not intending to leave the Emirates you may find yourself driving through small Omani enclaves, especially if you are driving off-road near Hatta, through Wadi Bih, or on the East Coast. Short-term insurance for Oman can be easily arranged.

If you cross a formal border post, such as the one at Hatta, you will be charged a Dhs.20 to Dhs.30 'border toll' as well. Have cash on hand.

Buying A Vehicle

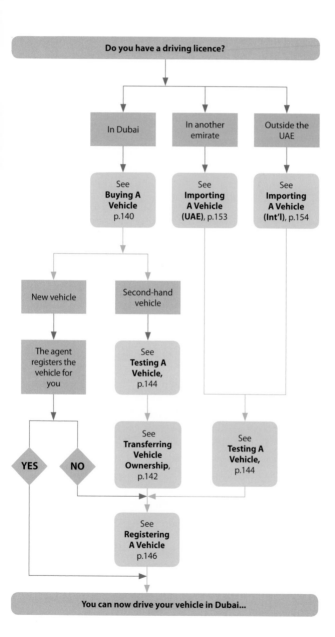

Do you have a driving licence?

In Dubai → In another emirate → Outside the UAE

In Dubai	In another emirate	Outside the UAE
See **Buying A Vehicle** p.140	See **Importing A Vehicle (UAE)**, p.153	See **Importing A Vehicle (Int'l)**, p.154

New vehicle → Second-hand vehicle

The agent registers the vehicle for you

See **Testing A Vehicle**, p.144

See **Transferring Vehicle Ownership**, p.142

See **Testing A Vehicle**, p.144

YES **NO**

See **Registering A Vehicle** p.146

You can now drive your vehicle in Dubai...

Vehicle

Driving

Vehicle

Buying A Vehicle

1 Overview

The process of buying a vehicle in Dubai is fairly straightforward.

A new vehicle is obviously more expensive than a second-hand one, but you won't have to deal with vehicle testing for two years, nor will you have to worry about the legitimacy of the sale.

2 Prerequisites

- Unless you're a cash buyer, you need to meet the requirements for auto finance through one of the UAE banks (see below). If you are buying the car through a dealer, they will assist with this procedure.

3 What To Bring

☐ Cash for purchase

Or, if financing:

☐ Passport (original and copy)

☐ Residence permit (original and copy)

☐ Driving licence (original and copy)

☐ Bank statements for the past three months, showing salary transfer

☐ Salary certificate from employer

☐ If financing is for a company car: valid trade licence (copy)

4 Procedure

New or used car dealer, or private sale:

- Find a vehicle you would like to purchase
- If the vehicle is second hand, have it tested
- Check with the Dubai Traffic Police that the vehicle is neither stolen nor has any liens or fines attached to it
- Obtain financing if necessary (at a bank or with the dealer)
- After you have purchased the vehicle, you will need to insure it and register it with the Dubai Traffic Police

The above procedures will probably be done for you if you purchase the vehicle from a dealer.

5 Related Procedures

- Transferring Vehicle Ownership, p.142
- Testing A Vehicle, p.144
- Registering A Vehicle, p.146

Tip | Buy Or Sell

There is another more straightforward way to buy or sell a used vehicle privately. Once you have arranged car insurance (either through transfer or a new policy), the buyer and seller simply need to meet at one of the 10 external police desks listed on p.295 bringing the documents listed on the left. The whole process can then be completed very quickly.

If buying privately, it is recommended that you have the car independently inspected before the handover procedure. A number of garages, including EPPCO Tasjeel (see. p.299), AAA Service Center (04 285 8989, www.aaadubai.com) and Max Garage (04 340 8200, www.maxdubai.com), offer pre-purchase inspections and the service should cost around Dhs.300.

Info | Fine Online

You can check whether there are any outstanding fines against a vehicle by entering the registration plate number online at www.dubaipolice.gov.ae.

Tip | Licence Plates

If you are buying a used car and are completing the whole process at one of the 10 external police desks (p.295) it may not be necessary to get new licence plates. In most cases the plates are simply transfered to the new owner.

Info | Special Licence Plate Number?

The Traffic Police set aside licence plates with desirable or short number combinations, and sell them for anywhere between Dhs.1,000 and Dhs.35,000. If you are interested in purchasing one of these plates, visit the Administration Department in the Traffic Police HQ or log on to www.dubaipolice.gov.ae.

Vehicle

Driving

Vehicle

Transferring Vehicle Ownership

1 Overview

⚠ To register a second-hand car or motorcycle in your name, you must first officially transfer vehicle ownership. A Dhs.3,000 fine is imposed on both the buyer and seller if a vehicle is sold unofficially (ie. if ownership is not transferred through the Traffic Police).

⚠ Before purchasing a second-hand vehicle, check with the Traffic Police to ensure there are no outstanding fines or defaulted loan payments, and the car is not wanted or stolen.

2 Prerequisites

- Buyer is resident in Dubai
- All outstanding fines have been paid
- Insurance is valid for a minimum of 13 months

3 What To Bring

Buyer
- ☐ Passport and Dubai driving licence (original and copy)
- ☐ Vehicle registration card (original)
- ☐ Original licence plates
- ☐ Vehicle permit application form
- ☐ No objection letter from the finance company (if applicable)
- ☐ Insurance certificate (original)
- ☐ Transfer of loan by the finance company or bank (if applicable)

Seller
- ☐ Seller must be present to sign documents or bring a sale deed letter from a car showroom or dealer
- ☐ Passport (original and copy)
- ☐ Residence permit (original and copy)

Fee
- ☐ Dhs.20 – transfer fee for light vehicle or motorcycle

4 Procedure

Insurance
- The first step is to take a copy of the vehicle registration card to the seller's insurance provider
- The seller terminates the insurance policy and either requests a refund or transfers the policy to the buyer

  📄 If valid for more than six months, insurance should be refundable.

- If the insurance policy is not transferable, the buyer must obtain their own insurance cover from any insurance provider

Location RTA licensing offices, Various (see p.298)

Hours Sun – Thurs 07:00 – 14:30

istration
- Both parties go to a vehicle licensing centre or the Traffic Police Headquarters
- At the typing booth, the clerk will fill out the vehicle permit application form for you
- Submit all documents at the registration counter where a check for outstanding fines will be run
- Seller must pay all outstanding fines before proceeding

Buyer
- Pay the transfer fee to the cashier
- Submit all documents and the receipt at the customer service counter
- Wait for your name to be called
- The new registration card will be issued within 5 – 10 minutes
- Send a copy of the new registration card to your finance company

Seller
- Photocopy the new registration card and send it to your insurance company as proof that the car has been sold and ownership officially transferred. The insurer may also request a copy of the buyers' insurance certificate

5 Related Procedures

- Registering A Vehicle, p.146
- Paying Fines, p.160

Tip Quick Vehicle Ownership Transfer

For convenience, there are several external police desks around Dubai that offer the ownership transfer service at no extra cost. All transfer procedures will be performed, including checking for outstanding fines. Licence plates and the vehicle registration card will be issued on the spot. See the table on p.295 for a list of these service centres.

Info Vehicle Insurance

The insurance provider will need to know the make, model, year of manufacture and chassis number of the vehicle. Annual insurance policies are 13 months in length, covering the one month grace period the Traffic Police allows you after your registration expires.

Rates depend on the age and model of the car as well as your previous insurance history, and normally range from 4 – 7% of the car's listed value. Cars older than five years are insured at a rate of 5% of the listed value. Fully comprehensive and personal accident insurance is strongly advised.

Rates also depend on whether agency repairs are specifically requested. Normally, agency repairs are only offered on vehicles less than three years old.

Vehicle

Driving

Testing A Vehicle

1 Overview

This is an annual procedure for all vehicles older than two years. As well as being carried out by Dubai Traffic Police, vehicle testing has been outsourced to EPPCO Tasjeel, Emarat Shamil and Tamam. There are five Tasjeel and two Shamil testing stations in Dubai where you can have the vehicle tested and registered. The following procedure refers to Eppco Tasjeel, but the Shamil service is virtually the same. Shamil also offers a VIP service where they will collect the car, test, register and return it to you for Dhs.200, including the set costs below. See p.299 for a list of the testing station locations.

The technical inspection involves the following:

- Brake test
- Exhaust test
- Visual inspection (body and frame)
- Light test
- Side slip test
- Shock absorber test
- Brake test and brake quality test
- Exhaust test
- Road test (engine performance and gears)

2 Prerequisites

- Vehicle is older than two years

3 What To Bring

☐ Vehicle registration card, or

☐ Export/import documents

Normal Test
☐ Dhs.73 – light vehicle or motorcycle testing fee

☐ Dhs.75 – heavy vehicle testing fee

☐ Dhs.50 – second vehicle retest within 31 days

☐ Dhs.73 – vehicle retest after 31 days

Auction Test Fee
☐ Dhs.250 – testing fee

4 Procedure

Location EPPCO Tasjeel or Emarat Shamil, Various (see p.148)

Hours Various

- Drive to the registration lane
- Submit your registration card or export/import documents at the check-in booth
- The registration card will be punched and returned to you
- Pull into any available testing bay and park your vehicle
- Remove all valuables
- Leave the key and registration card with the inspector
- Go to the main building and wait for your name to be called
- When your name is called, pay the test fee at the counter
- You will receive a test result certificate
- Return to your vehicle and remove the licence plates, if they are not the new licence plates
- Proceed with vehicle registration (see Registering a Vehicle, p.146, or Renewing Vehicle Registration, p.151)

Failed Test
- If your vehicle fails the inspection, have it repaired and retested within 31 days for no additional fee
- If the vehicle fails a second time, the second retest within the first 31 days costs Dhs.50
- If the vehicle is retested after the first 31 days, the original testing fee of Dhs.73 will be charged

Vehicle

Driving

Tip **Pre-Inspected Second-Hand Vehicles**

All vehicles for sale at Dubai Municipality's Used Car Complex in Al Awir have been pre-inspected by EPPCO Tasjeel.

Tip **Temporary Insurance**

While driving with blue temporary export licence plates, regular insurance may not be valid. Special temporary insurance may be purchased for a period of three days for export within the UAE and 14 days for international export.

Vehicle

Registering A Vehicle

1 Overview

In order to obtain licence plates for the vehicle, the car must first be insured and registered with the Dubai Traffic Police. There are no longer any restrictions on the number of cars anyone may register.

Dealer Purchase If you have purchased a new vehicle from a dealer, the dealer will register the car for you. You do not need to test a new vehicle for the first two years, though you must re-register it after one year. In some cases, second-hand dealers will register the car for you.

⚠ If you purchase a second-hand vehicle, the registration date is not necessarily the anniversary of the date of purchase.

⚠ Make sure that the particulars on the application form, customs certificate, contract and insurance are the same as those that appear in your passport.

2 Prerequisites

- Buyer is resident in Dubai
- Insurance is valid for a minimum of 13 months
- Vehicle has been tested (see Testing a Vehicle, p.144)

Imported Vehicle
- Vehicle conforms to Gulf specifications (see Importing A Vehicle (International), p.154)
- Vehicle has been cleared through customs, or
- If transferred/imported from another emirate, vehicle registration has been cancelled in that emirate

3 What To Bring

☐ Vehicle insurance certificate (original, valid 13 months)

Your vehicle needs to be insured before it can be registered. You can arrange this through the dealer or it can be done independently. If you do not have an insurance policy, insurance providers have booths at the testing/registration centres.

☐ Vehicle transfer or customs certificate (if applicable)

☐ Proof of purchase agreement (original)

☐ If second-hand or imported, current registration card

☐ If imported, blue temporary licence plates

Private Vehicle
☐ Valid Dubai driving licence (original and copy), or

☐ Home country driving licence (original and copy)

☐ Passport (original and copy)

The above items are only necessary if you do not already have a Traffic Police file.

nmercial Vehicle ☐ Valid trade licence (original and copy)

nported Vehicle ☐ Application form from the RTA

☐ Blue temporary export licence plates

☐ Vehicle clearance certificate or customs papers

☐ GCC specification letter (if applicable)

☐ Proof of residence in Dubai – tenancy contract, DEWA or Etisalat bill (original)

Fees ☐ Dhs.10 – typing fee

☐ Dhs.70 – long number plates, or

☐ Dhs.50 – short number plates

☐ Dhs.420-Dhs.490 – annual vehicle registration fee (depending on size of plates) or

☐ Dhs.165 – annual motorcycle registration fee

☐ Dhs.20 – import registration fee (if applicable)

4 Procedure

ocation EPPCO Tasjeel or Emarat Shamil, Various (see p.148)

Hours Various

istration • Take the passed test certificate (see Testing A Vehicle, p.144), the old licence plates (if not new Dubai plates) and the insurance papers to the typing counter

• Your application form will be typed for you; pay Dhs.10 at the same counter

• At the Traffic Police Counter, submit all documents and the licence plates

• Your application will be validated and entered into the system

• Go to the cashier and pay the registration fee, the licence plate fee and any outstanding fines (cash or credit card)

• Wait for your name to be called

• You will receive your vehicle registration card and insurance papers

Licence Plates • Go to the last police counter

• Submit the receipt and vehicle registration card

• You will be given new plates and a date sticker for the rear licence plate; your registration card will be returned to you

• Affix the sticker to the licence plate

• Mount the plates on your vehicle

• Keep the vehicle registration card and the insurance documents in the car at all times

5 Related Procedure

• Paying Fines, p.160

EPPCO Tasjeel Centres		www.eppcouae.com
Light Vehicles, 4WD & Motorbikes		Map ref
Al Qusais	04 267 3940	6-H5
	Al Muhaisnah 4	
	Sat – Thurs 07:00 – 21:00	
Sheikh Zayed Rd	04 347 6620	2-D4
	Jct 4, next to Dubai Traffic Police HQ	
	Sat – Thurs 07:00 – 21:00	
Jebel Ali	04 883 0110	6-H5
	Shk Zayed Rd, JAFZA, Way 18	
	Sat – Thurs 07:00 – 15:30	
Used Car Complex & Pre-Auction Testing		
Al Awir	04 333 1510	5-C8
	Ras Al Khor Rd	
	Sat – Thurs 07:00 – 21:00	
Heavy Vehicles (2.5+ tons)		
Warsan	04 333 6470	Off Map
	Dubai Hatta Rd	
	Sun – Thurs 07:00 -21:00	

Emarat Shamil Centres		www.shamil.ae
Light Vehicles, 4WDs & Motorbikes		Map ref
Adhed	04 398 6006	5-C2
	Opp. Port Rashid, Bur Dubai	
	Sat – Thu 08:00 – 20:00	
Nad Al Hamar	04 289 4440	5-D7
	Nr. Coca Cola building, Rashidiya	
	Sat – Wed 08:00 – 13:00; 16:00 – 20:00	
Al Muhaisna	04 267 1117	6-H5
	Nr. Cattle Market, Al Qusais	
	Sat – Thu 08:00 – 20:00	

Tip Registration Service Companies

For those who do not wish to register the vehicle themselves, some companies offer a full registration service for a fee (in addition to the normal registration costs). They will need the vehicle's registration card, the insurance papers (with 13 months' validity) and cash for the fees and fines.

- AAA: 04 285 8989
- EPPCO Tasjeel: 800 4258
- Midland Cars: 04 396 7521/2
- Emarat Shamil: 800 4559

Tip Additional Insurance

As your vehicle insurance is most likely valid only for the UAE, it's advisable to take out additional insurance for the country to which you'll be travelling.

Setting Up Your Salik Account

1 Overview

If you intend to use Dubai's toll roads (there are four toll gates: Sheikh Zayed Road in Al Barsha near Mall of the Emirates, and in Al Safa, near the Safa Park exit, Garhoud Bridge and Al Maktoum Bridge), you must purchase a Salik tag. The tag must be attached to your windscreen and is read by radio frequency as you pass a toll gate. You'll be charged Dhs.4 each time you cross a toll gate, but if you travel between the two toll gates on Sheikh Zayed Road during one trip (and in the space of an hour) you will only be charged once. If your tag is out of credit you will be fined Dhs.50 for each gate you pass through. If you do not have a tag and you cross a toll gate, you have two days to purchase a tag before you will receive a Dhs.100 fine – the fine increases by Dhs.100 each time you offend.

2 Prerequisites

- You are the owner of a vehicle (Salik tags should come with rental vehicles and toll fees will be charged to your account)
- You intend to use Dubai's four toll roads

3 What To Bring

Fee ☐ Dhs.100 (Dhs.50 Salik credit and a Dhs.50 fee)
☐ Registration card
☐ Driving licence (original and copy)
☐ Licence plate number

4 Procedure

Location RTA Licensing Departments (p.298), petrol stations and some branches of Emirates Bank and Dubai Islamic Bank.

Hours Various

- Complete the application and hand it in along with the Dhs.100 fee
- You will receive a welcome pack that will include your tag
- Fix the tag to your windscreen (some vehicles require special mounting locations – see www.salik.ae for more details)
- You can use the toll roads immediately

Tip Salik Online

Registering online will allow you to view Salik violations and top up your account. If you would like to verify a Salik offence, you can see an image of your vehicle crossing a toll gate. You will need your Salik tag number, your licence plate number, the date you purchased your tag and the same mobile number you used on your Salik application, to set up an account.

Vehicle

Driving

Applying For A Tourism Certificate

1 Overview

If you wish to leave the UAE by car, you will need to apply for a tourism certificate. as the officials at border control may ask to see it when you are leaving and re-entering the UAE. The countries you intend to drive to may also request to see the tourism certificate when you apply for a visa. As the vehicle licence number may be entered into your passport together with the visa, you will then only be able to enter that country with that specific vehicle.

Contact the relevant embassy or the UAE Automobile & Touring Club (296 4019, www.aaauae.com/atcuae) to enquire whether this certificate is required.

2 Prerequisites

- Valid registration card
- Private vehicle, registered in the name of the driver
- Driving licence number of the driver, if the vehicle is not registered in his/her name

3 What To Bring

- ☐ Vehicle registration card
- ☐ Passport (original and copy)
- ☐ Application form
- ☐ Letter of no objection from the vehicle finance company if your car is financed or from the vehicle owner
- ☐ Driving licence (copy and original)
- Fee ☐ Dhs.80 – service charge

4 Procedure

Location Dubai Traffic Police, Various (see p.296)

Hours Sun – Thurs 07:30 – 14:30

- Submit documents in person at the vehicle permits section
- Pay the service charge to the cashier
- A tourism certificate will be issued immediately
- Cancel the tourism certificate upon your return to the UAE

Renewing Vehicle Registration

1 Overview

Car registration must be renewed on an annual basis with the Traffic Police. Re-registration involves a vehicle test, performed by EPPCO Tasjeel or Emarat Shamil while you begin the paperwork process.

There is a four-day grace period after your registration has expired in which to have your car re-registered.

2 Prerequisites

- Vehicle has been tested (see Testing A Vehicle, p.144)

3 What To Bring

☐ Vehicle registration card

☐ Vehicle insurance certificate (valid for at least 13 months)

Private Car ☐ Passport copy

Company Car ☐ Valid trade licence (copy)

Fees ☐ Dhs.10 – typing fee

☐ Dhs.360 – vehicle registration fee (light vehicle)

☐ Dhs.735 – vehicle registration fee (heavy vehicle)

☐ Dhs.130 – motorcycle registration fee

☐ Dhs.73 – overdue registration penalty charge per quarter (if applicable)

4 Procedure

Location EPPCO Tasjeel or Emarat Shamil, Various (see p.299)

Hours Various

- Take the passed test certificate (see Testing A Vehicle, p.144), the old licence plates (if old style) and the insurance papers to the typing counter
- Your application form will be typed for you; pay Dhs.10 at the same counter
- At the Traffic Police counter, submit all documents and the licence plates (if not new plates)
- Your application will be validated and entered into the system
- Go to the cashier and pay the registration fee, the licence plate fee and any outstanding fines (cash only)
- Wait for your name to be called
- You will receive your vehicle registration card and insurance papers
- Submit the receipt and vehicle registration card

Vehicle

Driving

Licence Plate
- You will be given new plates and a date sticker for the rear licence plate; your registration card will be returned to you
- Affix the sticker to the plate
- Mount the plates on your vehicle
- Keep the vehicle registration card and insurance documents in the car at all times

5   Related Procedure

- Paying Fines, p.160

Tip   **Fast Track**

You will find the following services at these outlets:

Al Ghandi Shamel
- Vehicle testing
- New vehicle registration
- Vehicle renewal
- Insurance
- Fine payment
- Certificates issued
- On-site testing for heavy mechanical equipment
- Manufacturing and supply of number plates
- Vehicle testing for auction purposes
- Mobile vehicle testing
- Temporary registration for vehicles to be exported
- Testing and renewal of motorbike registration

EPPCO Tasjeel
- Manufacturing, issuing, removal and affixing of number plates
- Export and import documentation
- Insurance booths
- Mobile vehicle inspection and registration unit

Emarat Shamil
- Vehicle testing
- Renewal of registration
- Payment of fines
- International driving licences
- Ownership cards

Importing A Vehicle (From Another Emirate)

1 Overview

Dubai residents may not own vehicles registered in another emirate. Vehicles may be purchased in other emirates, but must be imported into Dubai and registered with the RTA. Note that the Traffic Police refers to this procedure as 'vehicle export'.

If you purchase a new vehicle in another emirate, the dealer may obtain blue temporary export plates from the police for you before you register the car with the RTA.

2 Prerequisites

- Owner is resident in Dubai
- Vehicle is registered in another emirate

3 What To Bring

- ☐ Passport (original and copy)
- ☐ Residence permit (original and copy)
- ☐ Blue temporary export licence plates (provided by the police of the other emirate)
- ☐ No objection letter from the financing agency or bank (if applicable)

Fees
- ☐ Dhs.60 – temporary licence plate fee (if applicable)
- ☐ Dhs.50 – testing fee
- ☐ Dhs.420-Dhs.470 – vehicle registration fee

4 Procedure

Location Traffic Police of other emirate

Hours Various

- Obtain blue temporary export licence plates from the police of the emirate in which the vehicle was purchased
- Affix the licence plates and take the vehicle to any EPPCO Tasjeel or Emarat Shamil centre (see p.299)

These plates are valid for three days, and allow you to drive in Dubai until your vehicle is officially registered with the RTA.

5 Related Procedure

- Have the vehicle tested and registered (see Testing A Vehicle, p.144, & Registering A Vehicle, p.146)

Vehicle

Driving

Vehicle

Importing A Vehicle (International)

1 Overview

Any vehicle may be imported to Dubai from another country with relative ease. Once the initial step of obtaining a vehicle clearance certificate has been obtained from the Customs Authority of any UAE port, the vehicle must be registered with the RTA (see Registering A Vehicle, p.146).

You will be given blue temporary export licence plates, then you must obtain an NOC from the Ministry of Finance and Industry. Individuals may only import one vehicle for personal use.

Charges Note that customs duty will be charged at a rate of 5% of the Dubai market value of the vehicle. The customs authorities will determine the value of the vehicle upon arrival.

2 Prerequisites

- Owner is resident in Dubai
- Vehicle complies with GCC specifications and is a left-hand drive

3 What To Bring

- ☐ Passport (original and copy)
- ☐ Residence permit (original and copy)
- ☐ Vehicle papers
- ☐ Bill of entry

Fees
- ☐ 5% customs duty (cash or cheque)
- ☐ Dhs.60 – blue temporary export licence plates
- ☐ Dhs.10 – registration fee
- ☐ Ports Authority vehicle handling and storage fee is as follows:

  RORO(Roll-on Roll-off) handling fee depends on the weight of the vehicle. For vehicles up to 1.5 tonnes the fee is Dhs.138. For vehicles up to 5 tons the fee is Dhs.193.

  Storage is free for the first 15 days, after which vehicles weighing up to 1.5 tonnes are charged Dhs.10 per day and vehicles up to 5 tonnes Dhs.12 per day.

4 Procedure

- Ship the vehicle to Dubai
- When the vehicle arrives at the port, collect the delivery order from the shipping agent

If possible, have the delivery order issued in the name of the person who will register the car.

Location   Ports & Customs Vehicle Department, Port Rashid (Map Ref 7-D1) &
Jebel Ali (Map Ref 1-C3)

Hours   Sun – Thurs 07:30 – 15:00; Closed on Fridays

Clearance
- Submit the delivery order, vehicle papers and passport copy to the Customs Authority
- Except for new cars brought in by car dealers, all cars are inspected by customs and an inspection report is produced
- The customs duty will be calculated
- Pay the customs duty and fee (cash or cheque) at the customs clearance counter and get a receipt
- A vehicle clearance certificate will be issued

Location   Dubai Customs Inspection Office, Port Rashid   Map ref 7-D1

Hours   Sun – Thurs 07:30 – 15:00; Closed on Fridays

Temporary
- Submit all documents at the customs office
- Next to the Traffic Police desk, obtain temporary insurance for your vehicle
- The RTA will provide you with blue temporary export licence plates valid for three days
- Take the vehicle to be registered with the RTA (see Registering a Vehicle, p.146)

Location   Industry Department, Ministry of Finance & Industry   Map ref 8-F1

Hours   Sun – Thurs 10:00 – 14:00

NOC
- Take all paperwork provided by the Customs Authority and Dhs.200 to the counter on the ground floor
- The no objection certificate will be issued within five minutes

5   Related Procedure

- Registering A Vehicle, p.146

Tip   Import Assistance

It's a good idea to have the clearing and forwarding company handle the import procedures for you, if possible.

Info   GCC Specifications

Vehicles manufactured between 1987 and 2000 imported by individuals or private car showrooms will need a no objection certificate from the Ministry of Finance and Industry to confirm that the vehicle complies with GCC specifications.

Vehicle

Driving

Exporting A Vehicle

1 Overview

Before exporting a vehicle to another country or emirate, vehicle registration must first be cancelled with the RTA by the owner in person.

Testing If the vehicle has never been tested by the RTA, or if the registration has expired, the vehicle must be inspected prior to export to ensure that the chassis (body) number corresponds with the engine number.

2 Prerequisites

- Vehicle has no outstanding fines or loans

3 What To Bring

Testing If a test is required, take the vehicle to be exported
☐ Vehicle registration card

Fee ☐ Dhs.25 – testing fee

Cancellation ☐ Vehicle registration card

☐ Licence plates (no car necessary)

☐ Passport copy of person who will receive the car in other country/emirate (if applicable)

☐ Settlement of loan certificate (if applicable)

☐ If temporary plates are needed, temporary insurance papers valid for three days if exporting to another emirate, and 14 days if exporting overseas

Fees ☐ Dhs.10 – export fee

☐ Dhs.10 – transfer to another individual fee

☐ Dhs.10 – typing fee

☐ Dhs.60 – blue temporary licence plate fee (if applicable)

4 Procedure

Location EPPCO Tasjeel, Emarat Shamil, Various (see p.299)

Hours Sun – Thurs 07:00 – 21:00; Sat 07:00 – 14:00

Testing
- Take the vehicle to any EPPCO Tasjeel or Emarat Shamil centre
- Tell the registration officer that you wish to have an export test done
- Submit your vehicle registration card and export documents
- The registration card will be cancelled
- Pull forward to any available testing bay and park the car

Vehicle

Driving

- Remove all valuables
- Leave the key and registration card with the inspector
- Remove the licence plates
- Go to the main building and wait for your name to be called
- A visual test of the vehicle and all paperwork will be performed
- Pay the testing fee
- You will be issued a test result certificate

gistration
ncellation
- Go to the typing counter
- A vehicle permit application form will be prepared for you
- Pay the typing fee
- Submit the vehicle registration card, insurance certificate, licence plates and receipt at the Traffic Police counter
- Pay fees and fines (if applicable) at the cashier
- You will receive blue temporary export licence plates, which you must mount on your vehicle

 These plates are valid for a maximum of three days if you are exporting to another emirate, and 14 days for overseas export.

- The police will give you a transfer document (export form) in the buyer's name
- Vehicle registration is cancelled automatically
- If you are exporting the vehicle to an international destination, take the vehicle to the shipping agency

Vehicle

Driving

Tip | **Export To Another Emirate**

If you are exporting the vehicle to another emirate, contact the Traffic Police in the other emirate to determine import requirements first.

Tip | **Export To The UK**

If you are planning to export your vehicle to the UK, keep the Dubai export plates on the vehicle. This will allow you to avoid having to register the car and pay taxes on it for six months.

Tip | **Hiring A Car, Relying On A Driver**

If you hire a car, it's essential that you receive it in good condition – with brakes that work, a spare tyre and so forth – and that it comes with valid registration papers and full insurance. Likewise, if you book with a tour operator that provides a driver, it's important to verify that their drivers are well-trained and well-versed in safe driving practices.

Traffic Accidents

1 Overview

If you are involved in a traffic accident in which no one is injured and vehicle damage is minor, move your vehicle to the side of the road in order to avoid blocking traffic. Note that car repair companies cannot accept an order without an accident report so you must call the police.

If the other driver drives off without stopping and waiting for the police, go straight to the nearest police station and file a report. If you are not at fault (and presumably you wouldn't be as it's the other driver who drove off) you will be given a green form to take to your insurance provider.

If your car is damaged while parked (if you notice scratches on the side while parked at a shopping centre, for instance) call the police if the damage is bad, or go to the nearest police station to file a report. You will be issued a certificate, called a damage report, at a cost of Dhs.50, which you can then submit to your insurers. It's best to do this as soon as possible after noticing the damage.

2 Prerequisites

- Any damage whatsoever to the vehicle

3 What To Bring

- ☐ Valid driving licence
- ☐ Vehicle registration card

4 Procedure

- Determine whether anyone has sustained injuries
- Call the Dubai Police operations room on 999 to report the accident and request an ambulance if necessary
- Wait for the police to arrive
- Provide your driving licence and vehicle registration card
- Insurance • Present your insurance papers if you're driving a car that is registered outside the UAE (in Oman or Saudi Arabia, for example)
- Do not argue over responsibility; the police will hear both sides and determine liability
- The police will document all details and give each party a copy of the accident report
- If you receive a pink form, you are at fault
- If you receive a green form, you are not at fault

- If necessary, contact a recovery company to tow away your vehicle (see below)
- Submit the accident report to your insurance provider in order to repair the vehicle

The police may retain your driving licence until you obtain the necessary documentation from the insurance company demonstrating that the claim is being processed. If this is the case, you will be issued a notice from the police that will serve as a temporary licence, and the insurance provider will give you a letter entitling you to retrieve your licence from the police.

- Take the car to the designated garage for repair

Law **Repairs**

By law, no vehicle can be accepted for repair without an accident report from the Traffic Police. Insurance companies tend to have an agreement with a particular garage to which they will refer claimants. The garage will carry out the repair work and the insurance company will settle the claim for you.

Info **Breakdowns**

In the event of a breakdown, you will find that passing police cars will stop to help, or at least to check your documents. For assistance, contact:

AAA Service Centre	04 285 8989
Dubai Auto Towing Services	04 359 4424 (Pager 91146488)
IATC Recovery	800 5200

Vehicle Towing

By law, no vehicle can be towed by another vehicle, other than those specifically designed for that purpose. In other words, you are not allowed to tow your friend's car with a tow-rope and must instead contact a registered towing company to assist you. This does not apply to off-road driving.

Tip **Bird's Eye View**

Log on to www.dubaitourism.co.ae which has webcams set up at strategic points so that you can view current traffic patterns and hopefully avoid getting stuck in a traffic jam.

Traffic Accidents & Fines

Paying Fines

1 Overview

The Dubai Traffic Police fine drivers for traffic infractions such as speeding, parking illegally and driving recklessly. Note that unless you are pulled over and fined on the spot, you will not know you have been fined, nor will you know how many black points you have against your licence until you enquire with the Traffic Police. Fines issued on the spot show up on the traffic department's system within 24 hours.

Before renewing your vehicle registration, you will have to pay all outstanding fines that are logged under the ID number that appears on your vehicle registration card. The simplest method to determine how much you owe is to log on to www.dubaipolice.gov.ae and click on Online Services. You can search for fines by entering in your car registration number, your driving licence number or your traffic file number. Alternatively, call 800 7777 and follow the voice prompts.

2 Prerequisites

• You have been fined for a traffic infraction

3 What To Bring

☐ Original vehicle registration card or driving licence
☐ Cash for the amount you've been fined
☐ Dhs.10 – administration fee

4 Procedure

• Follow any of the methods listed below:

Fine Payment Options

Walk-In	Location	Comment
Counter Enquiry & Payment	Fines Section at any Traffic Police Department, or a Tasjeel or Shamil centre	Various locations in Dubai (see p.299). This is the only way you can pay for fines incurred in other emirates too.
Public Enquiry & Payment Machines (touchscreens)	Traffic Police offices, some shopping malls	24-hour payment at Lamcy Plaza, Jumeirah Plaza, Union Coop Safa Park and Al Ghusais
Online		
Dubai Traffic Police Website	www.dubaipolice.gov.ae	View and pay your fines by credit card. You may enquire about fines, but payment can only be made for fines incurred in Dubai

Traffic Accidents & Fines

Tip — Traffic Fine Notification

If you are issued an electronic fine (being caught speeding on camera, for instance), the fine will be entered into the traffic system within 24 hours. A hand-written fine such as a parking ticket will take a little longer to be logged in the system.

You can register online to enquire about any fines you may have received by logging on to www.dubaipolice.gov.ae. You can also SMS the word 'fine', followed by a space and the numbers on your licence plate, space, 2 (for the category your car falls in – 2 is for private vehicles), and the letter on your licence plate (anything from A to G), to 4488.

Towed Car

If your car is towed away, call the Dubai Police on 800 7777 to find out where to pay the fine and where your car has been impounded.

Tip — Long-Term Parking Card

Frequent users of public paid carparks can purchase a subscription card from Customer Service at the Road & Transport Authority. Call 800 9090 for details.

Info — Black Points

Black points are issued to holders of Dubai driving licences who break the law while driving. If you receive a total of 12 points within 12 months, your licence is withdrawn and you must pass a strict test before it is reissued.

See p.162 for a list of black point offences.

To determine the number of black points on your licence, check the receipt when you pay your traffic fines or call 800 7777.

Info — Parking Fines

The Road & Transport Authority has installed parking meters in many central carparks, main roads and central streets. If you are fined for not paying for parking time, pay the fine as follows:

- Online, at a police station or at Empost outlets
- Show the violation notice and pay the fine (cash only)
- Alternatively, pay outstanding fines plus an additional overdue penalty charge when you renew your vehicle registration

Law — Keep Your Licence With You!

If you are pulled over and do not have your driving licence with you, you may be fined Dhs.100.

Traffic Fines & Violations

Violations	Charges	Points
Driving a vehicle without a permit from the licensing authority	Dhs.200	3
Driving in a reckless manner (racing)	Dhs.2,000	12
Reckless driving	Dhs.2,000	12
Driving under the influence of alcohol or drugs	Court decision	24
Causing death of others	Court decision	12
Causing serious injury	Court decision	8
Causing moderate injury	Court decision	6
Not stopping after causing an accident that resulted in injuries	Court decision	24
Failing to stop after causing an accident	Dhs.500	–
Exceeding maximum speed limit by more than 60km/h	Dhs.1,000	12
Exceeding maximum speed limit by not more than 60km/h	Dhs.900	6
Exceeding maximum speed limit by not more than 50km/h	Dhs.800	–
Exceeding maximum speed limit by not more than 40km/h	Dhs.700	–
Exceeding maximum speed limit by not more than 30km/h	Dhs.600	–
Exceeding maximum speed limit by not more than 20km/h	Dhs.500	–
Exceeding maximum speed limit by not more than 10km/h	Dhs.400	–
Driving below the minimum speed limit	Dhs.200	–
Driving recklessly and causing danger to the public	Dhs.1,000	12
Jumping a red traffic signal	Dhs.800	8
Causing serious damage to a vehicle	Court decision	6
Causing a car to overturn	Court decision	8
Overtaking on the hard shoulder	Dhs.600	6
Overtaking where prohibited	Dhs.600	6
Overtaking dangerously or on the right	Dhs.200	4
Dangerous overtaking by truck drivers	Dhs.800	24
Vehicles entering the road in dangerous manner	Dhs.600	6
Entering the road without making sure it is safe	Dhs.400	4
Driving in opposite direction to the flow of traffic	Dhs.400	4
Failing to observe traffic signs and instructions	Dhs.500	–
Not giving way to emergency/official vehicles	Dhs.500	4
Not giving way to an overtaking car	Dhs.200	–
Not giving way to vehicles coming from the left (not yielding)	Dhs.200	–
Not keeping a safe distance from other vehicles	Dhs.400	4
Failure to follow road safety rules when a vehicle breaks down	Dhs.200	–
Performing an illegal U-turn	Dhs.200	4
Turning incorrectly	Dhs.200	4
Swerving suddenly (erratic driving)	Dhs.200	4
Reversing in a dangerous manner	Dhs.200	–
Driving at night or in fog without using lights	Dhs.200	4
Not signalling when turning or changing lanes	Dhs.200	3
Evading a traffic policeman	Dhs.800	12
Refusal to give name/address to a traffic policeman	Dhs.500	–
Not presenting vehicle registration when requested	Dhs.200	–
Not presenting driving licence when requested	Dhs.200	–
Driving a vehicle with an expired driving licence	Dhs.200	3
Not carrying driving licence or registration	Dhs.100	–
Driving with a licence from a foreign country	Dhs.400	–
Violating the terms of your driving licence	Dhs.300	–
Allowing others to drive a vehicle for which they are unlicensed	Dhs.500	–
Driving without wearing medical glasses or lenses	Dhs.100	–

Traffic Fines & Violations

Violations	Charges	Points
Violating a 'no entry' sign	Dhs.200	4
Obstructing traffic	Dhs.200	–
Not conforming to loading and unloading regulations	Dhs.200	4
Failure to ensure that the car is parked safely	Dhs.200	–
Parking in a 'no parking' area	Dhs.200	2
Unnecessarily parking in loading and offloading areas	Dhs.200	–
Parking the vehicle on the left side of the road (hard shoulder)	Dhs.200	–
Misuse of parking spaces	Dhs.200	3
Parking on a pavement	Dhs.200	3
Parking beside or behind parked vehicles (double parking)	Dhs.300	–
Parking in front of water hydrants or in a handicapped zone	Dhs.1,000	4
Stopping in the road for no reason	Dhs.500	4
Stopping in a yellow box	Dhs.500	–
Stopping vehicle on the left side of the road in prohibited places	Dhs.500	–
Stopping a vehicle dangerously or blocking traffic	Dhs.200	3
Allowing children under 10 years old to sit in the front seat	Dhs.400	4
Not wearing a seat belt while driving	Dhs.400	4
Littering road from a vehicle	Dhs.500	4
Using mobile phone or handset while driving	Dhs.200	4
Not giving way to pedestrians	Dhs.500	6
Stopping vehicle on pedestrian crossing	Dhs.500	–
Pedestrians crossing on roads or unmarked crossings	Dhs.200	–
Not wearing a helmet when riding a motorcycle	Dhs.200	4
Carrying more passengers than permitted	Dhs.200	3
Transporting passengers by vehicle undesignated for this purpose	Dhs.200	4
Carrying and transporting passengers illegally	Dhs.200	4
Use of horn in prohibited areas	Dhs.200	2
Use of horn in restricted areas in a disturbing manner	Dhs.100	2
Leaving a vehicle on the road with its engine running	Dhs.300	–
Using interior lights for no reason while driving	Dhs.100	–
Tinting windows beyond permitted percentage	Dhs.500	–
Driving a vehicle that causes pollution	Dhs.500	–
Driving a vehicle emitting excessive noise	Dhs.500	–
Vehicle unfit to be driven (not road worthy)	Dhs.200	–
Driving a vehicle that is not road worthy	Dhs.200	–
Driving with unfit tyres	Dhs.200	–
Lights not functioning	Dhs.200	6
Indicators not functioning	Dhs.100	2
Absence of red light at the rear of vehicle	Dhs.100	–
Driving a vehicle without a permit from the licensing authority	Dhs.200	–
Failure to adhere to authorised tariffs	Dhs.200	6
Failure to follow lane discipline in a light vehicle	Dhs.200	2
Failure to follow lane discipline in a heavy vehicle	Dhs.600	6
Driving without number plates	Dhs.1,000	24
Driving with one number plate	Dhs.200	2
Violation of laws of using commercial number plates	Dhs.200	–
Failure to fix number plates in designated places	Dhs.200	2
Unclear number plates	Dhs.200	3
Differences between number plates for cab and trailer	Dhs.200	–
Not using rear and side lights on a trailer	Dhs.200	–

Traffic Fines & Violations

Violations	Charges	Points
Faulty lights on the back or sides of a container	Dhs.200	–
Towing a vehicle, boat or trailer improperly	Dhs.300	–
Leakage or falling load from vehicle	Dhs.3,000	12
Overloaded or protruding load on light vehicles	Dhs.200	3
Overloaded or protruding load from a heavy vehicle	Dhs.500	6
Failure to fix a sign indicating licensed overload	Dhs.200	3
Loading a light vehicle in a way that may pose a danger to others	Dhs.200	3
Loading a heavy vehicle in a way that may pose danger to others	Dhs.500	6
Using vehicle for purposes other than designated	Dhs.200	4
Attaching indecent materials or images to the car	Dhs.200	–
Use of rotating multicoloured lights	Dhs.200	–
Modifying a vehicle's engine without permission	Dhs.400	–
Modifying a vehicle's chassis without permission	Dhs.400	–
Changing a vehicle's colour without permission	Dhs.400	–
Failure to have a vehicle inspected after modification	Dhs200	–
Failure to renew vehicle registration after expiry	Dhs.400	–
Placing marks on the road that may damage the road or block traffic	Dhs.500	–
Using training vehicles outside of specified timings	Dhs.200	–
Using training vehicles in undesignated areas	Dhs.200	–
Teaching driving in a training vehicle that doesn't have a learning sign	Dhs.500	–
Teaching driving in a non-training vehicle	Dhs.500	–
Carrying passengers in a training vehicle	Dhs.200	4
Taxis, with designated pick-up areas, stopping in undesignated places	Dhs.200	4
Driving a taxi without a permit	Dhs.200	4
Taxi refusing to carry passengers	Dhs.200	4
Opening left door of a taxi	Dhs.100	3
Failure to display a taxi sign where required	Dhs.200	–
Not conforming to specified colour of taxi or training vehicles	Dhs.200	–
Not displaying approved tariffs in a public vehicle	Dhs.200	–
Failure to keep taxis and buses clean inside and outside	Dhs.200	–
Smoking inside taxis and buses	Dhs.200	–
Failing to use internal lights in buses at nights	Dhs.100	–
Taxi driver wearing unspecified or unclean uniform	Dhs.100	–
Heavy vehicle without a vertical exhaust pipe	Dhs.200	–
Uncovered load in trucks	Dhs.3,000	–
Not fixing reflectors to the rear of trucks and heavy vehicles	Dhs.200	–
Driving a heavy vehicle that does not comply with safety and security conditions	Dhs.500	–
Driving a heavy vehicle in prohibited areas	Dhs.200	4
Operating industrial, construction and mechanical vehicles without permission from the licensing authority	Dhs.500	–
Failure to display allowed load capacity of a truck on both sides	Dhs.100	–

Dry Cleaners p.74
Divorce Lawyers p.108

Written by residents, the Dubai Explorer is packed with insider info, from arriving in the city to making it your home and everything in between.

Dubai Explorer – Live • Work • Explore
The Complete Residents' Guide

A FIRM OF TALENTED AND DIVERSE LAWYERS
A FIRM WITH DEPTH OF KNOWLEDGE AND STRENGTH IN THE MARKET PLACE
A FIRM THAT BUILDS LASTING RELATIONSHIPS

COMREHENSIVE CLIENT FOCUSED LEGAL SERVICES

ABU DHABI | DUBAI

www.hadefpartners.com

Personal Life

Overview

Overview

Overview

The following personal procedures are almost always handled by the individual rather than your sponsor. Whereas in the past people have returned to their home countries to get married or give birth, it has become a lot more common to remain in Dubai for these milestones.

The procedure for getting married differs according to nationality and faith. Muslim, Hindu, Christian and civil weddings are covered here; if you need further assistance your embassy should be able to help, see p.283.

If you decide to have your baby in Dubai, there are some excellent hospitals and medical professionals here. This section outlines the procedure and paperwork involved.

The tragic event of a death is further aggravated by the amount of bureaucracy involved; all authorities require letters of no objection for each step in the long process, along with numerous document cancellations. This is one area where you might get some assistance from your sponsor or embassy.

Numerous new schools have opened in Dubai in the last few years, so finding school places are less of a challenge. However, your school of choice may still have a long waiting list. This chapter lists the procedures involved with enrolling your child at nursery, primary, secondary school and university.

Finally, this chapter deals with personal banking, getting a liquor licence, and various procedures involved in bringing your pet to Dubai, registering it, sterilising it and taking it back to your home country.

Some of the procedures may require attested documents – refer to Notarising & Attesting Documents on p.9 for more information.

Overview

Personal Life

Marriage

1 Overview

Many expats choose to get married in their home country, but this section covers Dubai-based wedding procedures for Muslim, Catholic, Anglican and Hindu ceremonies.

In a nutshell:

- If you are Muslim, you can marry at the Dubai Court
- If you are Catholic or Anglican, you can marry at a church
- If you are a Hindu (of Indian nationality), you can marry at the Hindu Temple

If you choose not to have a religious wedding, and you are not a Muslim, you may be able to get married at your embassy. Embassies that perform weddings include India, Italy, Egypt, South Africa and Sri Lanka. Those that don't include USA, Canada, Australia, Lebanon and Pakistan.

Law Legal Marriages

In nearly all cases, a marriage that is legally performed in Dubai will be recognised elsewhere in the world, but it's always best to check. You may also need to inform your embassy of your intention to marry. The British embassy in Dubai, for example, will display a 'notice of marriage' in the embassy waiting room for 21 days prior to the marriage (along the same lines as 'the banns' being published in a parish newsletter for three successive Sundays). Afterwards, providing no one has objected, they will issue a 'certificate of no impediment' that may be required by the church carrying out your ceremony.

Tip Getting Married

Dubai is a very popular destination for weddings – whether for tourists or residents – and there are a number of luxury hotels just waiting to play host. For more information on where to host your reception, where to get your dress and where to have your cake made, see the Residents chapter of the *Dubai Explorer – The Complete Residents' Guide* available in all leading bookshops and supermarkets.

Marriage – Hindu

1 Overview

The procedure listed below is for Indian citizens. The marriage is conducted at the Hindu Temple, by the maharaj. The temple is run in conjunction with the Indian consulate and marriages performed here are recognised by the government of the UAE. There is no fee for this service.

2 Prerequisites

- Both parties are Hindu
- Both parties are resident in Dubai

3 What To Bring

- ☐ Completed application forms
- ☐ Both parties' passports (original and copy)
- ☐ Parents of both parties' passports (copy)
- ☐ Attested affidavit from the Indian embassy that both partners are free to get married

4 Procedure

Location Hindu Temple   Map ref 8-F1

Hours Sat – Thu 09:00 – 13:00; 16:00 – 20:00

- Submit all documents to the Hindu Temple's Marriage Committee for approval
- A decision will be made within one week
- Upon approval, set a date for the ceremony when both the temple and maharaj are available
- You may appoint a maharaj of your choice
- After the ceremony, you will be issued with a marriage certificate
- The marriage certificate should be attested at the Dubai Court as well as at your embassy (see Notarising & Attesting Documents p.9)

Waiting Time One week

5 Related Procedures

- Applying For A Residence Permit – Family, p.37
- Transferring From Father To Husband Sponsorship, p.41

Marriage

Personal Life

Marriage

Marriage – Anglican

1 Overview

Anglican marriages are conducted according to the rites and ceremonies of the Church of England, and are recognised in the UAE. You can have an Anglican ceremony at the Holy Trinity Church in Dubai, the Christ Church in Jebel Ali or at St Martin's in Sharjah.

Anglican marriages must take place in church, but can be followed by a service of blessing in a location of your choosing (hotel, golf club ,or a resort for example). Be sure to speak with the chaplain prior to making any arrangements or bookings.

2 Prerequisites

- At least one partner is baptised. Evidence of baptism is required
- Neither partner is Muslim, nor should the father of either the bride or groom be Muslim
- Attested proof from the embassy that each partner is unmarried
- The couple must attend marriage preparation sessions at the church
- Minimum age: 18

3 What To Bring

- ☐ Both passports (original and copy)
- ☐ Residence permits (copy) where appropriate
- ☐ Evidence of baptism (original certificate or record of baptism from the church)
- ☐ One passport photo each
- ☐ Two witnesses over the age of 18
- ☐ A certificate of no impediment (banns certificate) where appropriate
- ☐ Completed and signed forms collected from the chaplain's office regarding the following:
  - Intent of marriage (application)
  - Confirmation that neither you nor your father is Muslim
  - Certificate from each partner stating that each is single and free to marry (can be provided by your parents or parish priest and must be attested by your embassy)

If you have previously been married:

- ☐ Divorce certificate (final decree) or
- ☐ Death certificate of your previous partner

Fees
- ☐ Dhs.2,250 – for visitors to Dubai (non-residents)
- ☐ Dhs.1,500 – Dubai residents
- ☐ Dhs.650 – to register the marriage with the Dubai Courts (if required)

4 Procedure

Location Holy Trinity Church (Map ref 8-E7), Christ Church (Jebel Ali, Map ref 2-F4), St Martins Church (Sharjah, off map)

Hours Sat – Thu 09:00 – 17:00, Fri 17:00 – 19:00 (only for marriage consultations)

- Submit all documents (in due time) at the chaplain's office
- Meet with the chaplain to discuss your plans
- Set a date for the marriage ceremony
- Attend at least three sessions of pre-marital counselling
- The ceremony will take place at the church, or location of your choosing, where the two witnesses must sign the marriage register
- After the ceremony, you will receive two marriage certificates signed by the chaplain
- The certificate must be translated into Arabic
- The four documents (two marriage certificates, two Arabic versions of the marriage certificate) should be attested at the Dubai Court as well as your embassy. All of the churches can now do this for you at a cost of Dhs.650. The court will retain one English copy and one Arabic copy and you will keep the one certified English marriage certificate and the Arabic translation

Waiting Time Up to one month

5 Related Procedures

- Applying for a Residence Permit – Family, p.37
- Transferring from Father to Husband Sponsorship, p.41

Personal Life **Marriage**

Marriage

Marriage – Muslim

1 Overview

A Muslim groom can marry a bride (Muslim, Christian or Jewish) at the Dubai Court, also known as the Sharia court. A non-Muslim man cannot marry in this court.

Filipino citizens should contact their embassy in Abu Dhabi before having the marriage certificate authenticated at the Dubai Court.

2 Prerequisites

- Groom is Muslim
- Bride is Muslim, Christian or Jewish
- Approval of the bride's father or closest male relative
- At least one partner is resident in Dubai
- The couple must have a pre-marital health examination (see opposite)

The bride's father or relative must either be present, or must give official approval (see below).

3 What To Bring

- ☐ Both passports (original and copy)
- ☐ At least one residence permit (copy)
- ☐ Proof that groom is Muslim (i.e. birth certificate)
- ☐ Two male Muslim witnesses or four Muslim female witnesses
- ☐ Power of attorney letter (if applicable; see below)

The father or closest male relative of the bride must attend to show his consent to the marriage. If the father of the bride cannot attend the ceremony, he must send a power of attorney or his approval in writing. The approval must be attested and names of the bride and groom clearly mentioned in the document.

Fees ☐ Dhs.60 – service charge

4 Procedure

Location Al Mankhool Medical Centre   Map ref 7-D3

Hours Sun – Thurs 07:15 – 22:00, Sat 08:15 – 12:30

- Call the clinic (04 398 7333) to make an appointment
- Go to the first cashier's counter and submit all documents and pay Dhs.250 per person
- The clinic will provide you with a temporary health card which you must keep in order to collect the results

- Both of you will be interviewed and have blood samples taken
- Return at least three days later for the medical certificate

ocation   Dubai Court Marriage Section   Map ref 8-F6

Hours   Sun – Thurs 07:30 – 13:30; 17:00 – 20:00

- Bring all witnesses with you
- Submit all documents for verification
- The judge will marry you immediately

5 Related Procedures

- Applying for a Residence Permit – Family, p.37
- Transferring from Father to Husband Sponsorship, p.41

Tip   **Pre-Marital Health Examination**

A new law was passed in 2008 that requires partners to have a pre-marital health examination before they tie the knot in Dubai. It is not usually required for Christian and Hindu weddings. The tests are meant to spot any genetic defects or diseases that could be passed on to children. Couples can have the tests performed at the Al Mankhool Medical Centre (04 398 7333).

Marriage

Personal Life

Marriage

Marriage – Roman Catholic

1 Overview

Catholic marriages are conducted at St. Mary's Church, and are recognised by the government of the UAE.

2 Prerequisites

- At least one partner is Roman Catholic, and at least one is resident in Dubai
- The couple has attended four sessions of the marriage preparation course at the church
- Proof (with seal) from home church that each partner is unmarried
- Females should be over 18 and males should be over 21

3 What To Bring

- ☐ Both passports (original & copy)
- ☐ At least one Dubai residence permit (copy)
- ☐ Baptism certificates (original)
- ☐ Confirmation certificate
- ☐ A letter from the couple's parents or a letter from a person who knows the couple stating there are no objections to the marriage
- ☐ If one partner is not Catholic, his/her birth certificate
- ☐ A letter from the home country parish priest stating that the partner is free to marry
- ☐ If one partner is not Catholic, a statement from the embassy here or in the home country that he/she is free to marry
- ☐ If a partner is under 21, letter of consent from the parents
- ☐ Two witnesses, over 18 years old, that the bride and groom know

Fees ☐ Church donation

4 Procedure

Location St. Mary's Church   Map ref 8-E6

Hours Wed – Mon 08:00 – 12:30; 16:00 – 19:30, Fri closed

- Complete the application form at the priest's office
- Present all relevant documents
- Attend a marriage preparation course (every day except Fridays, Saturdays and Sundays)
- You will receive a marriage preparation certificate
- If no objections are registered, arrange a date for the ceremony
- Witnesses must sign the marriage register during the ceremony

- The church will issue you with a marriage certificate
- The marriage certificate should be attested at the Dubai Court and your embassy

5 Related Procedures

- Applying For A Residence Permit – Family p.37
- Transferring From Father To Husband Sponsorship p.41

Divorce

1 Overview

In accordance with the constitution of the UAE, family law (which governs matrimonial matters such as divorce) will either be governed by UAE law – which is Sharia law – or by the laws of the individuals' originating country. Therefore, if an English couple, residing in Dubai, approach the Dubai Courts for a divorce, the matter can either be decided by Sharia (UAE) or English law. If the parties are from different countries, the law applicable will be the law under which their marriage was solemnised.

Normally, the court will look into the possibility of reconciliation before granting a divorce. This means that before filing for divorce, you can approach the Family Guidance and Reformation Centre which functions under the Department of Justice at Dubai Courts. Anyone experiencing marital problems or any family dispute is able to approach this organisation. The other party in the dispute will be called in and the counsellors will try to help you reach an amicable settlement. If the matter is not resolved, the Guidance Centre may refer the matter to the court for legal proceedings to take place.

In divorce proceedings the jurisdiction will be one of the following:

- The court under whose jurisdiction the marriage took place
- The court under whose jurisdiction the spouses last resided together
- The court under whose jurisdiction the respondent is currently living

In deciding on the custody of any children, the court's paramount concern will be the child's welfare. In Sharia law and most other laws, the custody of the child will be the mother's right while the child is a minor, unless there are compelling reasons to decide otherwise.

2 Prerequisites

- Attempts have been made to reach an amicable settlement, but one or both parties wish to file for divorce
- Both parties are resident in Dubai

3 What To Bring

- ☐ Passport (original and copy)
- ☐ Residence visa (original and copy)
- ☐ Marriage certificate attested by UAE Embassy in country in which the marriage was solemnised and the certificate issued

If the parties wish their case to be decided in accordance with the laws of their countries of origin, they will need to produce a copy of the relevant law, duly attested by the Ministry of Justice of their home country and by the UAE Embassy in that country.

Divorce petition based on the law the parties have chosen to have their case decided under

Any invoices, receipts or other documentary evidence related to any financial claims either party wishes to make

Any witnesses

4 Procedure

- A divorce petition can be presented by either spouse against the other directly or through a lawyer
- Once the case is filed, the court will fix a date for the hearing and issue a summons to the address provided by the petitioner
- Both parties will be given the opportunity to produce witnesses and the court will provide a translator so witnesses can give a deposition in their mother tongue
- The court of First Instance acts as the Family Court
- The decision of the court of First Instance can be appealed in the Appeal Court
- The Appeal Court's decision can be challenged by filing a Second Appeal before the Supreme Court (Court of Cessation). The Supreme Court's decision is final and binding

Tip | Expert Advice

It's highly recommended that you appoint a lawyer to represent your case – firstly, because you may not be familiar with the intricacies of the legal procedures to be followed and, secondly, because court proceedings are conducted in Arabic. For a list of legal consultants, see p.279.

Divorce

Personal Life

Birth

Having A Baby

1   Overview

Dubai residents have the choice of delivering in a public or a private hospital. You will be charged for maternity services at public hospitals, although they are less expensive than private hospitals. In both private and public hospitals, husbands may be present during the delivery, upon approval of the attending doctor. It is also possible to have an epidural.

Health Insurance
Even if you are on a health insurance plan, it may not cover maternity costs. Those that do normally have a waiting period of 10 months to one year from the date that you join the plan before they will cover your costs. Check with your provider.

Citizenship
Expat children born in the UAE retain the citizenship of their parents. Check with your embassy to find out what the regulations are for citizens born abroad.

Public Hospitals
You must have a valid health card to deliver in a public hospital (see Obtaining a Health Card & Taking the Medical Test, p.26). There are two public hospitals that have specially equipped maternity sections: Al Wasl Hospital and Dubai Hospital. Women living in Bur Dubai, Satwa, Jumeira, Safa, Rashidiya, Hatta and Nad Al Sheba will be assigned to Al Wasl. Women living in Deira will be assigned to Dubai Hospital. If there are any complications during your labour, you will be transferred to Al Wasl Hospital.

Antenatal Care
You will be encouraged to have regular antenatal check-ups in the hospital at which the delivery will take place. Public hospitals may be reluctant to reveal the baby's gender.

Info   Marriage With Children

To give birth in Dubai you must be married. If you are pregnant and unmarried you may want to return to your home country to give birth; if you do remain in Dubai you should get married as soon as possible.

Info   Terminations

Elective abortions for married or unmarried women are illegal, although medical complications or abnormalities can justify a termination of pregnancy.

Having A Baby

1 Overview

During your pregnancy, you will need to have numerous tests, checks and scans on a regular basis (usually monthly at first; then weekly as your due date approaches). You can pay for your antenatal visits as a package (upfront) or on a visit-by-visit basis.

2 Prerequisites

- Parents-to-be are married
- Parents are residents (if delivering in public hospital)

3 What To Bring

- ☐ Health card (public hospitals)
- ☐ Registration card (private hospitals)
- ☐ Passport copy of both parents (original and copy)
- ☐ Attested marriage certificate
- ☐ Fees (see Maternity Package Prices overleaf)

4 Procedure

Public Hospital
- Call or visit for an appointment
- On the day of your visit, submit your passport copy, health card and marriage certificate
- Pay the package fees (see Maternity Package Prices overleaf)
- You will be assigned to a gynaecologist and given an appointment card. You need to bring the card with you on every visit
- After your initial consultation you will have regular check-ups (up to 12 visits). At each visit you will have the necessary prenatal tests and checks
- The doctor will advise you of your approximate due date, and closer to that date you will be given an admission date. You will also be given a list of things to bring at time of admission
- After the birth, you will be given a date for a follow-up check for both you and your baby

Private Hospital
- On your first visit to the private hospital, you will be given a registration card that you should bring to subsequent visits.
- After the baby is born, the hospital will require the necessary documentation to prepare the baby's notification of birth – you should bring these documents with you to the hospital (passport copy of mother and father, and marriage certificate)

5 Related Procedure

- Obtaining A Birth Certificate, p.183

Birth

Personal Life

Birth

Antenatal Package Prices

1 | Overview

Prices for antenatal and delivery packages vary greatly depending on the hospital and the circumstances, and therefore the figures below are for guidance only.

Public Hospitals

Antenatal care package price: Dhs.2,500 (includes 12 scheduled visits and all routine tests. You will be charged extra for any additional services or tests).

Normal delivery package price: Dhs.2,000 (Dhs.3,000 if you want a private room. Fee includes routine delivery and tests, two days in hospital, plus a follow-up with gynaecologist and paediatrician).

Caesarean section package price: Dhs.4,000 (Dhs.5,000 if you want a private room. Fee includes surgery and anaesthetist fees, routine tests, four days in hospital, plus follow-up with gynaecologist and paediatrician).

Other costs: In the case of a twin pregnancy, an additional Dhs.1,000 is charged for the second twin. Circumcision is charged at Dhs.500.

Private Hospitals

Antenatal care package price: Dhs.5,000 – Dhs.5,200 (includes 12 scheduled visits and all routine tests. You will be charged extra for any additional services or tests).

Normal delivery package price: Dhs.9,750 – Dhs.10,500 (includes routine delivery and tests, a private room, a follow-up with gynaecologist and paediatrician as well as a visit from the paediatrician one week after delivery, and a post-partum visit with the gynaecologist). Epidural is not included in the package, and is charged at Dhs.2,250.

Caesarean section package price: Dhs.19,000 – Dhs.22,000 (Fee includes surgery and anaesthetist fees, routine tests, four days in a shared room, follow-up with gynaecologist and paediatrician, visit from the paediatrician one week after delivery, and a post-partum visit with the gynaecologist).

Other costs: In the case of a twin pregnancy, an additional Dhs.1,800 – Dhs.2,850 is charged for the second twin. Circumcision is charged at Dhs.900 – Dhs.1,100. If your husband stays in the room with you overnight, there is an extra charge of around Dhs.125 per night, plus the cost of his meals.

Tip | Doctor, Doctor

One of the hardest things about moving to a new country is getting familiar with your surroundings and finding new professionals that you can trust. Whether you are looking for a GP, gynaecologist or paediatrician the Residents chapter of the *Dubai Explorer – The Complete Residents' Guide*, available in all leading bookshops and supermarkets, can point you in the right direction.

Obtaining A Birth Certificate

1 Overview

If your child is born in Dubai, you will automatically get a birth notification letter (in Arabic) from the hospital. You will need to get this stamped by the Ministry of Health before you can apply for the birth certificate – some hospitals will be able to get this stamped for you.

The full procedure for obtaining a birth certificate is detailed below, but there is an easier option. Medi Express (04 272 7772, www. mediexpress.ae) can complete the whole process for you and all documents should be ready in three days. The company will charge Dhs.415 – this includes the full cost of obtaining a birth certificate and a Dhs.130 service charge.

Note that non-Emirati children born in the UAE are not eligible for a UAE passport. Children born here assume their parents' nationality.

It is a good idea to get the birth certificate translated into English, which can be done on site at the typing office.

2 Prerequisites

• The child was born in Dubai

3 What To Bring

☐ Both parents' passports (originals and copies)
☐ Both parents' residence permits (originals and copies)
☐ Attested marriage certificate
☐ Hospital birth records ('birth notification') stamped by Ministry of Health

Fees
☐ Dhs.50 – Arabic birth certificate
☐ Dhs.15 – translation fee
☐ Dhs.50 – English birth certificate
☐ Dhs.120 – English attestation fee (Ministry of Health)
☐ Dhs.150 – attestation fee (Ministry of Foreign Affairs)

4 Procedure

Arabic Birth Certificate
• The hospital in which the baby was delivered will issue a notification of birth certificate
• Some public hospitals, such as the Dubai Hospital, have a Ministry of Health counter that will issue the Arabic birth certificate.

Location
Preventive Medicine Department, Al Baraha Hospital   Map ref 9-B2
(Al Bahara Hospital is commonly referred to as the Kuwaiti Hospital)

Department of Health and Medical Sciences   Map ref 7-C4

Hours Sun – Thurs 07:30 – 13:00

- Submit the birth notification and all documents at the birth certificate office
- Pay the fees at the same office
- The UAE birth certificate will be ready for collection one to two days later
- Have the Arabic spelling of the name checked for errors

English Birth Certificate

- Collect an application form from the birth certificate office (first floor of Building 2)
- Have it typed in English at one of the typing booths in the portacabins within the hospital grounds
- Submit the translated document to the birth certificate office at the Preventive Medicine Department (upstairs in Building 2)
- The official birth certificate will be endorsed immediately

Attestation

- Submit both the Arabic and English birth certificates to the doctor in charge of attestation
- The certificate will be stamped and signed, then must be countersigned by another official
- A birth certificate office official can direct you to both offices
- Pay the attestation and translation fees at the Attestation Counter
- You will be given the attested English and Arabic birth certificates immediately

Waiting Time

2 – 3 days, although the process is being streamlined and you may find that you will receive your certificates immediately

5 Related Procedures

- Registering A Newborn Child, p.43
- Applying for A Residence Permit – Family, p.37

Tip Public vs Private

When you become a resident in Dubai you will be issued with a health card (see p.26) and therefore entitled to treatment at the public hospitals, for an affordable fee. However there are also a number of private hospitals that offer an excellent level of care. For more information on the various hospitals in Dubai refer to the Health section of the *Dubai Explorer – The Complete Residents' Guide* available in all leading bookshops and supermarkets.

Birth

Personal Life

1 Overview

There is unfortunately a great deal of paperwork surrounding a death. It should be decided as soon as possible whether the body will be buried in Dubai or in the deceased's home country. If the body is to be flown out of the UAE, additional permits are necessary before departure.

You will need to get numerous no objection certificates (NOCs) from government officials – these are needed mostly to show that the deceased had no pending legal or civil actions, and that all financial obligations have been settled. You will have to get NOCs from the deceased's sponsor, the Dubai Police, Immigration, the Labour Department, the embassy and the Dubai Municipality.

Death

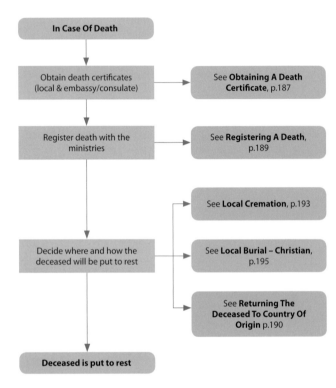

In Case Of Death

Obtain death certificates
(local & embassy/consulate)
→ See **Obtaining A Death Certificate**, p.187

Register death with the
ministries
→ See **Registering A Death**, p.189

Decide where and how the
deceased will be put to rest
→ See **Local Cremation**, p.193

→ See **Local Burial – Christian**, p.195

→ See **Returning The Deceased To Country Of Origin** p.190

Deceased is put to rest

Death

Personal Life

Obtaining A Death Certificate

1 Overview

The first administrative step in dealing with a death is to get a death certificate, which is needed before you can send the body home or arrange a local burial.

If the death occurs in a hospital, they will arrange for the transport of the body to Rashid Hospital. You will have to continue the procedure from there on.

2 Prerequisites

- A death has occurred

3 What To Bring

- ☐ Passport and visa/residence permit of the deceased (original and copy)
- ☐ Police report
- ☐ Death report from the hospital
- ☐ Death certificate declaration

Fees
- ☐ Dhs.60 – death certificate fee
- ☐ Dhs.100 – English translation fee (optional)
- ☐ Up to Dhs.700 – embassy/consulate certificate and registration fee

4 Procedure

Location District Police, Various (see p.295)   Map ref Various

Hours 24 hours

Notification
- Notify the police in your district
- On arrival, the police will make a report
- The police will arrange for an ambulance
- The body will be transported to Rashid Hospital (no charge)

Location Rashid Hospital Mortuary   Map ref 8-F6

Hours Sun – Sat 07:00 – 15:30 (in some cases until 22:00)

Death certificate declaration
- The hospital will determine the cause of death and issue a report, confirming the death. A post-mortem examination is not routinely performed unless foul play is suspected. If the family wants a post-mortem, a written request should be submitted to the Medical Superintendent at Police HQ
- Submit all documents (original passport and copy) and the fee
- The hospital will issue a 'death certificate declaration' (not to be mistaken for the death certificate itself)

- Ensure the actual cause of death is stated on the declaration and that the police stamp the declaration at the hospital

Location	District Police, Various (see p.295)

Map ref **Various**

Hours 24 hours

Police NOC
- Submit all documents
- The police will issue a no objection letter addressed to Al Baraha Hospital, Preventive Medicine Department
- If the deceased is to be sent to the home country, request no objection letters addressed to the airport, the mortuary and the hospital at this time (see Returning the Deceased to Country of Origin, p.190)

Location Al Baraha Hospital Preventive Medicine Department   Map ref **9-B2**

Hours Sun – Thurs 08:00 – 14:00

Death Certificate
- Submit all documents
- A death certificate will be issued in Arabic
- If the deceased is being sent home, the death certificate must be translated into English or the language required by the home country. See directory on p.279 for legal consultants

Location Embassy/Consulate, Various (see p.283)   Map ref **Various**

Hours Sun – Thurs 08:00 – 13:00 (varies)

Embassy Death Certificate
- Notify the embassy or consulate of the death
- The embassy will cancel the passport and register the death in the deceased's country of origin
- An 'embassy death certificate' will be issued
- If you wish to fly the deceased home, request an NOC from the embassy

5   Related Procedure

- Registering a Death, p.189

Registering A Death

1 Overview

Once the official and embassy death certificates have been issued, the death must be registered with the concerned authorities in Dubai.

Keep copies of documents, including the deceased's cancelled passport, with you for this and all procedures that follow.

2 Prerequisites

- Death certificates have been collected (see Obtaining A Death Certificate, p.187)

3 What To Bring

- ☐ Original cancelled passport
- ☐ Local death certificate (Arabic) (original & copy)
- ☐ Embassy/consulate death certificate (original & copy)
- Fees ☐ Dhs.20 – Ministry of Health registration fee
- ☐ Dhs.50 – Ministry of Foreign Affairs attestation fee
- ☐ Dhs.100 – Immigration Department cancellation fee

4 Procedure

Location Ministry of Health   Map ref 8-E4

Hours Sun – Thurs 08:00 – 14:30

- Submit all documents and pay the fee
- The ministry will register the death

Location Ministry of Foreign Affairs   Map ref 8-H3

Hours Sun – Thurs 08:00 – 12:00

- Submit all documents and pay the fee
- The original certificate will be attested and handed back to you

Location Immigration Department   Map ref 7-B4

Hours Sun – Thurs 07:30 – 14:30

- Submit all documents and pay the fee
- The deceased's visa will be cancelled immediately

5 Related Procedures

- Returning the Deceased to Country of Origin, p.190
- Local Cremation, p.193
- Local Burial – Christian, p.195

Death

Personal Life

Death

Returning The Deceased To Country Of Origin

1 Overview

If you are sending the body back home, you will need to think about transport arrangements, getting the necessary paperwork in order and embalming the body. Embalming is done at Maktoum Hospital.

Your embassy or consulate may offer assistance with parts of this procedure.

DNATA (04 211 1111) is currently the only handling agent who can make the necessary transport arrangements for you. If desired, a family member can accompany the body, although this is not a requirement.

In most cases, documentation must be translated into English (unless body is being transported to an Arabic-speaking country).

2 Prerequisites

- All relevant certificates have been collected (see Obtaining A Death Certificate, p.187)
- The death has been registered with the concerned authorities (see Registering A Death, p.189)

3 What To Bring

- ☐ Original cancelled passport and 7 copies
- ☐ Local death certificate (original and 7 copies)
- ☐ Embassy/consulate death certificate (original and 7 copies)
- ☐ Police Clearance certificate (original and 7 copies)
- ☐ NOC to embalm body (original and 7 copies)
- ☐ Embalming certificate (original and 7 copies)
- ☐ Accompanying passenger confirmed ticket and 2 copies
- ☐ Accompanying passenger passport photo (2)

Fees
- ☐ Dhs.1,000 – Dhs.3,000 cash (average cargo fees – this charge depends on the destination and can be more than Dhs.10,000)
- ☐ Dhs.1,010 cash – embalming fee
- ☐ Dhs.1,200 – coffin (approx)
- ☐ Dhs.110 – transportation fee (Medical Fitness Centre, 04 502 3910 07:00 – 17:00)

4 Procedure

Location DNATA Export Office, Cargo Village   Map ref 9-A7

Hours 24 hours

Trasnport Arrangements
- Contact the cargo department of the desired airline to reserve space

Death

Personal Life

- If the deceased will be accompanied, a flight ticket should be purchased from the ticketing section (04 316 6666)
- Contact the DNATA export supervisor to determine cargo fees
- If the casket will be unaccompanied, arrange for it to be collected at the destination. Prior to shipment, the person or undertaker must confirm by fax (04 282 2683) that they will accept the casket

Location	Cargo Village Police Station	Map ref **9-A7**
Hours	24 hours	
Police NOC	• Request an NOC to send the deceased out of the country	
	• Make 7 copies of this letter	

Location	Embassy/Consulate, Various (see p.283)	Map ref **Various**
Hours	Sun – Thurs 08:00 – 13:00 (varies)	
Embassy NOC	• Request an NOC to send the deceased out of the country	
	• Make 7 copies of this letter	

Location	DNATA Export Office, Cargo Village	Map ref **9-A7**
Hours	24 hours	
Confirmation	• Submit all documentation, including two copies of the confirmed flight ticket of accompanying person	

Location	District Police, Various (see p.295)	Map ref **Various**
Hours	Sun – Thurs 07:30 – 14:30	
Embalming NOC	• Request an NOC to embalm the body	

Location	Al Maktoum Hospital Mortuary	Map ref **8-H3**
Hours	Sun – Thurs 07:00 – 18:00; Sat 08:00 – 13:00	
Embalming	• Submit the NOCs from the police and the embassy, the death certificate and a passport copy	
	• An NOC will be issued to the hospital housing the deceased	
	• The deceased will be transported to Al Maktoum Hospital	
	• The body must be identified before and after embalming by the person making all arrangements and signing the documents	
	• The embalming process takes 2 – 4 hours	
	• The same person must collect the embalming certificate and wait at the mortuary until the body has been transferred to the Cargo Village	
	• The hospital will arrange transportation to the Cargo Village	

Location	Cargo Village	Map ref **9-A7**
Hours	24 hours	
Flight	• Delivery must take place at least four hours prior to departure	
	• The casket is weighed in the export cargo department and all paperwork processed in the office next door	
	• Pay the cargo fees (cash only)	

Death

Personal Life

Ensure the following documents (original) are accompanying the deceased

- Cancelled passport
- Local death certificate
- Translation of death certificate
- Embassy/consulate death certificate
- Police NOC
- Embassy NOC
- Embalming certificate
- All documents must be translated into English (unless body is being transported to an Arabic country).

5 Related Procedures

- Obtaining A Death Certificate, p.187
- Registering A Death, p.187

Info Transporting Ashes Back To Home Country

If the deceased has been cremated in Dubai, the ashes can be sent to the home country. Contact DNATA cargo on 04 211 1111 for further assistance or information.

Info Stillbirth

In the case of a stillbirth the process of registering the child's birth and death can be a very emotional task. You can contact the Stillbirth & Neonatal Death Society on 04 884 6309 for assistance and support.

Local Cremation

1 Overview

Deceased of any nationality or religion may be cremated in Dubai, but only in the Hindu manner.

2 Prerequisites

- The deceased must have been resident in Dubai
- All relevant certificates have been collected (see Obtaining A Death Certificate, p.187)
- The death has been registered with the concerned authorities (see Registering a Death, p.189)
- All financial obligations have been settled

3 What To Bring

- ☐ Death certificate
- ☐ Original cancelled passport and residence permit
- ☐ Written permission from the next of kin or sponsor
- ☐ Next of kin's passport (proof of relation)
- ☐ NOC from sponsor that all financial obligations have been settled
- ☐ Dhs.2,500 – cremation fee
- Fee ☐ Dhs.500 – deposit, paid upon submission of application and reimbursed on the collection of the ashes

4 Procedure

Location	Hindu Temple	Map ref 8-F1
Hours	Sat – Thurs 09:00 – 13:00; 16:00 – 20:00	
Application	• Collect a cremation application form	
	• Pay the cremation fee. A vessel will be arranged	
Location	Embassy, Various (see p.283)	Map ref Various
Hours	Sun – Thurs 08:00 – 13:00 (Varies)	
Embassy NOC	• Submit all documents	
	• The embassy may require an NOC from the deceased's relatives	
	• The embassy will issue an NOC for cremation	
Location	District Police, Various (see p.295)	Map ref Various
Hours	Sun – Thurs 7:30 – 14:30	
Police NOC	• Submit all documents and request an NOC for cremation	

Death

Personal Life

Location	Dubai Municipality Cemetery Office	Map ref 6-H7
Hours	Sun – Thurs 06:00 – 21:00
Cremation NOC	• Submit all documents and request an NOC for cremation
Location	New Sonapur (Hindu Cremation Ground)	Map ref off map
Hours	Sun – Thurs 09:30 – 15:00
Cremation	• Once all documentation is complete, the cremation will be organised within one day

5 Related Procedures

- Obtaining A Death Certificate, p.187
- Registering A Death, p.187

Info **Where Is Sonapur Crematorium?**

There is a crematorium in the municipality area called Muhaisnah (known locally as Sonapur, not to be confused with 'New Sonapur') which is situated between the Dubai Municipality labour accommodation and the Al Qusais labour accommodation.

There is also another crematorium and a Christian cemetery situated at New Sonapur, which is about 45km from Dubai World Trade Centre. Follow Sheikh Zayed Road towards Abu Dhabi and take Exit 13 (before the ninth bridge). When the road splits into two, keep left. After looping back round to go over the bridge, you will see signs for the Medical & Hazardous Waste Disposal Plant. Turn right just before the plant and you'll see the cemetery on your left after half a kilometre.

Personal Life Death

Local Burial – Christian

1 Overview

A local burial can be arranged at the Christian cemetery (04 337 0247) in Dubai. The charity-financed cemetery will assist you with burial arrangements. The graveyard is located at Jebel Ali and the land is provided by the Dubai Government.

2 Prerequisites

- Deceased was a member of any Christian community
- Deceased was resident in Dubai
- All relevant certificates have been collected (see Obtaining A Death Certificate, p.187)
- The death has been registered with the concerned authorities (see Registering A Death, p.189)

3 What To Bring

☐ Cancelled passport and residence permit (original and copy)

☐ Death certificate (original and three copies)

☐ NOC from sponsor that all financial obligations have been settled (original and copy)

☐ Dubai Police NOC (see below), three copies

☐ Dubai Municipality clearance letter (see below)

Burial Fees ☐ Dhs.1,010 – Dubai Municipality fee

☐ Dhs.1,100 – adult burial; Dhs.350 – child

4 Procedure

Location	Dubai Police Headquarters Map ref 10-D7
Hours	Sun – Thurs 07:30 – 14:30
Police NOC	• Submit all documents
	• The police will issue an NOC requesting that Dubai Municipality clears the burial
Location	Dubai Municipality Cemetery Office Map ref 6-H7
Hours	Sun – Thurs 06:00 – 21:00
Municipality Clearance Letter	• Submit all documents
	• Collect a clearance letter from the municipality
Location	Christian Cemetery Office Map ref 8-E6
Hours	Sun – Thurs 09:00 – 18:00
Burial	• Submit all documents
	• Contact the cemetery caretaker

Death

Personal Life

Death

- The caretaker will assist you in arranging a funeral
- Contact an undertaker or a carpenter to prepare a coffin
- You may arrange for a gravestone to be prepared, but only after six months
- Contact your church if you wish to hold a memorial service

5 Related Procedures

- Obtaining A Death Certificate, p.187
- Registering A Death, p.189

Info **Christian Cemetery In New Sonapur**

The Christian cemetery is situated at New Sonapur, about 45kms from Dubai World Trade Centre. Follow Sheikh Zayed Road towards Abu Dhabi and take Exit 13 (before the ninth bridge). When the road splits into two, keep left. After looping back round to go over the bridge, you will see signs for the Medical & Hazardous Waste Disposal Plant. Turn right just before the plant and you'll see the cemetery on your left after half a kilometre.

Info **Support Needs**

Culture shock and feeling miles away from home can make settling into your new life in Dubai somewhat challenging but there are a number of networks in Dubai set up to make the transition easier. Similarly if you have to cope with a bereavement help is at hand. For more information on support groups refer to the Residents chapter of the *Dubai Explorer – The Complete Residents' Guide* available in all leading bookshops and supermarkets.

Info **Muslim Burial Customs**

According to Islamic custom, the quicker a body is buried after death occurs, the better. In the UAE, a deceased Muslim person is often buried within 24 hours, although there are no hard and fast rules about the time limit.

Factors such as repatriation of the body to the home country, or the need for an autopsy after death, can be taken into consideration and allow for a delay in burial.

Local Burial – Muslim

1 Overview

Burial procedures for a Muslim have to be done quickly. Formalities such as getting the death certificate and cancelling the visa can be done after the burial (within one month of the death). Graveyards are situated in Sonapur, Al Qusais, Bur Dubai and Al Quoz.

2 Prerequisites

- Deceased was a Muslim and a resident in Dubai
- All relevant certificates have been collected (see below)
- Original passport of the deceased and two copies
- Death notification certificate (original and copy) from the hospital where the body is being kept

3 What To Bring

- ☐ Original passport (and photocopy) of guarantor or next of kin
- ☐ No objection certificate (NOC) from Dubai Police

4 Procedure

Location	Dubai Police Headquarters	Map ref 10-D7
Hours	Sun – Thurs 07:30 – 14:30	

Police Clearance Letter
- Submit all documents
- Original passport of the guarantor or next of kin will be retained by the police, and returned after all documentation is complete (within one month of death)
- The police will issue a letter (in quadruplicate) requesting Dubai Municipality to clear the burial

Location	Dubai Municipality Cemetery Office	Map ref 6-H7
Hours	Sun – Thurs 06:00 – 21:00	

Dubai Municipality Permission
- Submit a copy of the police letter – this is to obtain permission to dig the grave for burial
- The Kafan/Dafan Committee at Dubai Municipality will make arrangements for digging the grave, as well as prayers, kafan (coffin) and dafan (burial)
- Dubai Municipality will advise you when to release the body from the hospital

5 Related Procedures

- Getting A Death Certificate, p.187
- Registering A Death, p.189
- Registering A Death With Your Embassy or Consulate, See p.283

Death

Personal Life

Education

Enrolling In A School

1 Overview

There are no English-speaking government schools, and therefore expat children must attend private school. Some employers offer a schooling allowance as part of the remuneration package.

The year is split into three school terms: autumn (mid September to mid December), spring (early January to early April) and summer (mid April – early July). Most schools operate Sunday to Thursday from 08:00 to 13:00 or 15:00.

One of the biggest hindrances to enrolling your child in the school of your choice is long waiting lists. Schools may also charge a fee of Dhs.500 to Dhs.1,000 to join their waiting lists. You should enrol as early as possible and follow up regularly.

2 Prerequisites

- Student is between 3 and 18 years of age

3 What To Bring

For the School
- ☐ Student's and parents' passports (2 copies)
- ☐ Residence permit (2 copies)
- ☐ Student's birth certificate (2 copies)
- ☐ Eight passport sized photographs
- ☐ School records for the past two years (original and 2 copies)
- ☐ Current immunisation record and medical history (copy)
- ☐ Character reference from the previous school (if necessary)
- ☐ Dhs.300 – registration fee (this varies)

UAE Applicants
- ☐ Transfer certificate from the previous school

 You will need an original certificate from the old school addressed to the new school

External Applicants
- ☐ An official transfer certificate from the student's previous school detailing his/her education to date (original and 2 copies)

⚠ Original transfer certificates from any country other than UAE, Australia, Canada, USA, or western Europe must be attested by the Ministry of Education, Ministry of Foreign Affairs and the UAE Embassy in that country

The original document must contain the following details:

- Date of enrolment
- Year placement
- Date the child left the school
- School stamp
- Official signature

táaleem
inspiring young minds

Inspiring tomorrow's visionaries, today.

**Taaleem inspires young minds to discover
their talents and pursue their passions.**

The Taaleem family of schools:

Al-Mizhar, American Academy for Girls *Mirdif, Dubai*
American Curriculum (Girls only)
T + 971 (4) 288 7250 www.aag.ae

The Children's Garden *Green Community, Dubai*
Unique Tailor Made Multilingual Program
T + 971 (4) 885 3484 www.childrensgarden.ae

Dubai British School *The Springs, Dubai*
British National Curriculum
T + 971 (4) 361 9361 www.dubaibritishschool.ae

Greenfield Community School *Dubai Investments Park, Dubai*
IB Candidate School
T + 971 (4) 885 6600 www.gcschool.ae

My Nursery *Jumeirah, Dubai*
Bilingual Classical Arabic and English Curriculum
T + 971 (4) 344 1120 www.mynursery.ae

Raha International School *Al Raha Gardens, Abu Dhabi*
IB Candidate School
T + 971 (2) 556 1567 www.ris.ae

Uptown High School *Muhaisnah, Dubai*
IB Candidate School
T + 971 (4) 264 1818 www.uptownhigh.ae

Uptown School *Mirdif, Dubai*
IB World School
T + 971 (4) 288 6270 www.uptownprimary.ae

We encourage the apple of your eye
to become a visionary of tomorrow.

The Visionary

For more information visit www.taaleem.ae

- ☐ Original official transfer certificate
- ☐ The most recent report card (original)

4 Procedure

Contact the school, ask about waiting list

- If you have to put your child on a waiting list, investigate some alternative schools just in case
- Fill in the application form
- Fill in the student questionnaire (if applicable)
- Pay the required deposit
- If the student is accepted, pay the school registration fee
- Some schools require that prospective students sit an entrance exam, have a Ministry of Health physical examination, and undergo a family interview

5 Related Procedure

- Applying For A Residence Permit – Family, p.37

Info | **Special Needs**

If your child has physical or learning disabilities, there are several organisations you can contact in order to find out what activities or facilities are available to suit your child's special needs. Some mainstream schools will try to accommodate children suffering from dyslexia, ADHD and other more manageable challenges but you will need to discuss this with the school's administration.

The Al Noor Centre for Children with Special Needs (04 340 4844, www.alnooruae.org) provides therapeutic support and comprehensive training to special needs children of all ages. The Dubai Centre for Special Needs (04 344 0966, www.dcsneeds. ae) currently has around 130 students who follow individual programmes that include physiotherapy, speech and/or occupational therapy. The Rashid Paediatric Therapy Centre (04 340 0005, www.rashidc.ae) includes physical, occupational and speech therapy. Other support/activity groups include Riding for the Disabled (rdaddubai@hotmail.com), Dubai Autism Center (04 398 6862, www.dubaiautismcenter.ae) and the Dyslexia Support Group (050 652 4325).

Enrolling At Nursery/Pre-School

1 Overview

Most pre-schools accept children from the age of three. Nursery schools may take babies as young as three months, although most will only admit children once they are walking. Nurseries are generally open from 08:00 to 12:30 or 13:00, but many offer late hours (some even up to 19:00) and early drop-offs (07:30). Most nurseries are open five days a week.

2 Prerequisites

- Residency visa
- Child is of the right age

3 What To Bring

- ☐ Completed registration forms
- ☐ Photocopy of child's passport with valid residence visa (2 copies)
- ☐ Photocopy of birth certificate (2 copies)
- ☐ Passport photos (up to 8)
- ☐ Completed medical form
- ☐ Copy of immunisation records
- ☐ Registration fees (from Dhs.100 – Dhs.500, non-refundable)
- ☐ Medical fees (from Dhs.100 – Dhs.500, payable once a year)
- ☐ Term fees (from Dhs.3,000 – Dhs.7,000 per term)

4 Procedure

Contact the nurseries you are interested in

- Find out if there is a waiting list, and put your child's name on it
- Fill in the application/registration form
- Fill in the student questionnaire (if applicable)
- Pay the necessary deposit
- Upon confirmation, pay the term fees

Education

Personal Life

Education

Enrolling In University

1   Overview

More school-leaving students are choosing to remain in the UAE to study tertiary courses. The opening of Knowledge Village (www.kv.ae) in 2004 saw an influx of international educational organisations offering various courses.

One of the important factors to consider is the residency of the student: girls can remain on their father's sponsorship while they study, but boys may not be sponsored by their fathers after their 18th birthday, and therefore have to apply for a student visa (see below). The academic institution will assist with this.

2   Prerequisites

- Residency visa
- School leaving certificate from a UAE school or a recognised international equivalent
- Successful completion of the University's entrance assessment (if applicable)
- TOEFL certificate if English is not the student's first language – if you don't have this, you may be required to take an English test

3   What To Bring

- ☐ Completed application form
- ☐ Passport photographs (up to 8)
- ☐ Passport copy with valid residence visa page
- ☐ Non-refundable application fee
- ☐ High school certificate and academic record covering the last three years of school
- ☐ Letters of recommendation from teachers (stamped and sealed)

4   Procedure

- Visit the university to discuss entrance requirements and its courses
- Select courses and fill out registration form
- Pay the fees

Info   Student Visa

Universities usually offer sponsorship and provide a residence visa for international students coming to Dubai to study, or for male students over the age of 18 resident in Dubai. This is only valid while the student is studying, and does not permit employment. The cost of this visa is around Dhs.2,000 to Dhs.3,000 (which is borne by the student) plus a Dhs.3,000 to Dhs.4,000 refundable deposit.

Importing Pets

1 Overview

Pets may be brought into the UAE without quarantine as long as they are microchipped and vaccinated with verifying documentation, including a government health certificate from the country of origin (not from a private vet). You are not permitted to import cats or dogs under four months old into the UAE. Pets that are under four months old will be kept in quarantine until they are four months old. All pets must arrive as manifest cargo. The limit, although not official, is three pets per person and if documents are incorrect the animal will be confiscated and quarantined.

2 Prerequisites

- The animal should have a valid rabies vaccination done not less than 21 days before their arrival.
- Animals should be microchipped in order to enter Dubai and must have verifying documentation.

3 What To Bring

- ☐ Owner's passport (copy)
- ☐ Owner's residence permit or visit visa (copy)
- ☐ Owner's contact details: company name, telephone and fax numbers, PO box number
- ☐ Vaccination card (original and copy)
- ☐ Certificate for the rabies serum neutralisation test is required for some countries. Countries that do not need this include: Australia, Germany, New Zealand, Spain, UK and the USA – check www.uae.gov.ae/mafeservices for more details.
- ☐ Government health certificate from country of origin

Pets must arrive with all original documents, including the government health certificate from the country of origin, attached to the airway bill.

Fees ☐ Handling fee – Dhs.200

4 Procedure

Location Ministry of Environment & Water   Map ref 8-H5

Hours Sun – Thurs 07:30 – 14:30

Import Permit
- Fill in an application form for an import permit at the Ministry. You can also apply online (www.uae.gov.ae/mafeservices), you will need to create an account and fax or email copies of documents to 04 295 6945, animalquarantine@moew.gov.ae.
- Submit all relevant documents

Pets

Personal Life

- Either pick up the import permit the following day, or the Ministry will send it to you within one week
- The import permit is valid for one month only
- Make flight arrangements with the airline

Location   Cargo Village (arriving as manifested cargo)   Map ref 9-A7

Hours   24 hours

Pre-Arrival & Arrival
- Submit the import permit (copy) to the Import Office
- The airline will send a telex to Cargo Village prior to the pet's arrival
- When clearing the pets, you must be able to produce owner's passport (copy)
- Clearance can take between two and four hours
- There is a fee of Dhs.220

Permit Validity   One month

5   Related Procedures

- Vaccinating And Registering Pets, p.208
- Sterilising Pets, p.209

Info   **K9 Friends And Feline Friends**

The tireless efforts of these two non-profit organisations have improved the lives of many lucky dogs and cats in Dubai. If you would like to lend a hand, make a donation (cash, jumble sale items or even time), or adopt a pet of your own, you can get more information on their websites:

www.k9friends.com

www.felinefriendsuae.com

Tip   **Cats & Dogs**

If you are considering getting a cat or dog while you live in Dubai then K9 Friends and Feline Friends (see above) are the best bet. For more information on these associations as well as pet services check out the Residents chapter of the *Dubai Explorer – The Complete Residents' Guide* available in all leading bookshops and supermarkets.

Personal Life   Pets

Exporting Pets

1 Overview

A pet can be sent out of Dubai either accompanied by a person on the same flight, or unaccompanied as cargo depending on the airline and destination. Below is the basic procedure as required by the government, Emirates SkyCargo and DNATA, the cargo-handling agent for all airlines except for Emirates. Dubai Kennels & Cattery offer an export service (04 285 1646), as do IAL Pet Express (04 310 9455).

2 Prerequisites

- As per the laws of the country to which you are sending the pet

If you wish to avoid having your pet spend six months in quarantine on arrival in the United Kingdom, note that the authorities there require that a rabies blood test (RNATT) be done to test the levels of the rabies antibody in the pet's system. The test must be done in the correct sequence and no less than six months before the animal's arrival in the UK. If the test is negative or the procedure is not correctly followed your pet will be quarantined or sent back to the UAE to restart the process.

3 What To Bring

- ☐ A vaccination card, showing a rabies vaccination not older than one year and not less than 30 days
- ☐ Any other documentation required by the destination country (such as blood test results)
- ☐ A travel box, wooden or fibreglass, that meets airline specifications

Fee ☐ Variable

4 Procedure

Flight
- Contact the airline cargo department and inquire about country-specific pet import regulations
- Book flight for the pet. It is recommended that this is done at least one week in advance

Location Dubai Cargo Village   Map ref 9-A7

Hours 24 hours

Export Permit
- No more than seven days prior to departure, take the vaccination records, health certificate and passport copy to the Ministry of Environment & Water veterinarian at Cargo Village
- Pay Dhs.100
- You will be given a UAE health certificate, referred to as an export permit by some countries, which is valid for five days only

Pets

Personal Life

Pets

Location	DNATA Export Office or SkyCargo Export Office Map ref 9-A7
Hours	24 hours

Shipment
- Take the pet, travel box and all original documents to the export office
- Fill in a 'live animal declaration' form
- Complete an IDG and shipper's certificate
- The animal will be weighed and measured, and the export fee calculated
- Pay the fee (cash only for DNATA. Emirates SkyCargo also accept credit card payment)
- Collect the shipper's copy of the airway bill
- At least four hours before departure, take the pet and travel box to the Export Office
- All original documents must travel with your pet, attached to the air waybill

Procedure Timings   10 days

Many countries have slightly different import requirements when it comes to taking your pets out of the UAE. It helps to be aware of these as early as possible as some require action to be taken at least seven months before your pets arrive in their destination country.

Canada And United States
Pets must arrive with the original vaccination certificate and original UAE health certificate (see p.205). Quarantine for dogs that work with livestock may apply. Regulations do vary among the various states of America so enquire with the relevant authorities.

Europe (including France, Germany, Spain, Holland and Portugal)

All pets must arrive with an official EU veterinary health certificate. RNATT (rabies) blood tests are not required.

South Africa
South Africa requires that dogs have blood tests for five specific diseases done within 30 days of export, and that the results are negative for the diseases. The cost of these tests is around Dhs.1,000 per animal as the samples are sent to South Africa for testing. A two-week quarantine period also applies for dogs but not for cats.

United Kingdom
To avoid having your pets placed in quarantine for 6 months on arrival in the UK, they have to be microchipped, vaccinated against rabies and tested for the level of rabies antibodies in their blood. The positive test result for rabies antibodies must be obtained at least six months before the animals leave the UAE. If the test is negative, the animal must be revaccinated and retested a month later, so it's best to start this process well in advance.

You will also need written confirmation from a private veterinarian that the steps (microchipping, vaccination and testing) were carried out in the correct order. The letter must been on headed paper, signed and stamped. You also require an official veterinary certificate, from an authorised vet, which must be completed in block letters and in English.

Between 24 and 48 hours before departure the pets must be treated for internal and external parasites and confirmation that this has been done must be entered by the vet in the official EU veterinary health certificate.

A six month quarantine period applies if the blood test procedure is not done or if it has been done incorrectly.

Pets

Personal Life

Pets

1 Overview

Dogs and cats should be vaccinated annually. After vaccination you should apply for a municipality ID disc, which should be worn on the pet's collar at all times. Vaccinations can be done either by a private vet or by the Dubai Municipality Veterinary Section (04 289 1114).

⚠ The municipality controls the stray population by trapping and euthanasing cats and dogs. Pets without an ID disc, or without a current ID disc are treated as strays.

2 Prerequisites

- Pet is not yet vaccinated or registered

3 What To Bring

Fees
- ☐ Dhs.220 (cat), Dhs.250 (dog) – vaccination, tagging, microchipping and ID disc at the Dubai Municipality clinic
- ☐ Dhs.350 – vaccination at private veterinary clinic (approx)
- ☐ Dhs.250 – tagging and microchipping at a private clinic (approx)
- ☐ Dhs.75 – municipality ID disc at a private clinic

4 Procedure

Location Dubai Municipality Veterinary Section   Map ref 6-G9

Or a Private Clinic (various, see p.291)

Hours Sun – Thurs 07:30 – 14:00; 16:00 – 19:00

- Go to a veterinary clinic in Dubai or to the Municipality's Veterinary Section
- Your pet will be vaccinated
- Collect the vaccination certificate and apply for a municipality number disc
- Attach the tag to the pet's collar to protect it from being collected as a stray if it wanders. If your pet is wearing its tag and the municipality finds it, they will contact you immediately

Sterilising Pets

1 Overview

Sterilising (or 'desexing') your pets is strongly recommended, especially in this part of the world where there is a problem with strays and unwanted animals. Female pets are spayed (womb and ovaries are removed) and male pets are castrated (testicles are removed). Both operations are straightforward, carried out under general anaesthetic, and your pet will recover quickly. Sterilisation is highly recommended to reduce the number of unwanted animals that are forced to live on the streets. Once sterilised, your pet will also probably wander less, and therefore be less exposed to the dangers of traffic and disease.

You can have your pet sterilised either at a private veterinary clinic or at the Dubai Municipality Clinic (04 289 1114).

2 Prerequisites

- Pet is not yet sterilised
- Pet is the appropriate age (approximately six months for dogs, and five months for cats, although your vet will be able to recommend the best age for your pet)

3 What To Bring

nicipality Vet Fee ☐ Dhs.60 (regardless of size or gender of cat or dog)

Private Vet Fee ☐ Fee depends on weight and sex:
- Dogs: Dhs.450 – Dhs.760 (female); Dhs.300 – Dhs.450 (male)
- Cats: Dhs.300 – Dhs.380 (female); Dhs.195 – Dhs.265 (male)

4 Procedure

- Make an appointment
- Take your pet to the vets at the appointed time (usually in the morning)
- The animal will have a pre-op check (if you are at a private vet, they may ask you if there are any other minor procedures, such as nail clipping or teeth cleaning, you want to have done while your pet is under general anaesthetic. Such procedures will be charged extra)
- Leave your pet at the vet for the operation
- Collect your pet in the afternoon – at this point the vet will give you clear instructions for care during your pet's recovery

Pets

Personal Life

Banking

Opening A Bank Account

1 Overview

A Dubai bank account is a requirement for most residents and each bank has specific prerequisites.

General banking hours are from Sunday to Thursday, 08:00 – 15:30 and Saturday 08:00 – 14:00 but they do vary from bank to bank.

Most banks set a minimum account/balance limit – normally Dhs.5,000 for a savings or current account. If the balance drops below the minimum set by the bank, a fee of Dhs.30 – Dhs.100 is charged per month (depending on bank and account type)

All banks have different procedures – below is a general overview.

2 Prerequisites

- Residence permit or residency application in process (if applying for a savings account)

If your residency application is being processed, you may be able to open a savings account if your sponsoring company confirms your employment and the branch manager signs your application.

3 What To Bring

Private Account
- ☐ Passport (original and copy)
- ☐ Residence permit (original and copy)
- ☐ One form of local ID, such as a driving licence (original and copy)

Corporate Account
- ☐ Minimum balance amount (varies from bank to bank)
- ☐ Valid trade licence
- ☐ Proof of membership with the Dubai Chamber of Commerce & Industry
- ☐ Board resolution authorising the opening of the account
- ☐ Certified copies of the memorandum and articles of association

New Company
- ☐ List of directors
- ☐ Registration certificate from the Ministry of Economy & Commerce
- ☐ Passport copies of company owner(s)
- ☐ If you are about to establish your company in Dubai and you do not yet have all of the above documents, you will need a letter from the Dubai Department of Economic Development

4 Procedure

Location Banks (see p.276)   Map ref Various

Hours Sun – Thurs 08:00 – 15:30; Sat 08:00 – 14:00

As procedures and timings differ from bank to bank, please check with your bank for more information.

Banking

Personal Life

Applying For A Good Conduct Certificate

1 Overview

The two main reasons for needing a good conduct certificate are employment and emigration. This certificate is provided by the Criminal Investigation Department (CID) and confirms that you have no criminal record in the UAE.

Future potential employers may request that you supply this certificate before completing the recruitment process, and certain countries (USA, Canada, Australia) require this as part of the application for immigration process.

2 Prerequisites

- Applicant has been resident in Dubai for at least six months

3 What To Bring

- ☐ Passport (original and copy)
- ☐ Residence permit (copy)
- ☐ Two passport photos

Fee ☐ Dhs.110 – service charge

4 Procedure

Location CID, Dubai Police Headquarters   Map ref 10-D7

Hours Sun – Thurs 07:30 – 14:00

- Pick up the application form from the CID and have it typed out
- Submit all documents with the application form
- Give one set of fingerprints
- If you pass the background check, the certificate will be ready for collection after three days

Waiting Time Three days

Work

Personal Life

Liquor Licence

Applying For A Liquor Licence

1 Overview

The sale of alcohol is controlled in the UAE.

In order to purchase alcohol for home consumption, you first have to obtain a liquor licence. With your licence, you can buy a limited quantity of alcohol per month from one of two licensed companies; African and Eastern (A&E), or Mercantile Maritime International (MMI). Both have numerous branches around Dubai. For a list of locations, see p.288.

You can apply for your liquor licence at any branch of A&E or MMI and the process is quite streamlined and quick.

Monthly Quota When you receive your licence, you will be given a 'monthly quota' – the amount of alcohol you are allowed to buy in one month. The quota is based on your salary, age, job and the size of your family. It usually ranges from Dhs.500 upwards.

Licence Transfer Liquor licences are not transferable, so your friends are not permitted to buy alcohol using your licence. It is possible for a wife to buy alcohol on her husband's licence, but only if you apply for this. See the Info box opposite.

Validity One year

2 Prerequisites

- Applicant cannot be Muslim
- Applicant must be resident in Dubai
- Minimum monthly salary of approximately Dhs.3,000
- Minimum age of 21 years
- Married couple: only the husband may apply

The wife may apply with written agreement from the husband if the husband is Muslim and the wife is non-Muslim, or if the husband's sponsoring company does not support its employees applying for liquor licences due to religious reasons.

3 What To Bring

- ☐ Completed application form from one of the above liquor stores, signed and stamped by your employer. The application must be signed by the applicant, and it should bear the stamp of the company.
- ☐ Passport (valid for at least six months) and copy
- ☐ Residence permit (valid for at least three months) and copy

☐ One passport photo, with your full name written on the back

☐ One passport photo of wife (optional) – see info box below

☐ Tenancy contract (copy)

☐ Employment contract showing your monthly salary (copy)

☐ Letter of no objection from your employer (original)

Fee ☐ Dhs.160 – application fee

4 Procedure

Location Any A&E or MMI store (various, see p.288)   Map ref Various

- Get an application form from any A&E or MMI store
- Submit all documents
- Pay the fee
- The store will then process the application through the Dubai Police on your behalf and you will be given a date on which you can collect your licence

Waiting Time One week

Law Alcohol Use

- It is against the law to sell or offer alcoholic beverages to Muslims
- It is illegal to consume alcohol in public places, including in the desert or at the beach
- Driving under the influence of alcohol and public drunkenness are punishable offences; there is a ZERO TOLERANCE policy in effect and breaking the law will earn you a stint in jail
- During Ramadan, only tourist establishments are permitted to serve alcohol, and only after 18:00

Duty Free

This allowance is for non-Muslims only and is a generous four litres for alcoholic beverages, or 24 cans of beer (which must not exceed 355 millilitres per can).

Info Liquor Licence – Wife

A married couple can share one liquor licence if they first apply at MMI or A&E. You will need to provide a passport photograph of your wife, as well as a copy of her passport (with a valid residence permit), a completed application form and your current licence (if applicable). The liquor store will then process the application and she can then buy alcohol on your licence.

Liquor Licence

Personal Life

HADEF & PARTNERS

HIGHLIGHTS

KEEP ON TOP OF
LEGAL DEVELOPMENTS
IN THE UAE

Subscribe to our
monthly legal
newsletter by
registering on
our website.

Business

Overview

Overview

Business

Overview

In this chapter, various options for opening a business are outlined with a focus on the expat entrepreneur. A step-by-step guide through the trade licence application procedure is also included.

Overview & Main Institutions

Red-Tape gives a short introduction to business in Dubai, as well as the organisations you need to deal with, like the Department of Economic Development (DED), the Federal Ministry of Economy and Planning, the Dubai Chamber of Commerce & Industry (DCCI) and the Dubai Municipality.

Preparation & Selection

Outlines the different company forms that can be set up here and lists things to consider before applying for a trade licence.

Setting Up

Covers how to set up an LLC, a branch or representative office of a foreign company, a sole proprietorship and a professional civil company.

Immigration & Labour

How to open company files with the Ministry of Labour and Immigration. More info on applying for visas, see the Visas Section.

Commercial Agent

In most cases, a foreign company may have to appoint a commercial agent. This section explains how to do this.

Free Zones

Free zone regulations differ greatly from the rest of Dubai. There is an increasing number of free zones in Dubai, but we have focused on the main ones.

E-Government

The Dubai government supports business. For more information on the new 'e' drive, see p.xi in the introduction.

Info	e-Dirham

The e-Dirham card (www.e-dirham.gov.ae) is a prepaid electronic payment tool introduced by the Ministry of Finance and Industry. The card replaces the use of cash as payment for procedures at the Department of Economic Development and the Ministry of Finance. It can be deactivated in case of loss or theft by calling the Tele e-Dirham Service (04 800 2243). This service can also be used for balance enquiries, PIN changes, and many other transactions. To get a card, you'll need a residence permit as well as a valid trade licence. e-Dirham cards are available at several banks (see Directory, p.276).

Overview

Business

Overview

1   Overview

Financial Benefits
- No personal income tax
- No foreign exchange controls
- No restrictions on repatriating capital and/or earnings
- No corporate tax except for branches of foreign banks, courier companies and oil companies

Ownership

At least 51% participation by UAE nationals is the requirement for all UAE-established companies. See below for exceptions.

Exception

100% foreign ownership is permitted in the following cases:

- Companies located in UAE free zones
- Companies with activities open to 100% AGCC ownership
- Companies where wholly owned AGCC companies enter into partnership with UAE nationals
- Branches and representative offices of foreign companies registered in Dubai
- Professional or artisan companies practising business activities that allow 100% foreign ownership

Land Ownership

Currently, foreign companies and non-Nationals are not permitted to own commercial land in the UAE other than in free zones, where lease-hold ownership is offered. Commercial property must be either rented or leased, and rates tend to be high.

Labour Law

The UAE Labour Law deals with working hours, termination rights, benefits and repatriation, but is employer friendly in some aspects. Labour issues are administered by the Federal Ministry of Labour and Social Affairs. Trade unions don't exist and strikes are forbidden.

Copyright Law

Introduced in 1993, the UAE Copyright Law was most recently updated in 2002 with the development of Federal Copyright Law No.7. It protects the rights of creators, performers, producers of audio recordings and broadcasting/recording corporations.

Trademark Law

Trademark law was introduced in 1974 and updated in 1993. Trademark registration in the UAE is done through the Ministry of Economy & Planning and takes between 12 and 18 months.

Work Permits

The employer is responsible for all work permits and related immigration procedures for their employees including any costs. In a free zone, the free zone authority will handle all immigration procedures.

Employment Contracts

The Ministry of Labour provides a model labour contract in English and Arabic. The Arabic labour contract is enforceable in a court of law.

Employees

The ministry sets a maximum number of expatriate staff that may be hired according to the size of the business and the business activity.

Main Institutions

1 Overview

The Department of Economic Development, the Federal Ministry of Economy & Planning, and the Dubai Chamber of Commerce & Industry are the main authorities you will deal with when setting up a company in Dubai.

Dubai Department of Economic Development

This is the first port of call when setting up a business in Dubai. The Economic Department or DED, as it's known, issues trade licences and is an integral authority for businesses. Its office is always extremely busy, but there is an efficient queuing system. It has a comprehensive website (www.dubaided.gov.ae) which is worth checking out.

Ministry of Economy & Planning

The Ministry of Economy & Planning is the federal institution that oversees all economic activity in the UAE. It plays a supervisory and regulatory role in setting up all commercial companies. The head office is located in Abu Dhabi and, while there is a Dubai office, few new companies will need to make a visit. Foreign companies wanting to set up a branch in Dubai, as well as insurance companies, agents and brokers, must obtain approvals from this ministry.

The Ministry of Economy also handles the registration of commercial agents/agencies. Other responsibilities include issuing certificates of origin for National exports and the protection of trademarks.

Dubai Chamber of Commerce & Industry

The Dubai Chamber of Commerce and Industry, or DCCI, promotes commerce through various means, both locally as well as internationally. The Chamber also compiles all business-related data for the emirate, issues certificates of origin of commodities and other goods, nominates experts for goods surveying, receives commercial complaints, states and sets standards, defines commercial usage and terminology, and holds economic and commercial conferences.

Every commercial, professional and industrial company must register with the Chamber (very small businesses may be the exception).

Dubai Municipality

All companies outside of a free zone must gain approval from the Municipality for their premises before setting up; zoning regulations are both devised and enforced here.

The Municipality is responsible for Dubai's infrastructure and urban landscaping.

Free Zones

Free Zones are designed to encourage foreign investment and the rules and procedures for establishing companies differ from the rest of Dubai, particularly with regard to foreign ownership. Both labour and immigration laws vary slightly as well, easing requirements and reducing headaches for business owners, see p.264.

Overview

1 Overview

Variable Rules

While the information gathered in this book is as accurate as possible, anyone setting up a business in Dubai needs to be prepared for the unpredictable. Rules can vary and depend on nationality, business activity, capital amounts, partners and products, and the laws and/or regulations change on a regular basis.

Guidance

The procedures outlined in the following pages provide guidance as to the types of red-tape and formalities required when setting up various kinds of businesses in Dubai. Four options for non-GCC nationals have been covered alongside free zone set up: setting up an LLC, a branch of a foreign company, a sole proprietorship and a professional company.

First Steps – Helping Hand

In addition to the information in this book, the Department for Corporate Relations and the Investment Promotion Centre at the DED will lend an essential helping hand. In an effort to promote investment, particularly foreign investment, they will assist with the paperwork involved in obtaining a trade licence – the first step in setting up a business. For a commercial service fee of between Dhs.200 and Dhs.500, depending on the licence type, this very friendly, helpful and efficient department will guide you through the trade licence application procedure. This can significantly speed up the process and save a few headaches. The office is located in the DED head office, on the first floor.

How To Succeed In Business

Doing business in Dubai is a whole new ball game for new residents and learning the dos and don'ts of business etiquette is a must before you step into the boardroom. For more information on working and doing business in Dubai check out the Residents chapter of the *Dubai Explorer – The Complete Residents' Guide* available in all leading bookshops and supermarkets.

Selecting A Trade Licence Type

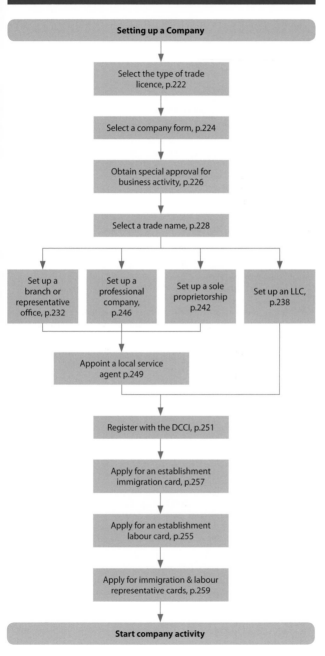

Setting up a Company

↓

Select the type of trade licence, p.222

↓

Select a company form, p.224

↓

Obtain special approval for business activity, p.226

↓

Select a trade name, p.228

↓

| Set up a branch or representative office, p.232 | Set up a professional company, p.246 | Set up a sole proprietorship p.242 | Set up an LLC, p.238 |

↓

Appoint a local service agent p.249

↓

Register with the DCCI, p.251

↓

Apply for an establishment immigration card, p.257

↓

Apply for an establishment labour card, p.255

↓

Apply for immigration & labour representative cards, p.259

↓

Start company activity

Overview

Business

Preparation & Selection

Selecting A Trade Licence Type

1 Overview

Trade Licence
All companies in Dubai must have a trade licence, as it determines which specific business activities a company is permitted to practise.

Licence Type
Three types of trade licence exist:

- Commercial Licence: issued for all business activities in general
- Professional Licence: issued for services as well as different professions
- Industrial Licence: issued for manufacturing activities

DED
The institution responsible for this stage of company establishment is the Dubai Department of Economic Development, as it issues the trade licence.

Free Zones
All free zone companies have trade licences provided by their free zone authority.

Special Approval
Depending on the business activity and the company form, approvals from other ministries may be necessary before the DED issues the trade licence (see Business Activities Requiring Special Approval table on p.226).

Company Forms
Before setting up a company, you will first have to decide which legal company form you would like. The form will depend on the business activity and the ownership of the company. For more information on the various options available, see Selecting A Company Form on p.224. The company form will influence which type of trade licence can be applied for.

Categories
All business activities in Dubai fall into one of the three categories of licence as listed above. The Licence Categories table on the facing page will assist you in determining which category your company will fall into.

> **Tip** **New Business Activities**
>
> If your business activity is not listed within the licence categories you will need to contact the Dubai Department of Economic Development to issue a new business activity. Submit a summary of your proposed business activity at the DED head office and it will be reviewed. They will inform you in two to three days whether this activity will be permitted.

Licence Categories

Licence	Business Activity
Commercial Licence	All trading activity (ie. buying and selling goods) for the purpose of profit • Banks • Media companies • Contractors • Insurance Agencies • Real Estate • Retail Companies • Supermarkets • Transport Companies
Professional Licence	Professions, services, craftsmen and artisans who practice a profession in which the service depends on physical or mental efforts rather than on capital. • Accountants • Advertising Agencies • Architectural Consultants • Auditors • Education and Welfare • Engineering Consultants • Exhibition Organisers • Legal Consultants • Medical & Health Services • Secretarial Services • Social Services • Technical Consultants • Translation Services • Veterinary Services
Industrial Licence	Industrial or manufacturing activity: any investment activity in order to discover natural resources or to transform raw material into fully manufactured or semi-manufactured products, or transform semi-manufactured products into fully manufactured products using mechanical power. • Agriculture • Building & Contracting • Construction • Discovery of Natural Resources • Electricity-related • Fishing • Gas & Water • Industrial

Preparation & Selection

Business

Info Heads Up On VAT

Plans to introduce VAT in the UAE have been on the table for sometime but, as of early 2009, no concrete plans have been put in place. If this is introduced, VAT could replace the customs duty that is currently charged on imports (also at 5%). Even locally manufactured goods may be subject to VAT and will be considered on a par with imported items, although it's possible that there will be exemptions on certain essential items.

Preparation & Selection

1 Overview

Legal Status

In order to practise an activity, the company must first have legal status. There are several company form options with corresponding legal status, and therefore different requirements. These differences are particularly important for foreign nationals wanting to start a business in the UAE, as they are restricted by the company form they are permitted to own and business activities they are allowed to practise.

Company Forms

Under UAE commercial law, there are seven broad company types, with different specifications in terms of shareholders, directors, minimum capital and corporate procedures. In general, for most forms, 51% UAE National participation is required.

Sole proprietorship and branches of foreign companies are also covered by commercial law, unlike professional companies, considered to be civil companies and falling under civil transactions law.

Free zone companies follow rules and regulations as set by the various free zone authorities.

Listed below are the main company forms available:

- Commercial companies:
  - General Partnership
  - Joint Participation
  - Limited Liability Company (LLC)
  - Partnership Limited By Shares
  - Private Joint Stock Company
  - Public Joint Stock Company
  - Simple Limited Partnership
- Professional Company
- Sole Proprietorship
- Branch or Representative Office of a Foreign Company
- Free Zone Companies:
  - Branch or Representative Office of a Foreign Company
  - Free Zone Establishment

 In this book, those company forms that are of most interest to expats have been described. Those that are outlined here are highlighted in blue in the table on the facing page.

Limitations

Limitations depend upon nationality:

- UAE Nationals: may conduct all commercial, professional and industrial activities
- GCC Nationals: may conduct most commercial, professional and industrial activities except the reserved activities for Nationals (according to Cabinet decision 6 of 2004)
- Other Nationals: limitations exist (see table)
- Foreign Companies: limitations exist (see table)

Preparation & Selection

Permission to set up such companies is subject to approval of the concerned authorities, depending upon the business activity. For example, media activities require approval of the Ministry of Information & Culture (see Business Activities Requiring Special Approval, p.226).

Joint Venture
A foreign party may enter a joint venture agreement for a specific one-off project without needing a separate licence. Business will be conducted under the name of the local entity holding a licence for this activity. Local participation must be greater than 51%, but profit and loss can be distributed according to the agreement signed.

Options According To Nationality

Nationality	Permissible Company Forms

UAE National	• Sole Proprietorship (Individual Establishment)
	• Commercial Companies:
	  • General Partnership Company
	  • Simple Limited Partnership Company
	  • Particular Partnership
	  • Public Joint Stock Company
	  • Private Joint Stock Company
	  • Limited Liability Company (LLC)
	  • Partnership Limited By Shares
	• Professional Company

GCC National	• Sole Proprietorship • Joint Participations • Limited Liability Company • Private Joint Stock Company • Public Joint Stock Company • Professional Company: may practise a specific profession without a local service agent
Non-GCC National	• Sole Proprietorship: may only practise professional activities with the assistance of a UAE National local service agent except in cases of legal, engineering or auditing consultancies • Limited Liability Company: may practise any commercial or industrial activity with one or more UAE National partners who own at least a 51% share of the company, except for the reserved activities of insurance, banking and investment. • Private Joint Stock Company: may practise any commercial or industrial activity, with one or more UAE National partners who own at least a 51% share of the company • Professional Company: may practise a profession with a UAE service agent or a UAE National partner • Public Joint Stock Company: Shareholders may decide to allow non-UAE nationals to become shareholders
Foreign Company	• Branch of a Foreign Company • Limited Liability Company: may practise any commercial or industrial activity, with one or more UAE National partners who own at least a 51% share of the company, except for the reserved activities of insurance, banking and investment • Private Joint Stock Company: may practise any commercial or industrial activity, with one or more UAE National partners who own at least a 51% share of the company • Public Joint Stock Company: Shareholders may decide to allow non-UAE nationals to become shareholders

Preparation & Selection

Business

Obtaining Special Approval For Business Activity

1 Overview

Certain business activities require additional approval from various ministries and/or other authorities. You will need a no objection letter (NOC) from the ministry before applying for a trade licence with the DED.

- Some business categories (eg. businesses engaged in oil or gas production and related industries) require more detailed procedures than a simple NOC letter
- Some trade activities (eg. jewellery and insurance) require the submission of a financial guarantee issued by a bank operating in Dubai

For more information, call the Contact Centre on 202 0200 or 7000 40000 to be connected to the relevant department (working hours: Sun-Thurs 07:30-14:30)

Business Activities Requiring Special Approval

Activity	Authority
Pharmacies	Ministry of Health
Music & Video Shops, Bookshops, Publishers and Printers, Newspapers, Magazines, Advertising and Translation Offices, News Agencies, Party Contractors, Calligraphers, Photographers, Computer Software Importers	Ministry of Information
Explosives & Arms	Ministry of Defence
Telecommunication & Wireless Systems	Ministry of Communication
Financial & Banking Institutions, Exchange Establishments, Money Brokers, Financial Investment Consultants, Investment Firms, Banking Investments	Central Bank
Private Clinics	Department of Health & Medical Services (Medical Committee)
Contracting Companies, Engineering Consultants, related Technical Services, Laboratories	Dubai Municipality
Travel Agents and Air Cargo Offices	Civil Aviation Department
Sea Freight, Passenger Charters, Cargo, Packing, Forwarding & Clearing Services	Seaports & Customs Authority
Lawyers, Legal Consultants, Fuel Stations	Ruler's Court
Nurseries, Private Schools, Institutes	Ministry of Education (Private Education Department)
New Industrial Projects and Expansions	Ministry of Finance & Industry (Industrial Directorate)
Chartered Accountants, Auditors	Ministry of Economy & Planning

Tip	**Get The Business Activity Right The First Time Around**

Once the Ministry of Economy & Planning has approved an activity, the DED will examine the activity according to its own guidelines. If incompatibilities exist, changes to the ministry's certificate may be necessary before you'll be given the trade licence.

As this can become costly, it's advisable to decide from the beginning exactly which activity the company is applying for, and verify that it is acceptable. Also keep long-term plans in mind; if the company will add a new activity at a later stage, it must provide proof that it has experience in that field, and further approval and payment will be necessary once again.

For additional information, have a look at the *Standard Classification of Economic Activities*, published by the DED & DCCI, listing the various acceptable business activity categories and their codes.

Preparation & Selection

1 Overview

If you are setting up a Dubai-based company outside a free zone, approval for the company name by the DED must first be obtained. A trade name can be reserved as part of the setting up procedure. Have a look at the various flowcharts in this section to determine the best time to apply for the trade name (see p.238, 242 and 246).

⚠ The DED has the right to reject a proposed trade name if the name does not comply with their prerequisites. Even if the trade name has already been reserved, the DED can request a name change if they feel it is not indicative of the type of activity declared. In 2009, the government announced that the word 'Dubai' could no longer be used in the names of private companies.

2 Prerequisites

- The name should be translated into Arabic
- The name should not contain the word 'Dubai'
- It should be indicative of the business activity (but not always enforced)
- It should not conflict with Arabic and Islamic traditions and values
- It should not involve any of God's names and descriptions, or have any Islamic indication
- It should be consistent with true state of affairs

3 What To Bring

☐ Completed Trade Name Application Form (BR/1) collected from the DED reception desk. Alternatively, you can download the form from their website: www.dubaided.gov.ae

Fees
☐ Dhs.2,000 per year, if a local company chooses a foreign trade name

☐ Dhs.1,000 additional per year to add the word(s) 'International', 'Middle East' or 'Global'

☐ Dhs.2,000 additional per year to add the word(s) 'UAE' or 'Gulf'

☐ Dhs.2,000 per year for name including abbreviations

☐ Dhs.1,000 per year to use a foreign name of a company using a trade name or trade mark of an international company

📄 There is no fee for a foreign trade name given to branches of foreign companies & representative offices, or to Arabic trade names.

📄 Fees referred to above apply to new licences and to changes of trade names.

☐ Dhs.100 – trade name registration fee

☐ Dhs.200 per year – trade name reservation

4 Procedure

Location   DED   Map ref **8-H4**

Hours   Sun-Thurs 07:30-14:30

- Submit the application form at the Licensing Department and collect a receipt with a collection date
- Return to the same department on the specified date; if the name is approved, collect a payment voucher
- Pay the application fees at the Cashier
- Return to the Licensing Counter and collect the approval receipt

5 Related Procedures

- Setting Up A Company, p.220
- Setting Up A Branch Or Representative Office Of A Foreign Company, p.232
- Setting Up A Limited Liability Company (LLC), p.238
- Setting Up A Sole Proprietorship, p.242
- Setting Up A Professional Company, p.246
- Free Zone Overview, p.264

Tip   **Selecting An Office Or Warehouse**

When applying for a trade licence, the rent agreement is normally required as part of the documentation. Ensure that you select a location for your premises in an area in which you are permitted to perform your business activity. Dubai has strict zoning rules that restrict where a company may open up an office or warehouse. Approval must be gained from the Planning Department and will depend on your business activity. To have a warehouse you must have an industrial licence – note that only 10 percent of the whole warehouse space is allowed to be used as an office.

Tip   **Don't Sign Yet!**

Don't sign a tenancy agreement for a warehouse or office before the DED has contacted the Municipality and approved it.

For more information, contact the Municipality's Planning Department in the DED Building (04 202 0105), or the Planning Department in the Dubai Municipality Building (04 206 3788).

If the property is leased from or granted by the Government of Dubai, you will also need a sub-lease no objection letter from the Real Estate Department.

Preparation & Selection

Business

Options For Non-Nationals & Foreign Companies

1 Overview

Foreign Company The most common ways a foreign company may enter the Dubai market are as follows:

- Give the 'agency' for its products/services to an agent (see Appointing A Local Service Agent, p.249)
- Set up a branch office or a representative office in Dubai (see Setting Up A Branch or Representative Office Of A Foreign Company, p.232)
- Set up a branch or representative office in a free zone (see Free Zone Overview, p.264)

Regional Company Some foreign companies choose to set up a free zone branch as the regional head office, plus have an agent in Dubai cover a specified region, such as Dubai, the Northern Emirates, or the entire UAE (see Appointing A Local Service Agent, p.249).

More Presence On the other hand, if a physical presence is necessary, options range from the establishment of a representative or branch office with 100% foreign ownership, an LLC with a maximum of 49% foreign equity, or the establishment of a professional or consultancy business under a local licensing regulation issued by the Dubai Government.

Setting Up A Company In Dubai

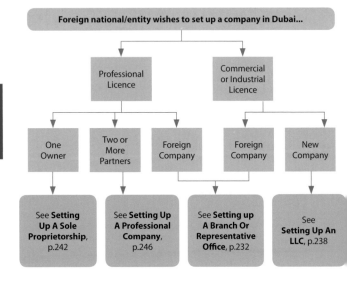

Foreign national/entity wishes to set up a company in Dubai...

Professional Licence

- One Owner → See **Setting Up A Sole Proprietorship**, p.242
- Two or More Partners → See **Setting Up A Professional Company**, p.246
- Foreign Company → See **Setting up A Branch Or Representative Office**, p.232

Commercial or Industrial Licence

- Foreign Company → See **Setting up A Branch Or Representative Office**, p.232
- New Company → See **Setting Up An LLC**, p.238

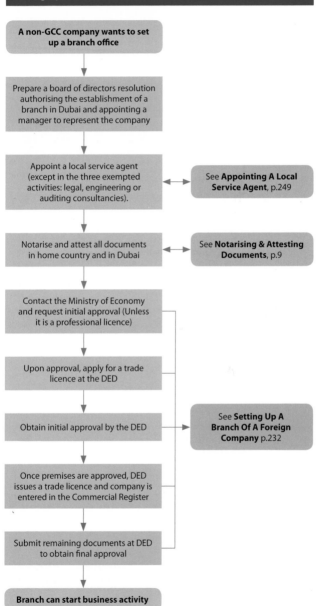

Setting Up A Branch Office

A non-GCC company wants to set up a branch office

↓

Prepare a board of directors resolution authorising the establishment of a branch in Dubai and appointing a manager to represent the company

↓

Appoint a local service agent (except in the three exempted activities: legal, engineering or auditing consultancies). ←→ See **Appointing A Local Service Agent**, p.249

↓

Notarise and attest all documents in home country and in Dubai ←→ See **Notarising & Attesting Documents**, p.9

↓

Contact the Ministry of Economy and request initial approval (Unless it is a professional licence)

↓

Upon approval, apply for a trade licence at the DED

↓

Obtain initial approval by the DED → See **Setting Up A Branch Of A Foreign Company** p.232

↓

Once premises are approved, DED issues a trade licence and company is entered in the Commercial Register

↓

Submit remaining documents at DED to obtain final approval

↓

Branch can start business activity

⚠ As this procedure depends on many variables, and rules and procedures change, visit the Corporate Relations Department at the DED for assistance (see p.219).

Setting Up

Business

Setting Up

Setting Up A Branch Office

1 Overview

Established foreign companies may set up a branch or a representative office of their firm in Dubai. The branch will be considered a part of the parent company, and not a separate legal entity.

The branch office is technically allowed to trade, but it will not always receive permission to import and export the company's products. The company will be encouraged to select a local distributor/agent to distribute its goods (see Appointing A Local Service Agent, p.249).

Service Agent
If the branch is 100% foreign owned, the company must appoint a local service agent (see Appointing A Local Service Agent, p.249). Exceptions to this rule are legal, engineering or auditing consultancies.

Comapny Register
In addition to having to find a sponsor, foreign companies setting up a branch in the UAE must gain approval from the Ministry of Economy & Planning and be registered in their Register of Foreign Companies before applying for a trade licence.

A representative office does not need to register with the Ministry of Economy & Planning.

All documents submitted to the Ministry of Economy must be in sets of two. One set will remain in the office in Dubai; one will be sent to the head office in Abu Dhabi.

Charges
Dhs.2,000 – any amendments in documentation

Documents produced outside the GCC must be authenticated by the UAE or GCC consulate or embassy in the company's home country, and notarised by the Ministry of Foreign Affairs in the UAE (see Notarising & Attesting Documents, p.9).

All documents should be submitted in Arabic. If written in a foreign language, an attested Arabic translation should be attached.

Before a brand of a foreign company may commence operations, it must do the following:

- Register in the Ministry's Register of Foreign Companies
- Be inscribed in the DED Commercial Register
- Obtain a trade licence from the DED

Representative Office
Unlike a branch office, a representative office is allowed to promote the activities of the parent company only, and not sell products itself.

It is permitted to practise promotional services for the company and the products, and also to facilitate contacting potential customers.

2 Prerequisites

- The branch may only engage in similar activities to the parent company, and only as stated in the licence

- Industry restrictions apply for companies practising the following business activities:
  - General trading
  - Import/export
  - Manufacturing
  - Insurance
  - Banking & other financial activities
- If the foreign company (without any registration in the UAE) is engaging in any commercial activity, it must appoint a local trade agent to import, export or sell its products in the UAE (see Appointing A Local Service Agent, p.249)
- The branch may not import parent company products
- Depending on the activity, additional special approval from the concerned authorities may be necessary (see Obtaining Special Approval For Business Activity, p.226)
- Trade Name must be the same as the name of the parent company (See Selecting A Trade Name, p.228)

3 What To Bring

Initial Approval

Ministry of Economy & DED

(Ministry of Economy: branch office applications only)

- ☐ Articles and memorandum of association of parent company (copy)
- ☐ Board of Directors' resolution from parent company authorising establishment of a branch office in Dubai and appointing the branch office manager
- ☐ Power of attorney from parent company authorising branch office manager to conduct all affairs of the branch office and sign on behalf of the branch office
- ☐ Audited financial statements of the parent company for the past two years
- ☐ Certificate of corporation stating company's form and capital (certificate of registration of parent company from the authority that regulates registration and incorporation of companies in that country, stating the company is validly incorporated and continues to exist)
- ☐ If applicable, a list of parent company's branches in the UAE and name of the local agent for each branch

If the company has no other branches in the UAE, a letter to certify this.

- ☐ Manager's passport (copy)

Initial Approval

Ministry of Economy (in addition to above)

(Branch office applications only)

- ☐ Application form in Arabic (typed)
- ☐ Local service agency agreement and documents proving the

agent is a UAE national or the company is fully UAE owned (see Appointing A Local Service Agent, p.249)

☐ Profile of the company – list of previous experience and activities in the field in which it is applying for in the UAE

☐ Licence issued and ratified by licensing authority in home country (copy)

Fee ☐ Dhs.5,000 (e-Dirham) – application fee

Additional Costs ☐ Dhs.50,000 Bank Guarantee

Initial Approval DED (in addition to above)

(Branch & representative office applications)

☐ Registration & Licensing Application Form ('BR/1') (typed)

☐ Trade Name Application Form if not already applied for ('BR/2') (typed) (see Selecting A Trade Name, p.228)

☐ Ministry of Economy & Planning Initial Approval Form (NOC)

☐ For representative office, certificate from the competent authority in the parent company's home country stating that the company has been registered for at least two years (translated by a certified legal translator)

☐ If an establishment or company was incorporated in the Jebel Ali Free Zone, certificate of formation (copy)

☐ If company was incorporated in another emirate, trade licence (copy) and Chamber certificate of all company branches (copy)

☐ If applicable, no objection certificate from the government authorities according to the type of commercial activity (see Obtaining Special Approval For Business Activity, p.226)

Fees ☐ Dhs.110 – initial approval fee

☐ Dhs.320 – trade name registration fee

Optional Fees ☐ Dhs.500 – express service fee

☐ Dhs.5,000 – representative office registration fee

Final Approval DED (in addition to above)

(Branch and representative office applications)

☐ DED initial approval

☐ DED trade name approval

☐ Ministry of Economy initial approval

☐ Tenancy contract of office premises including plot number (copy) (see Selecting An Office Or Warehouse, p.229)

☐ If premises will be leased from or granted by the Dubai Government, a sublease no-objection letter from the Department of Real Estate

☐ Company cheque (or personal cheque if the partner/owner is named on the trade licence) with the licence number and establishment's trade name on the back

Fee ☐ Dhs.200 – 'local fee'

☐ Dhs.500 – 'wastage fee'

☐ Dhs.3,000 – Ministry of Economy fee

☐ 5% of tenancy contract – Municipality tax

Ministry Approval Ministry of Economy

(Branch office applications only)

☐ Trade licence (original & copy)

☐ Commercial registration certificate (original & copy)

Fee ☐ Dhs.10,000 (e-Dirham) – registration fee

---

4 Procedure

Location Ministry of Economy & Planning   Map ref 9-A6

Hours Sun – Thurs 07:30 – 14:30

This section applies to branch office applications only.

Initial Approval
- Collect an application form from the Department of Commercial Affairs
- Complete the form, specifying the activity that the office or branch will undertake in the UAE
- Submit all documents for approval; pay the application fee at the same office
- Within one week the Federal Foreign Companies Committee will approve or decline the application
- If approved, an NOC (valid three months) will be issued specifying the approved activities
- Within these three months, the company must apply for the trade licence and commercial registration

Location DED Licensing Department   Map ref 8-H4

Hours Sun-Thurs 07:30-14:30

Initial Approval
- Submit all documents in order that the company be entered into the Commercial Register
- Go to the Licensing Counter on the first floor; take a ticket and wait for your number to be called
- Submit all documents and collect the application receipt (cash payment voucher) that will specify a date
- Return to the Licensing Counter on the specified date to check if the application received initial approval
- If it was approved, go to the Cashier and pay the fee
- Return to the Licensing Counter and collect the initial approval receipt and all documents submitted
- If the department rejects the application, you have 15 days from the notification date to submit a grievance

Initial approval is valid six months from date of approval. If you fail to renew the initial approval, it will expire within 10 days of the expiry date.

Setting Up

Business

Final Approval
- Go to the Dubai Municipality Planning Department Counter (first floor, DED) and request approval for the business premises
- Submit all required documents at the Licensing Counter; you will be given an application receipt and a date on which to return
- Return on the specified date to collect the 'fee payment voucher'
- Pay the fee at the Cashier and collect the licence

 You will receive two sealed copies of the licence, one to be used for inscription in the Commercial Register and the other for registration with the Dubai Chamber of Commerce (see Registering With The DCCI, p.251).

Commercial Register
- Commercial and industrial companies must register with the DED at the Commercial Registry; the charge varies from Dhs.700 to 1,200 (depending on the company type)

Location Ministry of Economy & Planning   Map ref 9-A5

Hours Sun-Thurs 07:30-14:30

This section applies to branch office applications only.

Final Approval
- Submit all documents and pay the certificate fee at the Commercial Affairs Department
- The certificate will be given to you within days

5 Related Procedures

- Applying For An Establishment Immigration Card, p.257
- Applying For An Establishment Labour Card, p.255
- Applying For Immigration & Labour Representative Cards, p.259
- Registering With The DCCI, p.251

Setting Up

Business

Setting Up An LLC

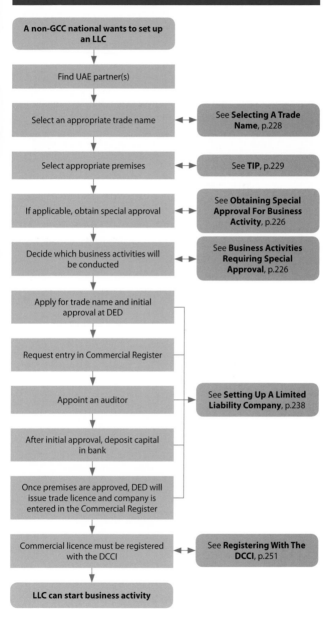

A non-GCC national wants to set up an LLC

↓

Find UAE partner(s)

↓

Select an appropriate trade name ←→ See **Selecting A Trade Name**, p.228

↓

Select appropriate premises ←→ See **TIP**, p.229

↓

If applicable, obtain special approval ←→ See **Obtaining Special Approval For Business Activity**, p.226

↓

Decide which business activities will be conducted ←→ See **Business Activities Requiring Special Approval**, p.226

↓

Apply for trade name and initial approval at DED

↓

Request entry in Commercial Register

↓

Appoint an auditor → See **Setting Up A Limited Liability Company**, p.238

↓

After initial approval, deposit capital in bank

↓

Once premises are approved, DED will issue trade licence and company is entered in the Commercial Register

↓

Commercial licence must be registered with the DCCI ←→ See **Registering With The DCCI**, p.251

↓

LLC can start business activity

⚠ As this procedure depends on many variables, and rules and procedures change, visit the Corporate Relations Department at the DED for assistance (see p.219).

Setting Up

Business

Setting Up

Setting Up A Limited Liability Company (LLC)

1 Overview

An LLC is a business structure that is a hybrid of a partnership and a corporation. Its owners are shielded from personal liability; the liability of the shareholders is limited to their shares in the company's capital.

Limitations
- Formed by a minimum of two, maximum of 50 people whose liability is limited to their shares in the company's capital
- Minimum share capital: currently Dhs.300,000 (US$ 82,000), contributed in cash or in kind, unless the activity is investment in and management of commercial, industrial and agricultural projects (when the minimum share capital is Dhs.3 million).
- Maximum foreign equity in the company: 49%
- Selling shares publicly is not permitted

2 Prerequisites

- Company auditor must be UAE accredited
- Trade name (ending with 'LLC') has been approved (see Selecting A Trade Name, p.228)
- Appropriate premises have been selected (preferably contract has not yet been signed)
- Depending on the activity, additional special approval from the concerned authorities may be necessary (see Obtaining Special Approval For Business Activity, p.226)

3 What To Bring

Registration & Licensing Application Form ('BR/1') (typed)

☐ Trade Name Application Form if not already applied for ('BR/2') (typed) (see Selecting A Trade Name, p.228)

Initial Approval
☐ If the LLC is established by a company, the company's memorandum (authenticated by a notary public) containing objectives and provisions for management, capital and distribution of company profits

No memorandum needed if established by an individual.

☐ If applicable, no objection certificate from the government authorities according to the type of commercial activity (see Obtaining Special Approval For Business Activity, p.226)

☐ Bank certificate certifying that all shares have been deposited

Fees
☐ Dhs.110 – initial approval fee

☐ Dhs.320 – trade name registration fee

Commercial Register
☐ DED initial approval

☐ Application form signed by manager/representative (two originals)

- ☐ Certificate (two copies) issued by manager and signed by company auditors stating that all shares are fully paid, their value has been deposited in a UAE bank, the shares have been valued and their value has been credited to the company assets
- ☐ Memorandum of association (original & copy – both authenticated)
- ☐ Auditors' trade licence
- ☐ Letter from the company's auditors stating that they are willing to act as auditors for the company

Fees
- ☐ Dhs.500 – licence registration fee

Document notarisation charges range from Dhs.750 (Export/Import LLC) to Dhs.7,500 (General Trading LLC) depending on business activity.

Final Approval
- ☐ DED initial approval
- ☐ DED trade name approval
- ☐ All documents mentioned above
- ☐ Tenancy contract of office premises including plot number (copy) (see Selecting An Office Or Warehouse, p.229)
- ☐ If premises will be leased from or granted by the Dubai Government, a sublease no objection letter from the Department of Real Estate
- ☐ Memorandum of Association Form ('Form 4') collected from the DED, signed by the company's shareholders and notarised at the Dubai Court
- ☐ A certificate from a UAE-licensed bank certifying that all the shares of the company have been deposited in cash
- ☐ If industrial activity, Ministry of Finance & Industry approval
- ☐ Notarised memorandum of association (copy)
- ☐ Application for entry in the Commercial Register (copy)
- ☐ Certificate issued by manager (as above), with date and number of commercial registration (copy)
- ☐ Manager's passport (copy)

Fees
- ☐ Dhs.200 – local fee
- ☐ Dhs.500 – wastage fee
- ☐ Dhs.3,000 – Ministry of Economy fee
- ☐ 5% of tenancy contract – Municipality tax
- ☐ Dhs.1,000 – charge per foreign partner
- ☐ Dhs.500 – DED express service fee (optional)

4 Procedure

Location DED Licensing Department — Map ref **8-H4**

Hours Sun – Thurs 07:30 – 14:30

- • Submit trade name application (see Selecting A Trade Name, p.228)
- • Notarise the company's Memorandum of Association (DED 'Form 4') at the Dubai Court desk in the DED

Setting Up

Trade Name
- Go to the Licensing Counter on the first floor; take a ticket and wait for your number to be called

Initial Approval
- Submit all documents and collect the application receipt (cash payment voucher) that will specify a date
- Return to the Licensing Counter on the specified date to check if the application received initial approval
- If approved, go to the Cashier and pay the fee
- Return to the Licensing Counter and collect the initial approval receipt and all documents submitted
- If the department rejects the application, you have 15 days from the notification date to submit a grievance

Initial approval is valid six months from date of approval. If you fail to renew the approval, it will expire within 10 days of the expiry date.

Location Banks (various) See p.276

Hours Various
- Deposit all capital, then request an undertaking from the bank that the deposited amount will only be released to the managers upon proof of company registration

Location DED Map ref 8-H4

Hours Sun – Thurs 07:30 – 14:30

Final Approval
- Go to the Municipality Planning Department Counter (first floor, DED) to request approval for the business premises
- Submit all required documents at the Licensing Counter; you will be given an application receipt and a date on which to return
- Return on the specified date to collect the 'fee payment voucher'
- Pay the fee at the Cashier and collect the licence

You will receive two sealed copies of the licence, one to be used for inscription in the Commercial Register and the other for registration with the Dubai Chamber of Commerce (see Registering With The DCCI, p.251).

Commercial Register
- Submit all documents and request inscription in the Commercial Register
- Once approval is granted, the company will be entered in the Commercial Register and have its Memorandum of Association published in the ministry bulletin

5 Related Procedures

- DCCI Membership Registration, p.257
- Applying For An Establishment Labour Card, p.255
- Applying For An Establishment Immigration Card p.257
- Applying For Representative Cards p.259

Setting Up A Sole Proprietorship

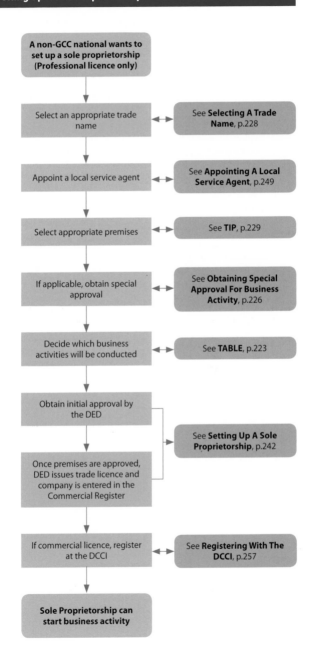

A non-GCC national wants to set up a sole proprietorship (Professional licence only)

Select an appropriate trade name → See **Selecting A Trade Name**, p.228

Appoint a local service agent → See **Appointing A Local Service Agent**, p.249

Select appropriate premises → See **TIP**, p.229

If applicable, obtain special approval → See **Obtaining Special Approval For Business Activity**, p.226

Decide which business activities will be conducted → See **TABLE**, p.223

Obtain initial approval by the DED

Once premises are approved, DED issues trade licence and company is entered in the Commercial Register

→ See **Setting Up A Sole Proprietorship**, p.242

If commercial licence, register at the DCCI → See **Registering With The DCCI**, p.257

Sole Proprietorship can start business activity

Setting Up

Business

Setting Up

Setting Up A Sole Proprietorship

1 Overview

A sole proprietorship is the most basic entity form where the owner has a trade licence in his name and is personally held liable for his accounts, i.e. he is responsible for the entity's financial obligations. The proprietor can conduct business in the commercial, professional, industrial, agricultural or real estate industry.

Nationals and GCC nationals are permitted to set up a sole proprietorship with few restrictions. Stricter conditions apply for non-GCC nationals. A non-GCC national setting up a sole proprietorship is restricted in the type of activities he may perform. The entity should be in a service or knowledge-based industry.

Validity
- Initial approval is valid six months from approval date
- If you fail to renew the initial approval, it will expire within 10 days of the expiry date

 Since this procedure depends on many variables, and rules and procedures change, we strongly recommend you visit the Corporate Relations Department at the DED for assistance (see p.219).

2 Prerequisites

- An appropriate trade name (see Selecting A Trade Name, p.228)
- Appropriate premises
- If applicable, special approval for business activity has been obtained (see Obtaining Special Approval For Business Activity, p.226)

GCC Nationals
- Must be resident in the UAE
- Must practise the activity on his own

Non-GCC Nationals
- Must appoint a local service agent (see Appointing A Local Service Agent, p.249)

3 What To Bring

UAE National
- ☐ Owner's passport with proof of naturalisation (copy)
- ☐ Manager's passport (copy)

GCC Nationals
- ☐ Owner's passport (copy)
- ☐ Certificate of good conduct from the relevant authorities of his GCC state
- ☐ Local agent's passport (copy)
- ☐ Investor's/manager's passport (copy)

Non-GCC Nationals
- ☐ Visit visa (copy)
- ☐ If he has a residence permit, a NOC from his sponsor

- ☐ Degree certificate, notarised, legalised and authenticated
- ☐ Work experience certificate if consultancy entity
- ☐ Certificate of good standing from a government body or the body governing the applicant's profession (if applicable)

Initial Approval
- ☐ Registration and Licensing Application Form ('BR/1') (typed – Arabic and/or English)
- ☐ Trade Name Application Form ('BR/2') (typed)
- ☐ If applying for a professional business licence, the resume of the applicant proving qualifications ('BR/3') (typed)
- ☐ If commercial or industrial activity, approval of the Ministry of Economy & Planning
- ☐ If applicable, no objection certificate from the government authorities according to the type of commercial activity (see Obtaining Special Approval For Business Activity, p.226)
- ☐ If applicant is under 21 years, permission from the court to practise business

Fees
- ☐ Dhs.110 – trade name registration fee
- ☐ Dhs.320 – initial approval fee
- ☐ Dhs.500 – DED express service fee (optional)

Final Approval
- ☐ Initial approval slip
- ☐ All documents mentioned above
- ☐ Tenancy agreement including plot number (copy) (see **Tip**, p.229)
- ☐ Sublease no-objection letter from the Department of Real Estate of Dubai Government if the premises will be leased from or granted by Government of Dubai
- ☐ If general trading, contracting or investing in commercial, industrial or agricultural holding & trust company, a bank certificate issued by the applicant's bank in Dubai stating the amount of capital deposited

Fees
- ☐ Dhs.200 – local fee
- ☐ Dhs.300 – wastage fee
- ☐ 5% of tenancy contract – Municipality tax
- ☐ Dhs.500 – registration fee

Local Agent
- ☐ 'Appointment of National Agent' contract duly authenticated by the notary public ('BR/13') (original & copy)
- ☐ For UAE agents without previous licences, agent's passport and UAE naturalisation identification (copy)
- ☐ Local service agency agreement (original) (see p.249)
- ☐ If the local service agent is an individual, his passport (copy)
- ☐ If the local service agent is a company, its memorandum of association (original and copy), trade licence (copy), passports and family books of all the members (or proof that the members are UAE Nationals) (copy)
- ☐ Director's passport (copy)

Setting Up

Business

4 Procedure

Location DED Licensing Department

Map ref 8-H4

Hours Sun – Thurs 07:30 – 14:30

Initial Approval

- At least one week prior to the proposed start of the permit's validity date, go to the Licensing Counter on the first floor of the DED. Take a ticket and wait for your number to be called
- Submit required documents and collect the application receipt (cash payment voucher) that will specify a pick-up date
- Return to the Licensing Counter on that date and check if the application was initially approved
- If it was approved, go to the Cashier and pay the fee
- Return to the Licensing Counter and collect the initial approval receipt and all documents submitted
- If the department rejects the application, you have 15 days from the notification date to submit a grievance

Initial approval is valid six months from date of approval. If you fail to renew the initial approval, it will expire within 10 days of the expiry date.

Final Approval

- Go to the Municipality Planning Department Counter (first floor, DED) to request approval for the business premises
- Go to the Inspection and Control Counter on the first floor, if there are other licences on the proposed premises
- Submit all required documents at the Licensing Counter; you will be given an application receipt and a date on which to return
- Return on the specified date to collect the 'fee payment voucher'
- Pay the fee at the Cashier and collect the licence

You will receive two sealed copies of the licence, one to be used for inscription in the Commercial Register and the other for registration with the Dubai Chamber of Commerce (see Registering With The DCCI, p.257).

Commercial Register

- Submit all documents and request inscription in the Commercial Register
- Once approval is granted, the company will be entered in the Commercial Register and have its Memorandum of Association published in the ministry bulletin

5 Related Procedures

- Applying For An Establishment Immigration Card, p.257
- Applying For An Establishment Labour Card, p.255
- Applying For Immigration & Labour Representative Cards, p.259

Setting Up A Professional Company

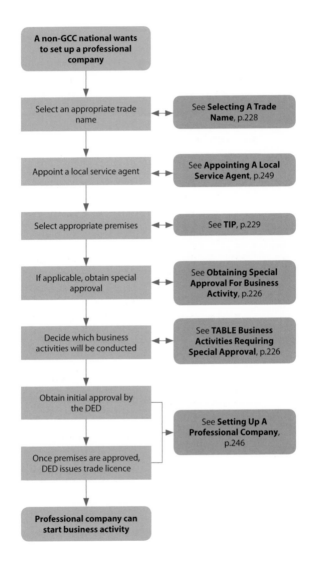

A non-GCC national wants to set up a professional company

↓

Select an appropriate trade name ⟷ See **Selecting A Trade Name**, p.228

↓

Appoint a local service agent ⟷ See **Appointing A Local Service Agent**, p.249

↓

Select appropriate premises ⟷ See **TIP**, p.229

↓

If applicable, obtain special approval ⟷ See **Obtaining Special Approval For Business Activity**, p.226

↓

Decide which business activities will be conducted ⟷ See **TABLE Business Activities Requiring Special Approval**, p.226

↓

Obtain initial approval by the DED

See **Setting Up A Professional Company**, p.246

↓

Once premises are approved, DED issues trade licence

↓

Professional company can start business activity

Setting Up

Business

Setting Up

Setting Up A Professional Company

1 Overview

Also referred to as a business partnership, professional business company, or consultancy business, this company type falls under the civil code, rather than under commercial law and is unique to the UAE. Such firms may engage in professional or artisan activities but the number of staff members that may be employed is limited and a UAE national must be appointed as a local service agent (see Appointing A Local Service Agent, p.249).

An important part in applying for the licence is showing evidence of the credentials and qualifications of the employees and partners. According to the DED, 'A professional is a person who independently practices a profession based on investing his intellectual powers and acquired information, which generates an income. In such work, he either depends on his own physical effort or uses the help of some tools and equipment, whether solely or with a maximum number of five workers.'

Buisness Activities
These companies usually practise in the following fields:

- Engineering and business consulting
- Graphic and architectural design
- Healthcare
- IT
- Teaching

Ownership
It may be 100% foreign owned, provided there is a local service agent.

Timing
- Initial approval is valid for six months from approval date
- If you fail to renew the initial approval, it will expire within 10 days of the expiry date

 Since this procedure depends on many variables, and rules and procedures change, we strongly recommend you visit the Corporate Relations Department at the DED for assistance (see p.219).

2 Prerequisites

- Trade name has been selected (see Selecting A Trade Name, p.228)
- Appropriate premises have been selected
- Depending on the activity, additional special approval from the concerned authorities may be necessary (see Obtaining Special Approval For Business Activity, p.226)
- Must appoint a local service agent (see Appointing A Local Service Agent, p.249)

Business

3 What To Bring

Initial approval Registration and Licensing Application Form ('BR/1') (typed – Arabic and/or English)

☐ Trade Name Application Form ('BR/2') (typed)

☐ If applying for a professional business licence, the resume of the applicant proving qualifications ('BR/3') (typed)

☐ If commercial and industrial activity, approval of the Ministry of Economy & Planning and the Ministry of Finance & Industry

☐ If established by a company, the company's memorandum of association

☐ If applicable, no objection certificate from the government authorities according to the type of activity (see Obtaining Special Approval For Business Activity, p.226)

Fees ☐ Dhs.320 – trade name registration fee

☐ Dhs.110 – initial approval fee

☐ Dhs.500 – DED express service fee (optional)

Final Approval ☐ Initial approval slip

☐ All documents mentioned above

☐ Tenancy agreement including plot number (copy)

☐ Sublease no-objection letter from the Department of Real Estate of Dubai Government if the premises will be leased from or granted by Government of Dubai

☐ Local Service Agency agreement and documents proving that the agent is a UAE National or the company is fully UAE owned (see Appointing A Local Service Agent, p.249)

Fees ☐ Dhs.100 – local fee

☐ Dhs.150 – wastage fee

☐ 5% of tenancy contract – Municipality tax

☐ Dhs.500 – registration fee

☐ Dhs.500 – charge per foreign company partner

4 Procedure

Location DED Licensing Department   Map ref 8-H4

Hours Sun – Thurs 07:30 – 14:30

Initial Approval
- Go to the Licensing Counter on the first floor of the Department; take a ticket and wait for your number to be called
- Submit all documents and collect the application receipt (cash payment voucher) that will specify a date
- Return to the Licensing Counter on the specified date and check if the application received initial approval
- If approved, go to the Cashier and pay the fee

Setting Up

Business

- Return to the Licensing Counter and collect the initial approval receipt and all documents submitted

- If the department rejects the application, you have 15 days from the notification date to submit a grievance

Initial approval is valid for six months from date of approval. If you fail to renew the initial approval, it will expire within ten days of the expiry date.

Final Approval

- Go to the Municipality Planning Department Counter (first floor, DED) to request approval for the business premises

- If there are other licences on the proposed premises, go to the Inspection and Control Counter on the first floor

- Submit all required documents at the Licensing Counter; you will be given an application receipt and a date on which to return

- Return on the specified date to collect the 'fee payment voucher'

- Pay the fee at the Cashier and collect the licence

You will receive two sealed copies of the licence, one to be used for inscription in the Commercial Register and the other for registration with the Dubai Chamber of Commerce (see Registering With The DCCI, p.251)

Commercial Register

- Submit all documents and request inscription in the Commercial Register

- Once approval is granted, the company will be entered in the Commercial Register and have its Memorandum of Association published in the ministry bulletin

5 Related Procedures

- Applying For An Establishment Immigration Card, p.257
- Applying For An Establishment Labour Card, p.255
- Applying For A Representative Card, p.259

Appointing A Local Service Agent ('Sponsor')

1 Overview

By law, foreign nationals wanting to set up companies such as a sole proprietorship, a branch of a foreign company or a professional company, must find a National agent and sign a local (national) service agency agreement with him. The local agent is usually referred to as a 'sponsor'.

The sponsor will not have any responsibility towards the business but is obliged to assist with all government related procedures such as obtaining government permits, trade licences, visas and labour cards. His signature will be required for most application forms.

Individual/ company Sponsor A sponsor may be a UAE national or a company fully owned by UAE nationals. The choice of sponsor can be of significant importance, especially for a bigger company. Appointing a sponsor who is considered prominent and influential can open many doors that may be difficult for others to open.

Local sponsors may be paid a lump sum and/or a percentage of the profits or turnover.

Finding the right sponsor There is a lot of trust involved in this system. Before choosing a sponsor, it is highly advisable to first find out about his/her reputation etc.

⚠ It is very difficult to break a local service agency agreement.

Validity One year, renewed automatically

2 Prerequisites

• The local service agent (sponsor) is a UAE national or a company 100% owned by UAE nationals

3 What To Bring

Contacts ☐ Local Service Agent Contract (attested by notary public) (original & copy)

In some cases the DED's 'Appointment Contract of a Local Service Agent' (Form 'BR/13') will be sufficient to make a contract. You can collect it from the DED or download it from www.dubaided.gov.ae. However, if a lot of money is involved and the agreements are more complicated, the owners may have a lawyer draft the contract which is more specific, especially regarding payment and other obligations.

Individual Agents ☐ Passport and UAE naturalisation identification (copy)

Company Agents ☐ Documents proving that the company is fully UAE owned

☐ Its memorandum of association and articles of association (attested) (original and copy)

☐ Trade licence (copy)

☐ Certificate of registration in the Commercial Register

☐ Passports and family books of all board members or partners (copy)

☐ Letter from the DED certifying that all partners of the selected company are UAE nationals

☐ If company incorporated in Dubai, the Chamber of Commerce (DCCI) certificate (copy)

☐ If company incorporated in another emirate, the memorandum of association (copy)

☐ An authorisation card

4 Procedure

Location DED Licensing Department   Map ref 8-H4

Hours Sun – Thurs 07:30 – 14:30

• Sign and notarise the contract

Legalising the contract if setting up a Branch or Representative Office of a Foreign Company

• Legalise it by the foreign office of the country from which the parent company originates

• Authenticate it by the UAE Embassy in that country

• Authenticate it by the UAE Ministry of Foreign Affairs

• Translate it into Arabic by a translator registered with the Ministry of Justice and sealed by the notary public of the Dubai Courts Department (copy)

• The contract is ready to be submitted with the other documents required for setting up a company

5 Related Procedures

• Setting Up A Branch of a Foreign Company, p.232

• Setting Up A Professional Company, p.246

Registering With The Dubai Chamber Of Commerce & Industry (DCCI)

1 Overview

In general, all commercial and industrial businesses in Dubai should be registered with the Dubai Chamber of Commerce and Industry. Companies in the free zones may register to be listed in the Chamber's Directory and use their services.

Validity One year

2 Prerequisites

- Company has a commercial or industrial trade licence
- Applicant has commercial or industrial premises in Dubai
- Applicant is already operating the business
- Applicant, in the 10 years prior to applying for membership, has not been declared bankrupt, or been convicted of theft, swindling, breach of trust, fraud or forgery

3 What To Bring

Licence (copy) issued and ratified by the licensing authority (DED, JAFZA, DAFZA, etc).

☐ Valid passport of the owner of the establishment (copy)

Non-National
☐ Valid residence permit (copy)

Local Agent
☐ Passport of the local agent (copy)

☐ Agency agreement (copy)

☐ Agency contract signed by the foreign company and the local agent (original and true copy)

☐ If the local agent is a company and registered as a member of the Chamber, a copy of the membership certificate with the DCCI

☐ If the local agent is not a registered member with the Chamber, a copy of the company's memorandum of association and professional licence, proving that all partners are Nationals

Sole Proprietor-ship
☐ Passport of the manager of the establishment, or the authorised signatory

☐ Power of attorney, duly notarised (copy)

☐ Authorised signature cards completed and signed by the licensee, the manager or the local agent

☐ Completed special data form, depending on the company's business activity ('Industrial Firms Data Form', 'Contracting Firms Data Form', 'Hotel Classification Form')

LLC or Professional Comapny
☐ Partnership contract (authenticated by the Notary Public at the Dubai Courts) (copy)

☐ If the partner is a company, the company memorandum (copy)

☐ If the partner company is a company incorporated in Dubai, the Chamber certificate (copy)

☐ If the partner company is a company incorporated in another emirate, the memorandum of association (copy)

If Partner is a Foreign Company

☐ An official certificate from the competent authorities with whom the foreign company is registered, showing that it is registered in that country in accordance with its laws, and stating the legal status of the company, its capital, the names of its officials, their functions and powers

☐ Resolution of foreign company's board of directors, with regard to opening a branch or representative office in Dubai, and the resolution to authorise the company's representative to apply for a licence, the documents having been ratified by the concerned government departments in the country of origin

☐ Passport copy of the company's representative

☐ Identical copy of the foreign company's memorandum of association and articles of association if it is a public or private joint stock company, authenticated by the concerned government department in the country of origin

☐ If company incorporated in the Jebel Ali Free Zone, the certificate of formation (copy)

☐ If company incorporated in another emirate, trade licence and the Chamber certificate (copy)

Branch of Foreign Company

☐ Passport of the manager of the establishment, or the authorised signatory

☐ Notarised power of attorney (copy)

☐ Authorised signature cards completed and signed by the licensee, the manager or the local agent

☐ Completed special data form, depending on the company's business activity

☐ An official certificate from the competent authorities with whom the foreign company is registered, showing that it is registered in that country in accordance with its laws, and stating the legal status of the company, its capital, the names of its officials, their functions and powers

☐ Resolution of foreign company's board of directors, with regard to opening a branch or representative office in Dubai, and the resolution to authorise the company's representative to apply for a licence, the documents having been ratified by the concerned government departments in the country of origin

☐ Passport copy of the company's representative

☐ Identical copy of the foreign company's memorandum of association and articles of association if it is a public or private joint stock company, authenticated by the concerned government departments in the country of origin

☐ Certificate of registration in the foreign companies register at the Ministry of Economy & Planning (copy) (except companies having professional licences and those incorporated in the free zones) (see Setting Up A Branch Of A Foreign Company, p.232)

4 Procedure

Location Dubai Chamber of Commerce   Map ref 8-C4

Hours Sun – Thurs 07:30 – 14:30

registration
- Collect 'Application for Membership' form from the Chamber of Commerce
- The licensee, the manager or any authorised person may submit the documents at the Chamber of Commerce or at the Department of Economic Development
- The Chamber will make a preliminary check of the paperwork, the credentials and the information
- The annual fee is calculated and a 'Fees Payment Order' will be attached to the application form
- Pay the fee at the Cashier

membership
- A Certificate of Membership will be issued at the company's request
- The company can also request an English version of the certificate or a 'To Whom It May Concern' certificate that certifies the membership with the Chamber

5 Related Procedures

- Applying For An Establishment Immigration Card, p.257
- Applying For An Establishment Labour Card, p.255
- Applying For Immigration & Labour Representative Cards, p.259

Setting Up

Business

Setting Up

New Company Immigration Requirements

1 Overview

Every company registered with the DED that has obtained a trade licence must register with the Immigration Department and the Ministry of Labour. By doing that, the company opens a file at the departments, allowing the company to use their services, such as obtaining work permits for employees and settling any labour related disputes.

Registration must be done as soon as the company receives a trade licence. The authorities will check whether the new business fulfils certain requirements and if it is a working company.

The company must apply for the following cards:

- Establishment immigration card
- Establishment labour card
- Representative card

Main institutions involved		
Establishment Documents	Institution	Page
Immigration Card	DNRD	257
Labour Card	Ministry of Labour	255
Representative Card	Ministry of Labour	259
	DNRD	259

 Go to these Ministries as early in the morning as possible to avoid the masses.

Prerequisites
- PO Box (see Applying For A PO Box, p.114)
- Company stamp
- Telephone number (see Applying For A Telephone Line, p.78)
- Fax machine

Applying For An Establishment Labour Card

1 Overview

As soon as a company obtains its trade licence, it must apply for an establishment labour card. This card is issued by the Ministry of Labour and allows a company to hire staff, obtain work permits and apply for visas on the employees' behalf. By holding this card, it means that the company is registered and has a file at the Labour office, with its own establishment number.

Validity As long as the company exists.

2 Prerequisites

- Company has received a trade licence
- Company has received an establishment immigration card (see p.257)

3 What To Bring

- ☐ Application form in Arabic with company stamp and signed by local partner or national agent (typed) (2 copies)
- ☐ Blank establishment labour card
- ☐ Blank signature authorisation card (2 copies)
- ☐ Passport of the authorised signatories and the owners of the company (all passport details on one A4 sheet) (copy)
- ☐ Trade licence (2 copies and original)
- ☐ If sponsor wants to give authority to other persons to sign, special Ministry of Labour form to give power of attorney to other signatories
- ☐ Passport of sponsor (2 copies)
- ☐ National book of sponsor (2 copies)
- ☐ Service agency agreement (copy)
- ☐ If owner a GCC national, tenancy agreement (attested by notary public)
- ☐ If there are several partners/owners, a letter from the DED listing the names of the partners
- ☐ If applicable, the memorandum of association (copy)
- ☐ An illustrated map of the company location
- ☐ Tenancy contract of the company premises

Fees ☐ Dhs.200 – signature authorisation card fee
- ☐ Dhs.100 – power of attorney form fee
- ☐ Dhs.1,000 – opening a company file fee
- ☐ Dhs.50 – typist fee
- ☐ Dhs.10 – Ministry of Labour envelope

Immigration & Labour

Business

4 Procedure

Location Ministry of Labour

Map ref 10-C9

Hours Sun – Thurs 08:00 – 19:00

- Go to a typing office, fill out the relevant documents and pay the fees with e-Dirhams
- An authorised person must sign the forms and seal each with the company stamp
- Submit all documents at the Ministry of Labour
- Collect the card at the same time
- Either the establishment labour card or a rejection will be sent to the PO Box within 10 – 12 days

5 Related Procedures

- Applying For An Establishment Immigration Card, p.257
- Applying For Immigration & Labour Representative Cards, p.259

Web Update

While Dubai's government is committed to cutting back on the red-tape involved in setting up in Dubai, both for individuals and businesses, changes in rules and regulations are inevitable. Therefore, if there have been any changes or additions to the procedures included in this book they will appear on the Explorer website. Just log on to **www.liveworkexplore.com** and click on the Red-Tape link. This page will tell you if there have been any changes to specific procedures – giving you the heads up before you head off to plough through Dubai's administrative maze!

Immigration & Labour

Business

Applying For An Establishment Immigration Card

1 Overview

Once a company has received the establishment labour card, it must open a file with the Immigration Department. The Immigration Card that is issued by the Immigration Department allows a company to recruit staff from abroad. Depending on the business activity of the company, it will also allow the company to apply for a 14-day transit visa (visa for a mission), visit visa and/or tourist visa for company clients and other business contacts. Some companies are not granted any visa privileges.

Validity One, two or three years, renewable

2 Prerequisites

- Company has received the trade licence

3 What To Bring

- ☐ Completed establishment card application form in Arabic and English with company stamp and signed by local partner or national agent (typed) (2 copies each)
- ☐ Completed establishment card (2 copies)
- ☐ Trade licence (2 copies)
- ☐ Passport of the authorised signatories and the owners of the company (all passport details on one A4 sheet) (copy)
- ☐ If applicable, local service agent's passport (copy)
- ☐ If applicable, local service agent agreement (copy)
- ☐ Power of attorney of authorised signatories, notarised by the Court
- ☐ If an LLC Company, a memorandum of association or a 'To Whom It May Concern' certificate from the DED listing the partners' names
- ☐ If applicable, the partnership agreement (copy)
- ☐ An illustrated map of the company location

Fee ☐ Dhs.200 – Dhs.300 per year – service fee (cash)

Renewal ☐ All of the above documents
☐ Previous establishment card

4 Procedure

Location Immigration Department   Map ref 7-B4

Hours Sun – Thurs 07:30 – 20:00

- Go to a typing office, fill out the relevant documents and pay the fees with e-Dirhams

Immigration & Labour

Business

- An authorised person must sign the forms and seal each with the company stamp
- Submit all documents at the Immigration Department
- Take a ticket with return date/time
- Collect establishment immigration card upon approval on that day

- To renew the card, follow the same procedure

5 Related Procedures

- Applying For An Establishment Labour Card, p.255
- Applying For Immigration & Labour Representative Cards, p.259

Info Staffing

For companies operating outside the free zones, the Ministry of Labour will set a maximum number of expatriate staff that may be hired, according to the size of business and business activity. In some cases, such as banks, the ministry will state the minimum percentage of employees that must be UAE Nationals. Actually recruiting your staff is a whole other kettle of fish – and there aren't always that many fish in the sea worth catching. Various agencies can assist with recruitment within the UAE (head-hunting firms are increasing in numbers) or internationally.

Immigration & Labour

Applying For Immigration & Labour Representative Cards

1 Overview

These two cards, sometimes also referred to as 'PRO cards', allow a selected individual to deal on behalf of the company with the Immigration and Labour Departments. Companies usually hire someone who specialises in these procedures. This person is called the PRO (Public Relations Officer).

Validity   Labour representative card: two years

Immigration representative card: one to three years

2 Prerequisites

- The company already has establishment labour and immigration cards
- The representative is employed by the company.

The PRO can work for several companies as long as he has the same sponsor.

3 What To Bring

For Both   ☐ Trade licence (copy)

☐ Representative's passport (copy)

☐ Representative's labour card (copy)

☐ Passport photographs of the representative (two)

Labour   ☐ Application form

☐ Establishment labour card

Fees   ☐ Dhs.400 – registration fee (e-Dirham)

☐ Dhs.10 – typing fee

Immigration   ☐ Application form

☐ Establishment immigration card

Fees   ☐ Dhs.200 – annual registration fee

☐ Dhs.100 – urgent fee (optional)

☐ Dhs.10 – typing fee

4 Procedure

Location   Ministry of Labour   Map ref 10-C9

Hours   Sun – Thurs 08:00 – 19:00

- Complete both the application form and representative card at a typing office
- Both the sponsor and representative must sign and stamp the forms

- Submit documents at the Labour Office
- Collect the representative card one week later

Location Immigration Department   Map ref 7-B4

Hours Sun – Thurs 07:30 – 14:30

- Complete both the application form and representative card at a typing office
- The sponsor must sign and stamp the forms
- Submit documents at the Immigration Department
- Return to collect the representative card

Free Zones Employees of companies in the free zones have different sponsorship options, depending on the free zone. An employee is sponsored by the free zone authority itself. In each case, the free zone authorities will handle the processing of your visa through the Immigration Department and, generally, they seem to be able to process your visa very quickly. Once Immigration has stamped your residence permit in your passport, some free zone authorities will issue a labour card. Both your permit and your labour card are valid for three years.

Info **Work Permits**

The employer is responsible for all the work permits and related immigration procedures, which unfortunately can be a tedious and lengthy process so you can expect your PRO to be very busy in the beginning. If you are setting up in a free zone, the free zone authority will handle all immigration procedures – this simplifies the setting-up stage dramatically but costs slightly more. The company must cover all costs – visa, medical test, and so on – when hiring a employee. But if your new employee happens to already be on a residence permit (ie. sponsored by their spouse), the costs (and hassle) are lower. So look out for those untapped wives and mothers!

Appointing A Commercial Agent

1 Overview

If a foreign company wants to supply goods and/or services from abroad without establishing a physical presence in Dubai, it can either do so through an appropriately licenced importer on a supply-of-goods arrangement (sale and purchase basis), or through a commercial agent/distributor for its goods and/or services in the UAE. The agent is entitled to statutory exclusive rights to distribute and market specific products and services within a specific territory. The company is not allowed to distribute these products in that territory. If the company does assist in a sale, its commercial agent is entitled to a commission.

 Such a commercial agency also covers franchises, distributorships and commission arrangements. The agent must register the agency agreement with the Ministry of Economy & Planning.

 Generally, entities established or formed in free zones can only sell goods in the UAE through UAE-based entities that have an appropriate licence to import into the UAE or through a commercial agent/distributor.

It can be difficult to terminate the agency agreement. Although the contract may be limited to a specific timespan, the agreement can be terminated in two ways:

- One can directly seek termination by going to the Commercial Agency Committee at the Ministry of Economy & Planning
- If you are not satisfied with the committee decision, you can also go directly to court and seek termination of the agency relationship. Note that one is not required to go to the committee before seeking a court decision

It is very important to select your agent carefully.

Generally, a commercial agency which is not registered at the Ministry of Economy & Planning will not be recognised and no actions will be entertained by the courts in respect of an unregistered agency.

A foreign company may seek the services of one agent for the whole of the UAE, or may appoint a different agent for each emirate or for each of its products.

2 Prerequisites

- The agent must be a UAE national or a wholly owned UAE entity incorporated in the UAE
- The agent must be listed in the register of commercial agents kept by the UAE Ministry of Economy and Planning

Agency agreement Must be in writing, and must include the following:

- The name, nationality and address of the agent and the principal

Commercial Agent

Business

- If the agent is a commercial company, the company's name, type (legal form), head office and UAE branch addresses, and its capital amount
- Listing of the products, commodities and services covered by the commercial agency
- The territory that the agreement covers
- The date on which the agreement is to come into effect
- The duration of the agency and provisions in the event of default
- The agency agreement must be notarised, legalised by the Foreign Ministry and authenticated by the UAE Embassy in the country in which it is executed

3 What To Bring

☐ Agent's trade licence and commercial register entry certificate (original and copy)

☐ Authenticated commercial agency agreement (original and copy)

Fee ☐ Dhs.400 (registration fee)

Company Agency
☐ Memorandum of association (certified copy plus one copy)

☐ Passport and family book of each partner (copy) or a certificate proving that the company is owned entirely by UAE nationals (original & copy)

Individual Agency ☐ Passport and family book of the trade agent (copy)

All documents must be translated into Arabic and certified.

4 Procedure

Location Ministry of Economy & Planning   Map ref 9-A6

Hours Sun – Thurs 07:30 – 14:30

Commecial Agreement
- Draft a notarised commercial agency agreement that includes the information outlined above
- Write the agreement in Arabic or have it translated into Arabic by a translator licensed by the UAE Ministry of Justice

Signing Outside the UAE
- Have a commercial agency agreement between agent and principal drafted in English and translated into Arabic by a translator licensed by the UAE Ministry of Justice
- Notarise the agreement here in Dubai, or in the country of the principal, and any documents that give the signatory authorisation to sign on the principal's behalf
- If notarised in the country of the principal, be sure the agreement is authorised at the UAE embassy in the country of the principal
- If drafted in Dubai, get it attested at the Ministry of Foreign Affairs
- Register the agency at the Ministry of Economy & Planning's Commercial Agency Register

Commercial Agent

Business

- Submit the above commercial agency agreement, application form and legal documents of agent and principal to the Ministry of Economy & Planning and pay the required fees
- The ministry will reply within 15 days of application
- If the registration is accepted, the agent will receive an authenticated certificate confirming the registration
- Details of the registration will be published in the Ministry's Official Gazette
- If registration is not accepted, the ministry must provide reasons for its refusal

5 Related Procedures

- Obtaining Special Approval For Business Activity, p.226
- Options For Non-Nationals & Foreign Companies, p.225

Free Zone

Free Zone Overview

1   Overview

In a concentrated effort to attract foreign investment, several free trade zones have been established in and around Dubai. Unique laws regarding ownership, taxation, recruitment of labour, and income repatriation apply to these areas. A further advantage of free zones is the assistance they provide in incorporating or setting up companies within them. Such benefits make these zones ideal for companies wishing to establish a distribution, manufacturing, storage or service base for trade outside of the UAE.

The Jebel Ali Free Zone (JAFZA), established in 1985, was the first such entity in the Emirates. Based on its success, other free zones have sprung up around Dubai, including the Airport Free Zone, Internet and Media Cities and Dubai Healthcare City, while Ajman, Fujairah, Hamriya, Sharjah and Abu Dhabi have all incorporated their own versions of this popular model. While each of these follows JAFZA's lead, they also have their own unique base of customers, services and benefits. This makes for a vast amount of flexibility and packages available to those wishing to set up businesses in the area.

The main UAE free zones are listed in the table opposite and a longer list can be found in the Directory (p.287). For the most up-to-date listing, visit www.uaefreezones.com.

Business Enviornment

Legally, companies based in free zones are seen as 'offshore', giving them the luxury of full ownership. In other words, no local sponsorship is required. There are many additional benefits, but the most attractive are tax exemption and 100% repatriation of profit and capital. Offshore status also means that companies wishing to trade in Dubai or the Emirates will often have to work through a commercial agent or distributor.

Licences Available At The Four Main Dubai Free Zones			
	Trade Licences	Service Licences	Industrial Licences	National Industrial Licences
JAFZA	Yes	Yes	Yes	Yes
DAFZA	Yes	Yes	Yes	No
DIC	Yes	Yes	No	No
DMC	Yes	Yes	No	No

Application Procedure

Most free zones are equipped with state-of-the-art facilities, and offer a great deal of administrative support. In some, companies can also purchase lease-hold property on which to build their own offices, warehouses or manufacturing centres. When setting up a company or office in a free zone, the applicant deals mostly with the free zone authority on the premises. For an administrative charge, they will assist with all government procedures, such as obtaining the necessary permits and visas. This cuts time significantly and saves a good deal of headache.

Company and Licence Types

The following companies can be set up in the free zones:

- Free zone establishment or company (a company incorporated in and regulated by a free zone)
- Branch of a foreign company
- Branch of a UAE company

A company must apply for a trade licence depending on the type of business activity. Not all free zones offer all types of licences. See the table on p.264 for a quick overview.

Free Zone Establishment

- 100% foreign owned
- Similar to an LLC
- Single shareholder option
- Minimum capital requirement
- Liability is limited to the amount of the paid capital

Main Free Zones In The UAE		
Abu Dhabi	Phone	Website
twofour54	02 401 2454	www.twofour54.com
Abu Dhabi Airport Free Zone	02 505 3403	www.adafz.ae
Ajman		
Ajman Free Zone Authority	06 742 5444	www.ajmanfreezone.gov.ae
Dubai		
Dubai Airport Free Zone (DAFZA)	04 299 5555	www.dafza.gov.ae
Dubai International Financial Center (DIFC)	04 362 2222	www.difc.ae
Dubai Internet City (DIC)	04 391 1111	www.dubaiinternetcity.com
Dubai Healthcare City (DHCC)	04 324 5555	www.dhcc.ae
Dubai Knowledge Village (DKV)	04 390 1111	www.kv.ae
Dubai Maritime City	800 4806	www.dubaimaritimecity.com
Dubai Media City (DMC)	04 391 4615	www.dubaimediacity.com
Dubai Silicon Oasis Authority (DSOA)	04 501 5000	www.dso.ae
Gold & Diamond Park	04 347 7788	www.goldanddiamondpark.com
Jebel Ali Free Zone (JAFZA)	800 52392	www.jafza.ae
Fujairah		
Fujairah Free Zone (FFZ)	09 222 8000	www.fujairahfreezone.com
Sharjah		
Hamriyah Free Zone	06 526 3333	www.hfza.ae
Sharjah Airport International Free Zone	06 557 0000	www.saif-zone.com
Ras Al Khaimah		
Ras Al Khaimah Free Trade Zone (RAK FTZ)	07 228 0889	www.rakftz.com
Umm Al Quwain		
Shk Ahmed Bin Rashid Port & Free Zone	06 765 5882	www.uaefreezones.com

Free Zone

Business

Free Zone

Setting Up In Jebel Ali Free Zone (JAFZA)

1 Overview

Laying claim to the largest man-made port in the world, the Jebel Ali Free Zone (JAFZA) was the first free zone established in the UAE. It is also the biggest, with well over 6,000 companies from some 110 countries. Most of the companies in JAFZA are involved with some form of distribution, but a number of manufacturers and a few service providers have chosen to take advantage of the site's facilities and services.

A massive and well-established infrastructure, and an enormous physical area a few minutes south of Dubai allows JAFZA to offer its customers a range of facilities, from individual office units to land sites where companies can construct their own offices, warehouses or manufacturing operations. Customers also have access to on-site staff accommodation, customs and banking, among other services and facilities, making it an attractive option for a diverse array of companies and establishments.

Setting up in the Jebel Ali Free Zone is designed to be a straightforward and relatively simple procedure. Requirements will differ slightly depending on the type of licence required.

Licence Type
Different types of companies will require different licences depending on the nature of their business. It should be noted that companies whose activities fall under different categories are required to carry separate licences for each.

Trading Licence
Allows the import, export, sale, distribution and storage of goods. Distribution of goods within the UAE may have to be made by an agent or distributor (see Appointing A Commercial Agent, p.261).

Industrial Licence
Allows the import of raw materials, manufacture of products and export of the finished goods. Distribution of goods within the UAE may have to be made by an agent or distributor.

Service Licence
Allows the holder to carry out specific services within the free zone as per their parent company, which must be registered in the UAE and have a valid UAE licence.

National Industrial Licence
Allows the import of raw materials, manufacture of products, and export of the finished goods.

Ownership must be at least 51% GCC national, and the value added in the free zone must be a minimum of 40%. This licence gives the holder the same rights as a local or GCC licence. These companies qualify for customs duty exemption on products imported into GCC states.

Free Zone Establishment or Free Zone Company
FZEs and FZCOs are separate legal entities regulated by the free zone authority which can be 100% foreign owned, with limited liability for their owners, and can operate independently from their shareholders. Such companies hold whichever of the above licence(s) are applicable to their business.

Validity
Licences are valid for one year, and are renewable annually for the extent of the company's lease, provided that certain requirements are met.

To hold any JAFZA licence, a company must have valid registration from either the DED (or equivalent authority) or the JAFZA Authority, or incorporation outside of the UAE. (individual or additional prerequisites are as follows.) Companies are also subject to applicable Federal and Municipal laws, as well as the rules and regulations of the free zone.

Trade Licence
- Company is a free zone establishment, was established outside the UAE or holds a valid licence from the DED

Industrial Licence
- Company is a free zone establishment or was established outside the UAE

Service Licence
- Company is already registered in the UAE as a service company
- Service provided must be the same as that named in the parent company's licence
- Provision of services will only be within the free zone

National Industrial Licence
- Company must be a manufacturing enterprise
- Company must be registered either outside or within the UAE
- Must be at least 51% UAE or GCC owned

At least 25% UAE ownership is required for a certificate of origin issued by the Ministry of Economy & Planning.

The UAE value-added input must be at least 40% of the total value of the product.

Free Zone Entity
- Minimum capital requirement: Dhs.1 million for a FZE, and Dhs.500,000 for a FZCO

Charges
- FZE – Dhs.10,000; FZCO – Dhs.15,000
- No licence from DED required
- Any activity, but only in the free zone and/or outside the UAE

3 What To Bring

☐ Completed 'Application for Licence' form (downloaded from www.jafza.co.ae/frame-app.htm)

☐ One page summary of proposed project

☐ Supporting documentation such as company or product brochures (optional)

4 Procedure

Location JAFZA Sales Department — Map ref 1-C4

Hours Sun – Thurs 07:30 – 14:30

Initial Approval
- Submit the application form and one page proposal

Free Zone

Business

- After an initial assessment, JAFZA will give provisional approval and detail which documents will be required next

Legal documents are required. All documents must be notarised by a notary public in the country of origin and attested by the local consulate or a recognised embassy.

- JAFZA will review availability of facilities and prepare a proforma lease agreement and possibly a personnel secondment agreement

FZE/FZCO
- Applicant must sign the proforma agreement
- Deposit share capital

Lease Agreement
- JAFZA will issue a certificate of formation and share certificates
- JAFZA prepares the final lease agreement
- Both parties sign the final agreement
- Applicant pays required licence and rental fees

Fees are contingent on licensing and leasing agreements.

- JAFZA prepares and issues the licence

- If required, the free zone will assist with immigration matters

Post Licencing
- If construction for factory, storage or other structure is involved, plans must be submitted after licence issued

Free Zone

Business

Setting Up In Dubai Internet City (DIC)

1 Overview

Dubai Technology, E-Commerce & Media Free Zone (TECOM), part of which also comprises Dubai Media City (DMC) (see Setting Up In DMC p.272) and Knowledge Village.

Dubai Internet City was heralded as the first information technology and telecommunications centre within a free trade zone when it opened in late 2000. Aimed at attracting and supporting information and communications technology companies, DIC has developed the Middle East's most advanced IT infrastructure, and has drawn IT giants such as Microsoft and IBM, as well as branch offices and smaller companies including local software developers and service providers.

Facilities are geared towards service and development companies; hence warehouses and manufacturing facilities are not available. Available office space starts at 600 square feet and optional land leases are available. Additionally, accommodation, retail outlets and restaurants are found within the confines of Internet City.

Situated 15 minutes from the World Trade Centre on Sheikh Zayed Road, new buildings are being quickly added to catch up with demand for office space.

DIC has gone to great lengths to insure a relatively hassle-free incorporation process.

Company
- Branch of a foreign company
- Branch of a UAE-based company (including other UAE free zone licensees)
- Free zone limited liability company (FZ LLC)
- Established by an individual
- Established by an entity (company)

2 Prerequisites

Company belongs to one of the following sectors:

- Business Services
- Consultancy
- IT Support
- Sales & Marketing/Regional Headquarters
- Software Development
- Web-based

Businesses from other related sectors may contact the DIC Commercial Division and explain how the company would fit into the DIC community.

Free Zone

Business

3 What To Bring

 Required documents will depend on the type of company to be incorporated.

☐ Completed application form collected from the DIC Commercial Division or downloaded from www.dubaiinternetcity.com (typed or hand-written; English/Arabic)

☐ The person signing the application form must be officially authorised to do so and must be able to show proof of this authority

☐ Business proposal with the following points clearly stated:

- Description of the business
- Products/Services
- Role of DIC location
- Marketing
- Target Marketing
- Market segment
- Competition
- Operating procedures
- Personnel
- CV of the owners, if individuals
- Financial data

☐ Company board resolution specifying the establishment of a branch/FZ company (FZ-LLC) in the Dubai Technology Electronic Commerce and Media Free Zone and appointing a manager (notarised)

Branch ☐ Manager's passport (copy)

☐ Memorandum/articles of association of the company (notarised) (copy)

☐ Specimen signature of the manager (notarised)

☐ If branch of a foreign company, current company registration certificate (copy) or certificate of good standing (original) (authenticated)

☐ If branch of a UAE company, current commercial registration and trade licence (copy)

FZ-LLC ☐ Proof of minimum capital requirement from a UAE registered bank (Dhs.50,000) (notarised)

☐ Manager's, director's and secretary's signature specimens (notarised) and valid passports (copy)

Individual ☐ Applicant's personal profile

☐ Banker's reference (original) (notarised)

☐ Business proposal

Multiple
- ☐ Current authenticated certificate of company registration (copy) or certificate of good standing (original)
- ☐ Memorandum and articles of association (authenticated)
- ☐ Power of attorney to a negotiator or legal representative
- ☐ Specimen of manager's signature
- ☐ Manager's valid passport (copy)

4 Procedure

Location   DIC, Commercial/Account Management   Map ref 3-B3

Hours   Sun – Thurs 08:00 – 17:00

- Submit the application for review
- If approved, DIC will issue a provisional approval letter listing the required legal documents and a submission deadline
- DIC will also issue a personnel sponsorship agreement (PSA), employment contract, specimen lease agreement, and general terms and conditions of the sponsorship agreement
- Submit all required legal documents
- DIC will review all documents
- Upon approval, DIC issues a final approval letter with the details of the office space, an invoice for the 20% deposit and licence fee, and a sample of the lease agreement
- Applicant pays fee upon acceptance of the PSA
- Upon payment, DIC will issue the lease agreement
- The authorised person has one week to sign the lease agreement and PSA
- DIC issues the licence

Info   Working As A Freelancer

The option to work as a freelancer is available only through the Media Business Centre (at Dubai Media City). The Freelance Permit identifies you as a sole practitioner, so you are able to conduct business in your own name, rather than under a company or brand name. Your permit includes a residence visa, shared fax, postal and other support services at the Business Centre, but you are not entitled to any employee visas.

Free Zone

Business

Setting Up In Dubai Media City (DMC)

1 Overview

Next to Dubai Internet City, Dubai Media City has been established to facilitate operations for all manner of companies in the media industry. In early 2001, Dubai Media City opened its doors, offering and guaranteeing (within the country's moral code) freedom of expression without censorship for its tenants. Since then, expansion has been rapid, adding several more media companies and facilities to accommodate them.

DMC offers clients access to a global interconnected network supporting print, television, radio, film and web-based media ventures within an attractive complex of inspired architecture featuring landscaped lakes and dining facilities. Additional free zone benefits of full foreign ownership and tax exemptions are also included as benefits of incorporating within Media City.

Target Companies Companies in the following fields are encouraged to become 'Media City Partners': broadcasting, communication, music, new media, post-production, production and publishing.

Licensing options:

- Branch of a UAE or non-UAE company
- New company: free zone establishment-limited liability company (FZE-LLC) with a minimum required paid up capital of Dhs.50,000
- Freelance Permit: sole practitioner based within the media business centre office (open or private serviced offices with administrative support)

2 Prerequisites

- Company activity belongs to any type of media discipline (i.e. communication, broadcasting, music, production, publishing, or new media)
- Company is not trading in goods (companies needing storage can rent a warehouse in Dubai)

3 What To Bring

☐ As always, all documents, especially copies, should be notarised and attested

Company Branch ☐ Completed application and partner registration forms downloaded from www.dubaimediacity.com

☐ Business plan/company profile/planned business proposal

☐ Partners' and manager's passports (copy)

☐ Banker's reference

☐ Power of attorney (if required)

□ Certificate of registration of the company and the trade licence

□ Memorandum and articles of association

□ Board resolution calling for establishment at Dubai Media City

Newly Incorporated Company

□ Completed application and partner registration forms downloaded from www.dubaimediacity.com

□ Business plan/company profile/planned business proposal

□ Partners' and manager's passports (copy)

□ Banker's reference

□ Power of attorney (if required)

4 Procedure

Location DMC Commercial/Account Management Map ref 3-A3

Hours Sun – Thurs 08:00 – 17:00

- Submit the application forms and attach all relevant documents listed above

- Book office space in one of the commercial buildings, or lease land for development

- Make necessary payments to secure office space within three days of the booking date

- Sign the lease agreement, and submit along with two post-dated cheques for the rent (the first dated as per the commencement date on the lease agreement for the first eight months of occupancy; the second post-dated for the remaining four months)

Info **New Free Zones**

Knowledge Village

There are a number of licensing options for educational facilities that want to set up in Knowledge Village, Dubai's educational free zone. You can set up a Free Zone Limited Liability Company (FZ LLC), a Branch of a Local or Foreign Company or you can apply for a freelance permit. For more information visit www.kv.ae.

Dubai International Financial Centre (DIFC)

DIFC is an onshore capital market and financial free zone that attracts international business and considers licence applications from financial institutions in banking services, capital markets, asset management & fund registration, reinsurance, Islamic Finance and back office operations. For more information visit www.difc.ae.

Free Zone

Business

MUSIC
DVDs
BOOKS
GAMES
ELECTRONICS
MULTIMEDIA
BOUTIQUE

Directory

Directory

Accountants – Chartered

AF Ferguson & Co	04 331 8856
AGN MAK Chartered Certified Accountants	04 228 3008
Ernst & Young	04 332 4000
Grant Thornton	04 268 8070
Griffin Nagda & Company	04 297 5010
Kant & Clients Auditors & Chartered Acountants	04 221 2168
Pricewaterhouse Coopers	04 304 3100

Airports

Abu Dhabi International Airport	02 505 5000
Abu Dhabi International Airport (Flight Enquiry)	02 575 7500
Abu Dhabi International Airport (Lost & Found)	02 505 2771
Al Ain International Airport	03 785 5555
DNATA Export Office	04 211 1111
Dubai Cargo Village	04 211 1111
Dubai International Airport	04 224 5555
Dubai International Airport (Flight Information)	04 216 6666
Dubai International Airport (Baggage Services, Lost Property)	04 224 5383
Dubai Airport Flight Information Voice Portal	04 216 6666
Dubai Meteorological Office	04 216 2218
Emirates	04 214 4444
Fujairah International Airport	09 222 6222
Ras Al Khaimah International Airport	07 244 8111
Sharjah International Airport	06 558 1111

Business Councils

American Business Council	04 331 4735
Australian Business in the Gulf (ABIG)	04 395 4423
British Business Group	04 397 0303
Canadian Business Council	04 359 2625
Denmark Business Council	04 222 7699
French Business Council	04 335 2362
German Business Council	04 359 9930
Iranian Business Council	04 344 4717
Pakistan Business Council	04 337 2875
South African Business Group	050 653 2469
Swedish Business Council	04 337 1410
Swiss Business Council	04 321 1438

Commercial Banks   @ E-Dirhams available

ABN AMRO Bank	04 351 2200
Abu Dhabi Commercial Bank @	800 2030
Abu Dhabi National Bank	04 343 3030
National Bank of Umm Al Qaiwain	04 397 5382
Arab Bank	800 27224
Arab Bank for Investment & Foreign Trade @	04 222 0152
Bank Melli Iran	04 201 5100
Bank of Sharjah	04 282 7278
Bank Pariba	04 424 8200

Commercial Banks (Cont'd)

Bank Saderat Iran	04 226 4805
Barclays Bank Plc	04 428 6000
Citibank	04 311 4000
Dubai Commercial Bank @	04 420 0119
Emirates Bank Group	04 316 0316
Habib Bank AG Zurich	04 221 4535
HSBC Bank Middle East	800 4722
Lloyds TSB Bank Plc	04 342 2000
Mashreq Bank @	04 424 4444
National Bank of Dubai	04 310 0101
National Bank of Ras Al Khaimah	04 213 0000
Sharjah Islamic Bank @	04 269 8339
Standard Chartered	800 4949
United Arab Bank @	04 222 0181

Courier Services

Aramex International	04 286 5000
DHL	800 4004
Empost	04 299 5333
Fedex UAE	800 4050
Memo Express	04 336 4400
Overseas Courier Services	04 262 5757
TNT Express	800 4333
UPS	800 4774

Hotels

Admiral Plaza	04 393 5333
Al Bustan Rotana Hotel	04 282 0000
Al Khaleej Palace Hotel	04 223 1000
Al Maha Desert Resort & Spa	04 303 4222
Al Manzil Hotel	04 428 5888
Al Murooj Rotana Hotel & Suites	04 321 1111
Al Qasr Hotel	04 366 8888
Ambassador Hotel	04 393 9444
Amwaj Rotana	04 885 0962
Arabian Courtyard Hotel & Spa	04 351 9111
Arabian Park Hotel	04 324 5999
Ascot Hotel	04 352 0900
Astoria Hotel	04 353 4300
Atlantis The Palm	04 426 1000
Bab Al Shams Desert Resort & Spa	04 809 6100
Burj Al Arab	04 301 7777
Capitol Hotel	04 346 0111
City Centre Hotel	04 294 1222
Comfort Inn	04 222 7393
Coral Deira	04 224 8587
Courtyard by Marriott Dubai Green Community	04 885 2222
Crowne Plaza	04 331 1111
Crowne Plaza Festival City	04 701 2222
Desert Palm Dubai	04 323 8888
Dhow Palace Hotel	04 359 9992
Dubai Grand Hotel	04 263 2555
Dubai International Hotel	04 224 4000
Dubai Marine Beach Resort & Spa	04 346 1111

Business

Directory

Hotels (Cont'd)

Dubai Palm Hotel	04 271 0021
Dusit Thani	04 343 3333
Emirates Towers Hotel	04 330 0000
Fairmont Hotel	04 332 5555
Four Points by Sheraton Bur Dubai	04 397 7444
Four Points by Sheraton Downtown Dubai	04 354 3333
Four Points by Sheraton Sheikh Zayed Road	04 323 0333
Grand Hyatt Dubai	04 317 1234
Grand Millennium Dubai	04 429 9999
Habtoor Grand Resort & Spa	04 399 5000
Hatta Fort Hotel	04 852 3211
Hilton Dubai Creek	04 227 1111
Hilton Dubai Jumeirah	04 399 1111
Holiday Inn Downtown	04 228 8889
Hyatt Regency Hotel	04 209 1234
Ibis Deira City Centre	04 292 5000
Ibis World Trade Centre	04 332 4444
Imperial Suites Hotel	04 351 5100
InterContinental Dubai Festival City	04 701 1111
Jebel Ali Golf Resort & Spa	04 883 6000
Jebel Ali Hotel	04 883 6000
Jumeira Rotana Hotel	04 345 5888
Jumeirah Beach Hotel	04 348 0000
JW Marriott Hotel	04 262 4444
Kempinski Mall of the Emirates	04 341 0000
La Maison d'Hôtes	04 344 1838
Le Meridien Dubai	04 217 0000
Le Meridien Fairway	04 608 5000
Le Meridien Mina Seyahi Beach Resort & Marina	04 399 3333
Lotus Hotel	04 227 8888
Marco Polo Hotel	04 272 0000
Media Rotana	04 435 0000
Metropolitan Hotel	04 343 0000
Metropolitan Palace Hotel	04 227 0000
Millennium Airport Hotel	04 282 3464
Mina A'Salam	04 366 8888
Mövenpick Hotel Bur Dubai	04 336 6000
Novotel Deira City Centre	04 292 5200
Novotel World Trade Centre	04 332 0000
One&Only Royal Mirage	04 399 9999
Park Hyatt Dubai	04 602 1234
Premier Inn Dubai	04 885 0999
President Hotel	04 334 6565
Qamardeen Hotel	04 428 6888
Radisson SAS Hotel, Dubai Deira Creek	04 222 7171
Raffles Dubai	04 324 8888
Ramada Hotel	04 351 9999
Regent Palace Hotel	04 396 3888
Renaissance Hotel	04 262 5555
Ritz-Carlton, Dubai	04 399 4000
Riviera Hotel	04 222 2131
Rydges Plaza Hotel	04 398 2222
Shangri-La Hotel	04 343 8888
Sheraton Deira	04 268 8888
Sheraton Dubai Creek Hotel & Towers	04 228 1111

Business

Directory

Directory

Hotels (Cont'd)

Taj Palace Hotel	04 223 2222
The Address, Downtown Burj Dubai	04 436 8888
The Carlton Tower	04 222 7111
The Harbour Hotel & Residence	04 319 4000
The Monarch Dubai	04 501 8888
The Montgomerie, Dubai	04 390 5600
The Palace	04 428 7888
The Westin Dubai Mina Seyahi Beach Resort & Marina	04 399 4141
Towers Rotana Hotel	04 343 8000
Traders Hotel, Deira	04 265 9888
Vendome Plaza Hotel	04 222 2333

Insurance Companies

Alliance	04 605 1111
Axa Insurance	800 2924
Eagle Star International Life	04 397 4444
Nasco Karaoglan Group	04 352 3133
National General Insurance Co	04 222 2772
New India Assurance Co	04 352 5563
Norwich Union Insurance (Gulf)	04 324 3434
Northern Assurance Co	04 331 8400
Oman Insurance Co	04 262 4000
Royal International Insurance Holdings	04 336 6551
Sedgewick Forbes Middle East	04 331 3265
United Insurance Brokers (UIB)	04 294 0842

Legal Consultants

Afridi & Angell	04 330 3900
Al Sharif Advocates & Legal Consultants	04 262 8222
Al Tamimi & Company	04 364 1641
Hadef Legal Consultants & Advocates	04 429 2999
Musthafa & Almana Associates	04 329 8411
Trench Associates	04 355 3146
Emirates Advocates	04 330 4343
James Berry & Associates	04 3317552
Key & Dixon	04 332 3324
Nabulsi Legal Consultants	04 222 3004
Simmons & Simmons	04 709 6600
Stockwell & Associates	04 228 3194
Trench & Associates	04 355 3146

Ports

Dubai Ports Authority	04 345 1545
Jebel Ali Port Authority	04 881 5555
Khor Fakkan Port	06 528 1327
Mina Saqr	07 266 8444
Mina Zayed Seaport Authority	02 673 0600
Port Fujairah	09 222 8800
Port Khaled	06 528 1327
Port Rashid Terminal	04 3453565
Sharjah Ports Authority	06 528 1327
Umm Al Quwain Port	06 765 5882

Business

Directory

Directory

Trade Centres & Commissions

Australian Trade Commission	04 508 7100
British Embassy – Commercial Section	04 309 4445
Canadian Trade Commission	04 314 5555
Catalonia Trade Office	04 343 8033
Cyprus Trade Centre	04 228 2411
Egyptian Trade Centre	04 222 1098
Export Promotion Council of Norway	04 353 3833
French Trade Commission	04 332 9040
German Office of Foreign Trade	04 397 2611
Guinea Conakry Trade Centre	04 224 9600
Hong Kong Trade Development Council	04 223 3499
Indian State Trading Corporation	04 227 1270
Indian Trade Centre	04 393 5208
Indonesian Trade Promotion Centre (ITPC)	04 227 8544
Italian Trade Commission	04 331 4951
Japan External Trade Organisation	04 332 8264
Korean Trade Centre	04 332 7776
Malaysia Trade Centre	04 335 5528
New Zealand Trade Office	04 331 7500
Philippine Trade Commission	04 223 6526
Polish Trade Centre	04 223 5837
Romanian Trade Representation	04 394 0580
Russian Trade Commission	04 223 1272
Singapore Trade Centre	04 222 9789
Spanish Commercial Office	04 330 0110
Sultanate of Oman Office	04 397 1000
Taiwan Trade Centre	04 3967814
Tajikistan Trade Office	04 266 6450
Thailand Trade Centre	04 228 4553
The Economic & Commercial Section of the Consulate General of China	04 344 8032
Tourism Authority of Thailand	04 266 1896
Trade Representative of the Netherlands	04 352 8700
USA Consulate General – Commercial Section	04 331 3584

Driving

Driving Institutes

Name	Branches	Phone
Al Ahli Driving Centre	8	04 3411500
Belhasa Driving Centre	18	04 324 3535
Dubai Driving Centre	13	04 345 5855
Emirates Driving Institute	35	04 263 1100
Galadari Motor Driving Centre	8	04 267 6166

New Cars

Alpha Romeo	Gargash Motors	04 340 3333
Audi	Al Nabooda Automobiles	04 347 5111
BMW	AGMC Dubai	04 339 1555
Cadillac	Liberty Automobiles	04 341 9341
Chrysler	Trading Enterprises	04 340 2445
Chevrolet	Al Ghandi Group	04 339 5555
Dodge	Trading Enterprises	04 340 2445
Ferrari	Al Tayer Motors	04 303 7070
Ford	Al Tayer Motors	04 303 7070
Isuzu	Genavco LLC	04 396 1000
Honda	Trading Enterprises	04 347 2212
Hummer	Liberty Automobiles	04 341 9341
Hyundai	Juma Al Majid	04 340 7070
Jaguar	Al Tayer Group	04 303 7070
Jeep	Trading Enterprises	04 340 2445
Kia	Al Majed Motors	04 347 7999
Lincoln	Al Tayer Group	04 303 7070
Land Rover	Al Tayer Group	04 303 7070
Lexus	Al Futtaim Motors	04 206 6666
Maserati	Al Tayer Group	04 303 7070
Mazda	Galadari Automobiles	04 299 4848
Mercedes	Gargash Motors	04 340 3333
Mercury	Al Tayer Group	04 201 1002
Mitsubishi	Al Habtoor Motors	04 269 1110
Nissan	Arabian Automobiles	04 295 2222
Opel	Liberty Automobiles	04 3419 341
Porsche	Al Nabooda Automobiles	04 321 3911
Saab	Gargash Motors	04 340 3333
Skoda	Autostar Trading	04 269 7100
Toyota	Al Futtaim Motors	04 310 6666
Volkswagen	Al Nabooda Automobiles	04 338 6999
Volvo	Trading Enterprises	04 340 2425

Used Cars

4x4 Motors – HQ	Al Awir	04 706 9666
Al Futtaim Automall	Al Quoz	04 340 8029
Auto Plus	Al Quoz	04 339 5400
Boston Cars	Al Awir	04 333 1010
Dynatrade	Al Awir	04 320 1558
Exotic Cars	Al Quoz	04 338 4339
House Of Cars	Sheikh Zayed Rd	04 343 5060
Motor World	Al Awir	04 333 2206
Off Road Motors	Al Quoz	04 338 4866
Quartermile – HQ	Al Quoz	04 339 4633
Reem Automobile	Al Wasl	04 343 6333
Sun City Motors	Al Barsha	04 269 8009
Tony Edwards Motors	Al Quoz	04 338 3887
Western Auto	Deira	04 297 7788

Driving

Directory

Directory

Nurseries & Pre-Schools

Alphabet Street Nursery	04 348 5991
Baby Land Nursery	04 348 6874
The Blossom Nursery	055 687 7379
British Orchard Nursery	04 398 3536
The Children's Garden	04 885 3484
Emirates British Nursery	04 348 9996
Jumeirah International Nursery School	04 349 9065
Kids Cottage Nursery School	04 394 2145
Kids' Island Nursery	04 394 2578
The Knightsbridge Nursery School	04 348 1666
Ladybird Nursery	04 344 1011
Little Land Montessori	04 394 4471
Little Woods Nursery	04 394 6155
The Palms Nursery	04 394 7017
Safa Kindergarten Nursery	04 344 3878
Seashells Nursery	04 341 3404
Small World Nursery	04 349 0770
Super Kids Nursery	04 288 1949
Tender Love & Care	04 367 1636
Yellow Brick Road Nursery	04 282 8290

Primary & Secondary Schools

American School of Dubai	04 344 0824
Cambridge High School	04 282 4646
Deira Private School	04 282 4082
Dubai College	04 399 9111
Dubai English Speaking School	04 337 1457
Emirates International School	04 348 9804
English College	04 394 3465
International School of Choueifat	04 399 9444
Jebel Ali Primary School	04 884 6485
Jumeira English Speaking School	04 394 5515
Jumeira Primary School	04 394 3500
School of Research Science	04 298 8776

Embassies

Embassies/Consulates

Australia	04 508 7100
Bahrain	02 665 7500
Canada	04 314 5555
China	04 394 4733
Czech Republic	02 678 2800
Denmark	04 348 0877
Egypt	04 397 1122
France	04 332 9040
Germany	04 397 2333
India	04 397 1222
Iran	04 344 4717
Ireland (Saudi Arabia)	+966 1 488 2300
Italy	04 331 4167
Japan	04 331 9191
Jordan	04 397 0500
Kuwait	04 397 8000
Lebanon	04 397 7450
Malaysia	04 337 2152
Mexico	04 394 5510
The Netherlands	04 352 8700
New Zealand	04 331 7500
Norway	04 353 3833
Oman	04 397 1000
Pakistan	04 397 0412
Philippines	04 254 4331
Qatar	04 398 2888
Russia	04 223 1272
Saudi Arabia	04 397 9777
South Africa	04 397 5222
Spain	02 626 9544
Sri Lanka	04 398 6535
Sweden	02 621 0162
Switzerland	04 329 0999
Thailand	04 348 9550
UK	04 309 4444
USA	04 311 6000

UAE Embassies Abroad

Algeria	+213 2 154 9677
Australia	+612 6 286 8802
Austria	+431 368 1455/56
Bahrain	+973 723 737
Belgium	+32 2 640 6000
Brazil	+55 61 248 0717
Canada	+1613 565 7272
China	+86 10 8451 4416
Egypt	+20 2 360 9722

Embassies

Directory

Directory

UAE Embassies Abroad (Cont'd)

France	+33 1 4553 9404
Germany	+49 228 267 070
Hong Kong	+85 22 866 1823
India, New Delhi	+91 11 687 2822
India, Mumbai	+91 22 218 3021
Indonesia	+62 21 520 6518
Iran	+98 21 878 8515
Italy	+39 6 3630 6100
Japan	+81 3 5489 0183
Jordan	+962 569 6634
Korea	+822 790 3235
Kuwait	+965 252 6356
Lebanon	+9611 85 7000
Libya	+218 21 483 2595
Malaysia	+60 34 253 5221
Morocco	+212 37 702 035
Oman	+968 600 302
Pakistan	+92 21 587 3819
Philippines	+63 2 818 9763
Qatar	+974 483 8880
Russia	+7 095 237 4060
Saudi Arabia	+966 1 482 6803
Singapore	+65 238 8206
South Africa	+27 12 342 7736
Spain	+34 91 570 1001
Sri Lanka	+941 565 053
Sudan	+249 11 471 094
Switzerland	+41 22 918 0000
Syria	+963 11 333 0308
Thailand	+66 2 639 9820
Tunisia	+216 1 782 737
Turkey	+90 312 447 6861
UK	+44 20 7581 1281
USA	+1 202 243 2400

UAE Tourist Offices Abroad

Australia & NZ	Sydney	+61 2 9956 6620
China	Beijing	+86 10 5979 2062
China	Guangzhou	+86 20 8760 7815
China	Shanghai	+86 21 5528 6900
Far East	Hong Kong	+852 2827 5221
France	Paris	+33 1 4495 8500
Germany	Frankfurt	+49 69 7100 020
India	Mumbai	+91 22 2282 8836
Italy	Milan	+39 2 8738 8132
Japan	Tokyo	+81 3 5367 5450
Kingdom of Saudi Arabia	Jeddah	+966 2 652 4283
Kingdom of Saudi Arabia	Riyadh	+966 1 217 7613
Russia, CIS & Baltic States	Moscow	+7 495 980 0717
Scandinavia	Stockholm	+46 8 411 1135
South Africa	Johannesburg	+27 11 785 4600
Switzerland & Austria	Ittigen-Bern	+41 31 924 7599
UK & Ireland	London	+44 20 7321 6110
USA	New York	+1 212 575 2262

Embassies

Directory

Dubai Red-Tape

Government Departments

Government Departments in Dubai

Awqaf & Minors Affairs Foundation	04 294 9494
Centre of Ambulance Services	04 429 4455
Community Development Authority	800 2321
Department of Economic Development	700 40000
Department of Health & Medical Services	04 337 1160
Department of Naturalisation & Residency	04 398 0000
Department of Tourism & Commerce Marketing	04 223 0000
Dubai Airport Free Zone Authority	04 299 5555
Dubai Chamber	04 228 0000
Dubai Civil Aviation Authority	04 216 2009
Dubai Civil Defence	04 261 1111
Dubai Consumer Protection (Himaya)	04 202 0299
Dubai Courts	04 777 7334
Dubai Culture	800 4003
Dubai Electricity & Water Authority	04 324 4444
Dubai Export Development Corporation	04 429 8888
Dubai Government Workshop	04 324 2222
Dubai Media Incorporated	04 336 9999
Dubai Municipality	04 221 5555
Dubai Municipality Public Health Department	04 223 2323
Dubai Police	04 609 6767
Dubai Ports, Customs & Freezone Corporation	04 345 5555
Dubai Public Prosecution	04 334 6666
Dubai Sports Council	04 324 4446
Dubai Statistics Centre	04 436 3300
Islamic Affairs & Charitable Activities	04 608 7777
Knowledge & Human Development Authority	04 364 0000
Land Department	04 222 2253
Roads & Transport Authority	800 9090
The Protocol & Guest House Department of Dubai	04 353 9999
UAE Central Bank Control & Inspection	04 393 9777
UAE Consumer Protection Department (CPD)	04 295 4000
Unified Labour Complaint	04 313 9900

Government Websites

Dubai e-Government	www.dubai.ae
e-Dirham (Ministry of Finance)	www.e-dirham.gov.ae
Dubai Government Departments & Related Organisations	
Department of Civil Defence	www.dcd.gov.ae
Department of Tourism & Commerce Marketing	www.dubaitourism.com
Dubai Chamber of Commerce & Industry	www.dcci.gov.ae
Dubai Civil Aviation	www.dubaiairport.gov.ae
Dubai Court	www.dubaicourts.gov.ae
Dubai Department of Economic Development	www.dubaided.gov.ae
Dubai Department of Health & Medical Services	www.dohms.gov.ae
Dubai Electricity & Water Authority (DEWA)	www.dewa.gov.ae

Government Departments

Directory

Government Websites (Cont'd)

Dubai Municipality	www.dm.gov.ae
Dubai Naturalization & Residence Department	www.dnrd.gov.ae
Dubai Police	www.dubaipolice.gov.ae
Dubai Ports & Customs	www.dxbcustoms.gov.ae
Dubai Ports Authority	www.dpa.co.ae
Dubai Traffic Police	www.dxbtraffic.gov.ae
Roads & Transport Authority	www.rta.ae
Emirates Internet & Multimedia	www.emirates.net.ae
Emirates Post	www.emiratespostuae.com
Etisalat	www.etisalat.ae/e4me.co.ae
Real Estate Department	www.realestate-dubai.gov.ae

Federal Government Departments & Organisations

General	www.uae.gov.ae
Ministry of Economy	www.economy.gov.ae
Ministry of Finance	www.fedfin.gov.ae
Ministry of Health	www.moh.gov.ae
Ministry of Information	www.uaeinteract.com
Ministry of Labour	www.mol.gov.ae

Ministries

Federal National Council	04 282 4531
Federation of UAE Chambers of Commerce & Industry	04 221 2977
General Secreteriat of UAE Municipalities	04 223 7785
Ministry of Agriculture & Fisheries	04 295 8161
Ministry of Communications	04 295 3330
Ministry of Defence	04 353 2330
Ministry of Economy & Commerce	04 295 4000
Ministry of Education & Youth	04 299 4100
Ministry of Electricity & Water	04 262 2000
Ministry of Finance & Industry	04 393 9000
Ministry of Foreign Affairs	04 222 1144
Ministry of Health	04 396 6000
Ministry of Information & Culture	04 261 5500
Ministry of Interior	04 398 0000
Ministry of Justice, Islamic Affairs & Endowments	04 282 5999
Ministry of Labour & Social Affairs	04 269 1666
Ministry of Planning	04 228 5219
Ministry of Public Works & Housing	04 269 3900
Ministry of State for Cabinet	04 396 7555
Ministry of Youth & Sports	04 269 1680
Protocol Department	04 253 1086
State Audit Institution	04 228 6000
UAE Central Bank	04 393 9777

Government Departments

Directory

Free Zones

UAE Free Zones

Free Zones in the UAE		www.uaefreezones.com
Abu Dhabi		
Abu Dhabi Ports Company (ADPC)	02 695 2000	www.adpc.ae
Abu Dhabi Airport Free Zone	02 505 3403	www.adafz.ae
Two Four 54	02 401 2454	www.twofour54.com
ZonesCorp (ZC)	02 550 0000	www.zonescorp.com
Ajman		
Ajman Free Zone	06 742 5444	www.ajmanfreezone.gov.ae
Dubai		
Dubai Airport Free Zone (DAFZA)	04 299 5555	www.dafza.gov.ae
Dubai Auto Zone	04 3337871	www.daz.ae
Dubai Biotechnology & Research Park (DuBiotech)	04 390 2222	www.dubiotech.ae
Dubai Flower Centre Free Zone	04 211 1111	na
Dubai Healthcare City (DHCC)	04 324 5555	www.dhcc.ae
Dubai International Financial Centre (DIFC)	04 362 2222	www.difc.ae
Dubai's International Media Production Zone (IMPZ)	04 391 1122	www.impz.ae
Dubai Internet City (DIC)	04 391 1111	www.dubaiinternetcity.com
Dubai Knowledge Village (DKV)	04 390 1111	www.kv.ae
Dubai Logistics City (DLC)	04 364 9999	www.dwc.ae
Dubai Maritime City	800 4806	www.dubaimaritimecity.com
Dubai Media City (DMC)	04 391 4615	www.dubaimediacity.com
Dubai Multi Commodities Centre (DMCC)	04 424 9600	www.dmcc.ae
Dubai Outsource Zone (DOZ)	04 367 6666	www.doz.ae
Dubai Silicon Oasis Authority (DSOA)	04 501 5000	www.dso.ae
Dubai Studio City (DSC)	04 391 4664	www.dubaistudiocity.ae
Gold & Diamond Park	04 347 7788	www.goldanddiamondpark.com
International Humanitarian City (IHC)	04 368 0202	www.ihc.ae
Jebel Ali Free Zone (JAFZA)	800 52392	www.jafza.ae
Techno Park (TP)	04 881 4888	www.technopark.ae
Fujairah		
Fujairah Free Zone (FFZ)	09 222 8000	www.fujairahfreezone.com
Ras Al Khaimah		
Ras Al Khaimah Free Trade Zone (RAK FTZ)	07 228 0889	www.rakftz.com
Sharjah		
Sharjah Airport International Free Zone	06 557 0000	www.saif-zone.com
Hamriya Free Zone	06 526 3333	www.hfza.ae
Umm Al Quwain		
Sheikh Ahmed Bin Rashid Port & Free Zone	06 765 5882	www.uaefreezones.com

Free Zones

Directory

Directory

Personal Affairs

24 Hour Pharmacies

Al Jameya Pharmacy	04 263 3677
Pharmacy Ibn Sina Central	04 355 6909
Safa Society Pharmacy	04 394 6618
Sondos Pharmacy	04 346 0660
Yara Pharmacy	04 222 5503

Alcohol/Liquor Stores

A&E

Al Karama	04 334 8056
Al Wasl	04 394 2672
Arabian Ranches	04 360 6620
Bur Dubai	04 352 4521
Deira	04 222 2666
Jumeira	04 349 0246
Marina	04 368 3981
Mirdif	04 288 2715
Ras Al Khaimah	07 236 334

MMI

Al Hamra (close to RAK Ceramics)	07 244 7403
Al Karama	04 335 1722
Al Wasl	04 394 0351
Bur Dubai	04 393 4361
Cellar Saver Bur Dubai	04 393 4361
Cellar Saver Karama	04 335 1722
Deira	04 294 0390
Green Community	04 885 4550
Ibn Battuta Mall	04 368 5626
Mall of the Emirates	04 341 0371
Sheikh Zayed Road	04 321 1223
Silicon Oasis	04 326 4583
Trade Centre Road	04 352 3091

Places Of Worship

Hindu Temple	04 353 5334
Holy Trinity Church	04 337 0247
St. Mary's Church	04 337 0087

Hospitals

Al Baraha Hospital – Emergency	04 271 0000
Al Maktoum Hospital	04 222 1211
Al Rafa Hospital for Maternity & Surgery	04 393 0340
Al Wasl Hospital – Emergency	04 219 3000
Al Zahra Hospital	06 561 9999
American Hospital – Emergency	04 336 7777
Belhoul European Hospital	04 345 4000
Belhoul Speciality Hospital	04 273 3333
Canadian Specialist Hospital	04 336 4444
Cedars Jebel Ali International Hospital	04 881 4000
Dubai Healthcare City	04 324 5555
Dubai Hospital – Emergency	04 219 5000
Emirates Hospital	04 349 6666

Hospitals (Cont'd)

Great Ormond Street Hospital for Children	04 362 4722
Gulf Speciality Hospital	04 269 9717
International Modern Hospital	04 398 8888
International Private Hospital Dubai	04 221 2484
Iranian Hospital – Emergency	04 344 0250
Jebel Ali Hospital	04 884 5666
Medcare Hospital	04 407 9100
Moorfield Eye Hospital	04 429 7888
Neuro Spinal Hospital	04 342 0000
NMC Hospital	04 268 9800
NMC Speciality Hospital	04 2679999
Rashid Hospital – Emergency	04 337 4000
The City Hospital	04 435 9999
Welcare Hospital – Emergency	04 282 7788
Zulekha Hospital	04 267 8866

Health Centres & Clinics

Abu Hail Clinic	04 266 1363,
Al Khawaneej Clinic	04 289 2092
Al Mamzar Medical Centre	04 296 7770
Al Mankhool Health Centre	04 398 7333
Al Qusais Clinic	04 261 2042
Al Rashidiya Clinic	04 285 7353
Al Safa Medical Centre	04 394 3468
Al Twar Medical Centre	04 261 2114
Al Badaa Health Centre	04 508 1000
Atlas Star Medical Centre	04 359 6662
Emirates Diagnostic Clinic	04 331 5155
German Heart Centre Breman	04 362 4797
German High Care Medical Center	04 362 2929
International Medical Centre	04 344 1142
Jumeirah American Clinic	04 344 4100
Medi Express	04 272 7772
Nad Al Sheba Clinic	04 336 3599
NMC Family Clinic	04 395 6660
Port Rashid Clinic	04 345 7043
Umm Suqaim Clinic	04 394 4456
Welcare Ambulatory Care Center	04 366 1030
Welcare Clinic Mirdif	04 288 1302
Welcare Clinic Qusais	04 258 6466
Zulekha Medical Centre	04 261 3004

Real Estate Agents

Al Futtaim Real Estate	04 211 9111
Arenco Group	04 355 5552
Asteco Property Management	04 403 7700
Betterhomes	04 344 7714
Cluttons	04 334 8585
Dubai Property Group	04 262 9888
Dubai Real Estate Corporation	04 398 6666
Global Capital Partners	04 438 0665
Landmark Properties	04 331 6161
Oryx Real Estate	04 351 5770
The Property Shop	04 345 5711

Personal Affairs

Directory

Real Estate Agents (Cont'd)

Sherwoods	04 343 8002
The Specialists	04 331 2662

Recruitment Agencies

Apple Search & Selection	04 329 8220
BAC Middle East	04 337 5747
Baker Regent	04 881 8282
Bayt	04 391 1900
Charterhouse Partnership	04 372 3500
Clarendon Parker	04 391 0460
Concur Consultants	04 813 5200
Grafton Recruitment	04 367 1939
Headway	04 398 7369
Hudson	04 705 0323
IQ Selection p.103	04 329 7770
Job Scan	04 355 9113
Job Track	04 397 7751
Kershaw Leonard	04 343 4606
SOS Agency	04 396 5600
Soundlines HR Consultancy	04 397 9064
Talent Management Consultancy	04 335 0999
TASC (Talent Asset Software & Consulting)	04 355 4242
Xpat Partners	04 341 8628

Removal Companies

Ahmed Saleh Packing & Forwarding	04 285 4000
Allied Pickfords	04 408 9555
Crown Relocations	04 289 5152
DASA International Movers	04 334 4545
Euro Movers	04 340 3920
Gulf Agency Company (GAC)	04 881 8090
Interem (Freight Systems Co Ltd)	04 807 0584
ISS Worldwide Movers	04 303 8651
Movers Packaging	04 267 0699
Southeast Shipping LLC	04 258 1815
Swift Freight International	04 881 9595
Writer Relocations	04 340 8814

Relocation Companies

Allied Pickfords	04 408 9555
Crown Relocations	04 289 5152
Daily's Relocation	04 343 7428
Dubai Luxury Homes	04 303 9300
Echo Xpats	04 391 2252
Enigma Relocation	04 394 6710
Equate Relocations	04 884 6051
Global Relocations	04 352 3300
Gulf Agency Company (GAC)	04 881 8090
Gulf Relocation Services	04 801 9210
In Touch Relocations	04 321 5701
Interem (Freight Systems Co Ltd)	04 807 0584
Southeast Shipping LLC	04 258 1815
The Specialists	04 329 5959
Writer Relocations	04 340 8814

Taxis

Al Marmoom Tourist Taxi	04 347 6650
Arabia Taxi	04 285 5566
Cars Taxis	04 269 3344
Dubai Airport Taxi	04 224 5331
Dubai Taxi Corporation	04 208 0808
Emirates Taxi (Limousines Only)	04 339 4455
Gulf Radio Taxi	04 223 6666
Metro Taxi	04 267 3222
National Taxis	04 339 0002

Telephone Codes

Abu Dhabi	02
Ajman	06
Al Ain	03
Dubai	04
Hatta	04
Fujairah	09
Jebel Ali	04
Sharjah	06
Umm Al Quwain	06
Ras Al Khaimah	07
Etisalat Mobile Telephones	050
du Mobile Telephones	055/056
Dubai number from outside the UAE	+971 4...
Mobile number from outside the UAE	+971 50/55...

Useful Numbers

Police/Ambulance/Emergency Hotline	999
Fire Department	997
DEWA	991
Dubai eGovernment	7000 40000
Dubai Rent Committee	04 221 5555
Directory Enquiries (Etisalat)	181
Directory Enquiries (du)	199
Etisalat	800 111 1050
du	800 112 2333
Mastercard International	04 391 4200
Visa International	04 331 9690
American Express	800 4931
Diner's Club	04 349 5800

Veterinary Clinics

Al Barsha Veterinary Clinic	04 340 8601
Al Safa Veterinary Clinic	04 348 3799
Al Zubair Animal Care	06 743 5988
Animal Care Centre Sharjah	06 543 6280
Deira Veterinary Clinic	04 258 1881
Energetic Panacea	04 344 7812
European Veterinary Center	04 343 9591
Jumeirah Veterinary Clinic	04 394 2276
Modern Veterinary Clinic	04 395 3131
Veterinary Hospital	04 344 2498

Personal Affairs

Directory

Directory

Dubai Chamber of Commerce & Industry (DCCI)

PO Box	1457	Map ref	8-G4
Tel	04 228 0000	Fax	04 202 8888
Location	Baniyas Rd, nr Sheraton Hotel, Deira Creek Side		
Timings	Sun – Thu 07:30 – 14:30; Sat 07:30 – 12:00 (Attestation)		
Web	www.dubaichamber.ae		

Branch	Details	Map Ref
Al Awir	04 333 1118 Emirates Rd Union Co-operative Society Sun – Thurs 08:00 – 16:00	5-C8
Al Twar	04 601 3316 Al Qusais Next to Ministry of Education Sun – Thurs 07:30 – 14:30	6-G6
DAFZA	04 299 4555 Dubai Airport Free Zone Al Tawar 3, Bldg W1 Sun – Thurs 08:00 – 16:00	6-F5
Dubai Economic Dept	04 202 0527 Baniyas Rd Land Department Building Sun – Thurs 07:30 – 14:30	8-G4
Dubai Industrial City	04 363 0405 Dubai Industrial City Building 1 Sun – Thurs 07:30 – 14:30	1-D6
Jebel Ali	04 202 8646 Main Gate – Entrance No.1, Jebel Ali Free Zone Sun – Thurs 08:00 – 15:00; Sat 08:00 – 13:00	2-E3

Dubai Courts

PO Box	4700	Map ref	8-F6
Tel	04 334 7777	Fax	04 334 4477
Location	Bur Dubai, nr Al Maktoum Bridge		
Timings	Sun – Thu 07:30 – 13:00, 16:00 – 20:00		
Web	www.dubaicourts.gov.ae		

Branch	Details	Map Ref
Al Barsha	04 311 1300 Dubai Traffic Department 07:30 – 13:00, 16:00 – 20:00	3-D4
Al Twar	04 263 9000 Al Qusais 07:30 – 13:00, 16:00 – 20:00	6-G6

Department of Economic Development (DED)

PO Box	13223	Map ref	8-H4
Tel	04 222 9922, 7000 40000	Fax	04 222 5577
Location	Opp Sheraton Dubai		
Timings	Sun – Thu 07:30 – 14:30		
Web	www.dubaided.gov.ae		

Dubai Electricity & Water Authority (DEWA)

PO Box	564	Map ref	7-D9
Tel	04 601 9999	Fax	04 324 9345 (Billing Dept)
Location	Za'abeel East, nr Wafi Mall		
Timings	Sun – Thu 07:30 – 20:30		
Web	www.dewa.gov.ae		

Branch	Details	Map Ref
Al Hudaibah	04 506 6666 Nr Mankhool Rd Sun – Thu 07:30 – 20:30	7-B2
Al Reef Mall	04 223 6681 Salahudeen Rd Sun – Thu 09:00 – 15:30	9-A4
Al Safa	04 266 2445 Opp Choithram Supermarket Sat – Thu 07:30 – 14:00	9-C5
Al Wasl	04 304 1301 Al Wasl Sun – Thu 07:30 – 20:30	5-A3
Ayal Nasser	04 271 7864 Nr Hyatt Regency Sat – Thu 07:30 – 20:30	8-H2
Burj Nahar	04 271 2478 Burj Nahar R/A Sun – Thu 07:30 – 20:30	9-A3
Hatta	04 852 3922 Hatta Sat – Thu 07:30 – 14:30	na
Habab	04 832 1226 Habab Sat – Thu 07:30 – 20:00	7-B1
Umm Ramool	04 285 9990 Umm Ramool Sun – Thu 07:30 – 20:30	6-E7
Al Aweer	04 333 5704 Union Co-operative, Opp Vegetable Market Sun – Thu 08:00 – 14:30	5-C8

Government & Municipality Offices

Directory

Directory

Dubai Municipality (DM)

PO Box	67	Map ref	8-H3
Tel	04 221 5555, 7000 40000	Fax	04 224 6666
Location	20 Baniyas Rd, Al Riqqa, Deira		
Timings	Sun – Thu 07:30-14:30		
Web	www.dm.gov.ae		

Branch	Details	Map Ref
Al Tawar Centre	04 263 8888 Al Qusais Sun – Thu 07:30 – 14:30	6-G6
Burial & Graveyard Services Unit	04 264 3355 Al Qusais Sun – Thu 06:00 – 21:00	6-H5
Customer Services Al Karama Centre	04 337 4800 Opp Emirates Post, Karama Sun – Thu 07:30 – 14:30	7-D4
Dubai Municipality Clinic	04 223 2389 Nr Al Ghurair Shopping Mall Sun – Thu 07:30 – 13:30	8-G3
e-library	04 348 2512 http://elibrary.dubai.ae 24 hours 7 days a week	4-F2
Rent Committee	04 221 5555 Dubai Municipality Bldg Sun – Thu, 07:30 – 14:30	8-G3
Used Car Complex	04 333 3800 Al Awir Sun – Thu 07:30 – 14:30	5-C8
Veterinary Services	04 289 1114 1.5 km from Mushriff Park Sun – Thu 09:00 – 20:00 Sun – Thu 07:30 – 14:30	6-G9

Government & Municipality Offices

Directory

Dubai Police

PO Box	1493	Map ref	9-D7
Tel	04 269 2222, 800 7777	Fax	04 221 5158
Emergency	999		
Location	Nr Al Mulla Plaza, Al Qusais		
Timings	24 hrs		
Web	www.dubaipolice.gov.ae		

Branch	Details	Map Ref
Airport	04 224 5555 Airport, Terminal 1	9-B9
Air Wing	04 224 4222 Cargo Area	6-F6
Al Hamriya Police Sub Station	04 266 7306 Al Hamriya	10-F2
Al Hibbab Police Sub Station	04 832 1333 Al Hibbab	2-E7
Al Muraqqabat	04 266 0555 Muraqqabat	9-B5
Al Qusais	04 263 1111 Al Qusais	6-G6
Al Rafaa	04 393 7777 Nr Peninsula Hotel	8-E1
Al Rashidiya	04 285 3000 Rashidiya	6-E7
Bur Dubai	04 398 1111 Trade Centre R/A	7-B4
Criminal Investigation Department (CID)	04 201 3400 Dubai Police HQ, Al Qusais	10-E7
Hatta	04 852 1111 Hatta	na
Jebel Ali	04 881 6111 Jebel Ali	2-E3
Nad Al Sheba	04 336 3535 Nr Racing Club	5-A7
Naif	04 228 6999 Naif Road	9-A2
Port Police Station	04 345 9999 Al Diyafah Rd	7-C1
Rashid Police Sub Station	04 337 4600 Nr Rashid Hospital	8-F6

Dubai Police

Directory

Directory

Dubai Traffic Police

PO Box	1493	Map ref	9-D7
Tel	04 269 4444, 800 4353	Fax	04 269 0053
Location	Al Qusais, nr Al Mulla Plaza		
Timings	Sun – Thu 07:30 – 14:30		
Web	www.dubaipolice.gov.ae		

Branch	Details	Map Ref
Bur Dubai Traffic Police	04 347 2222 Junction 4, Sheikh Zayed Rd Sun – Thu 09:00 – 21:00	3-D4

Emirates Post

PO Box	99999	Map ref	10-E6
Tel	04 262 2222	Fax	04 266 2929
Call Centre	600 5 99999		
Location	Deira		
Timings	Sun –Thu 08:00 – 20:00		
Web	www.emiratespost.co.ae		

Branch	Details	Map Ref
Abu Hail	04 269 4301 Sun – Thu 08:00 – 14:00	9-C2
Airport Free Zone	04 299 6130 Sun – Thu 08:00 – 14:00	9-D9
Al Awir	04 320 1447 Sun – Thu 08:00 – 14:00	5-C9
Al Barsha	04 323 5788 Sun – Thu 08:00 – 20:00	3-C4
Al Khor	04 222 1952 Sun – Thu 08:00 – 20:00	5-A3
Al Musalla	04 359 6699 Sun – Thu 08:00 – 14:00	8-F2
Al Quoz	04 338 8482 Sun – Thu 08:00 – 14:00	4-H4
Al Qusais	04 261 3307 Sun – Thu 08:00 – 14:00	6-G5
Al Ras	04 225 1298 Sun – Thu 08:00 – 14:00	8-F1

Branch	Details	Map Ref
Al Rashidiya	04 285 1655 Sun – Thu 08:00 – 20:00	6-F8
Al Riqqa	04 295 8978 Sun – Thu 08:00 – 20:00	8-H5
Al Shath	04 344 9317 Sun – Thu 10:00 – 22:00	4-G3
Al Tawar	04 261 2687 Sun – Thu 08:00 – 14:00	10-E9
Al Thanawiya	04 223 3656 Sun – Thu 08:00 – 14:00	8-G3
Cargo Village	04 286 5151 Sun – Thu 08:00 – 14:00	9-A8
Deira	04 203 1429 Sun – Thu 08:00 – 20:00	8-H3
DNATA	04 295 5343 Sun – Thu 08:00 – 14:00	8-H6
Dubai Airport	04 216 4994 24 hours, 7 days a week	9-B9
Exhibitions Centre	04 331 8399 Sun – Thu 08:00 – 14:00	7-A5
Free Zone	04 299 6130 Sun – Thu 08:00 – 20:00	3-B3
Hor Al Anz	04 262 9334 Sun – Thu 08:00 – 20:00	9-C4
International City	04 368 7162 Sun – Thu 10:00 – 22:00	na
Jebel Ali	04 881 6989 Sun – Thu 08:00 – 14:00	1-D4
Jumeira	04 344 2706 Sun – Thu 08:00 – 20:00	4-H3
Karama	04 337 1500 Sun – Thu 08:00 – 22:00	8-E5
Masfoot	04 852 3662 Sun – Thu 08:00 – 14:00	na
Satwa	04 344 0364 Sun – Thu 08:00 – 20:00	7-A3
Trade Centre	04 331 3306 Sun – Thu 08:00 – 14:00	7-A4
Umm Ramool	04 286 2782 Sun – Thu 08:00 – 14:00	6-E6

Emirates Post

Directory

Directory

Roads & Transport Authority (RTA)

PO Box	118899		Map ref	Off map
Tel	04 284 4444		Fax	04 206 5555
Call Centre	800 9090			
Location	Deira			
Timings	Sun – Thu 07:30 – 14:30			
Web	www.rta.ae			

Driving Licence Offices	Details	Map Ref
Al Barsha Licensing	04 347 6620 Al Quoz Industrial Area 3	3-D4
Al Safa Union Co-op	04 394 5007 Jumeira Sun – Thu 09:00 – 21:00	4-H3
Al Tawar Union Co-op	04 261 3100 Al Qusais Sun – Thu 09:00 – 21:00	10-F3
Deira City Centre	04 203 6666 Deira Sun – Thu 09:00 – 21:00	8-H7
Dubai Industrial City	04 364 3333 Jebel Ali Sun – Thu 08:00 – 14:00	2-E5
Dubai Media City	04 365 8505 Dubai Media City Sun – Thu 07:30 – 14:30	3-B3
Jumeira Plaza	04 349 1124 Jumeira Sun – Thu 09:00 – 21:00	5-B2
Parking Services		
Al Ghubaiba Office	04 393 7747 Al Ghubaiba 07:30 – 14:30	8-F1
Al Karama Centre	04 337 4800 Al Karama 07:30 – 14:30	7-D4
Al Tawar Centre	04 263 8888 Al Tawar 07:30 – 14:30	10-E8
Main Customer Service Centre	04 284 4444 Umm Ramool 07:30 –14:30	6-E6
Vehicle Licensing		
Al Awir Used Car Complex	04 333 1510 Ras Al Khor 07:30 – 20:00	5-C8
Dubai Cars & Automotive Zone (DUCAMZ)	04 333 5021 Ras Al Khor 07:30 – 19:30	5-B7
Main Customer Service Centre	04 284 4444 Umm Ramool 07:30 – 14:30	6-E6

Vehicle Registration	Details	Map Ref
Deira City Centre	04 203 6666 Port Saeed 09:00 – 21:00	8-H7
Main Customer Service Centre	04 284 4444 Umm Ramool 07:30 – 14:30	6-E6

Vehicle Testing & Registration		
Shamil Al Muhaisna	04 267 1117 Al Wusais 08:00 – 20:00	6-H6
Shamil Nad Al Hamar	04 289 4440 Nad Al Hamar 08:00 – 13:00, 16:00 – 20:00	5-D7
Tasjeel Al Aweer	04 333 1510 Ras Al Khor 07:30 – 19:30	5-C8
Tasjeel Al Barsha	04 347 6620 Sheikh Zayed Rd 07:00 – 21:00	3-D4
Tasjeel Al Qusais	04 267 3940 Al Muhaisnah 07:00 – 21:00	6-G6
Tasjeel Al Warsan	04 333 6470 Al Warsan 08:00 – 20:00	na
Tasjeel Jebel Ali	883 0110 Sheikh Zayed Rd 07:00 – 15:30	1-C5
Wasel Centre	04 324 5524 Al Jaddaf 08:00 – 20:00	5-D5

Vehicle Testing & Licensing – Dealers		
Al Futtaim (Honda)	04 206 6300 Dubai Festival City 08:00 – 19:30	5-D6
Al Futtaim (Toyota)	04 206 6666 Dubai Festival City	5-D6
Al Futtaim (Toyota)	04 295 4231 Deira 06:00 – 20:30	8-H7
Al Habtoor Motors (licensing only)	04 269 1110 Deira 08:30 – 19:00	8-H6
Arabian Motors (Nissan)	04 295 0333 Deira 06:00 – 20:30	9-A6
Galadari Motors	04 273 4995 Deira 08:00 – 17:00	9-A3
Gargash Enterprises	04 269 8777 Dubai – Sharjah Road 08:00 – 19:30	na
Swaidan Co (Peugeot)	04 266 7111 Deira 09:00 –13:00, 16:00 – 20:00	6-E6

Roads & Transport Authority (RTA)

Directory

Directory

du

PO Box	502666	Map ref	8-H4
Tel	04 390 5555	Fax	04 390 5554
Location	Building 14, Dubai Media City		
Timings	Sun – Thu 08:00 – 20:00		
Web	www.du.ae		

Branch	Details	Map Ref
Al Barsha	Mall of Emirates	3-D4
Al Rigga Road	Al Ghurair Centre	8-H4
Bur Dubai	Al Khaleej Centre	8-E2
Deira	Deira City Centre	8-H7
DIFC	Building 5	5-B4
Discovery Gardens	Ibn Battuta Mall	2-G3
Downtown Burj Dubai	The Dubai Mall	5-A4
Dubai International Airport	Terminal 1, Terminal 3	9-B2, 6-F6
Dubai Marina	JBR, Bldg 6, Sadaf	3-A3
Jumeira Beach Road	Jumeirah Centre	5-B2
Oud Metha	Lamcy Plaza	7-D6

Etisalat

PO Box	1150	Map ref	8-H4
Tel	101, 04 222 8111	Fax	105
For Non Etisalat Customer	800 101		
Location	Baniyas Rd, opp Sheraton Dubai Creek		
Timings	Sun – Thu 08:00 – 20:00		
Web	www.etisalat.co.ae		

Branch	Details	Map Ref
Al Baraha	04 271 3131 Al Baraha Business Centre Sun – Thu 08:00 – 20:00 Sat – 08:00 – 13:00	na
Al Khaleej	04 355 3333 Al Mankhool Rd, Bur Dubai Sun – Thu 08:00 – 20:00 Sat 08:00 – 13:00	8-E2
Al Tawar	04 261 4444 Al Qusais Sun – Thu 08:00 – 20:00 Sat 08:00 – 13:00	1-D3
Al Wasl	04 343 2000 Sheikh Zayed Rd, Jct 1 Sun – Thu 08:00 – 20:00, Sat 08:00 – 13:00	5- A3
Jebel Ali	04 881 6216 Jebel Ali Free Zone Sun – Thu 08:00 – 20:00 Sat 08:00 – 13:00	1-D3

du & Etisalat

Directory

Department of Naturalisation & Residency Dubai (DNRD)

PO Box	4333	**Map ref**	7-B4
Tel	04 398 0000	**Fax**	04 398 1119
Customer Service	04 313 9999 (24 hrs)		
Complaints	800 5111, www.amer.ae		
Location	Al Jaffiliya, nr Bur Dubai Police Station		
Timings	Sun – Thu 07:30 – 14:30		
Web	www.dnrd.gov.ae, http://ednrd.ae		

Main Branches	Details	Map Ref
Abu Hail Centre	04 269 6699 Al Hamriya Port Sun – Thu 07:30 – 14:30	10-F2
Dubai Airport Free Zone	04 202 7506 Al Quds Rd Sun – Thu 07:30 – 14:30	9-D8
Hatta	04 852 1718 Hatta 24 hrs	na
Jebel Ali	04 881 8777 Jebel Ali Sun – Thu 07:30 – 14:30	1-B4

Ministry of Economy & Planning

PO Box	3625	**Map ref**	9-A6
Tel	04 314 1555	**Fax**	04 358 1811
Location	Bur Dubai, nr Trade Centre		
Timings	Sun – Thu 07:30 – 14:00		
Web	www.economy.ae		

Ministry of Health/Dubai Dept of Health & Medical Services

PO Box	1853	**Map ref**	8-E4
Tel	04 396 6000	**Fax**	04 396 5666
Location	Opp BurJuman Centre, Trade Centre Rd, Karama		
Timings	Sun – Thu 08:30 – 14:30		
Web	www.moh.gov.ae, www.dohms.gov.ae		

Ministry of Labour

PO Box	5025	**Map ref**	10-G9
Tel	04 702 3333	**Fax**	04 266 8967
Location	Dubai – Sharjah Rd, nr Al Mulla Plaza		
Timings	Sun – Thu 08:00 – 19:00		
Web	www.mol.gov.ae		

Ministries

Directory

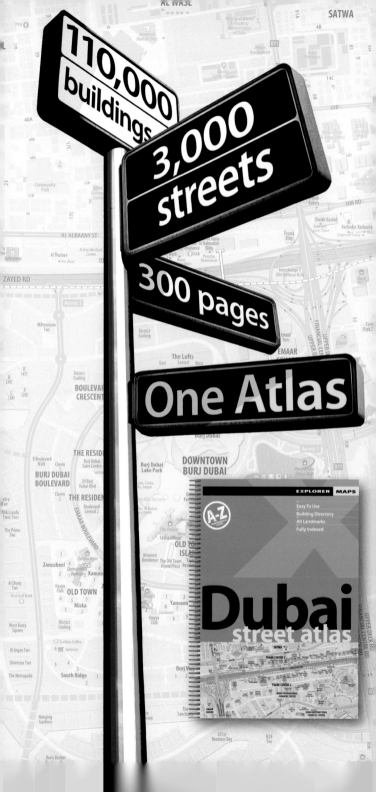

Maps

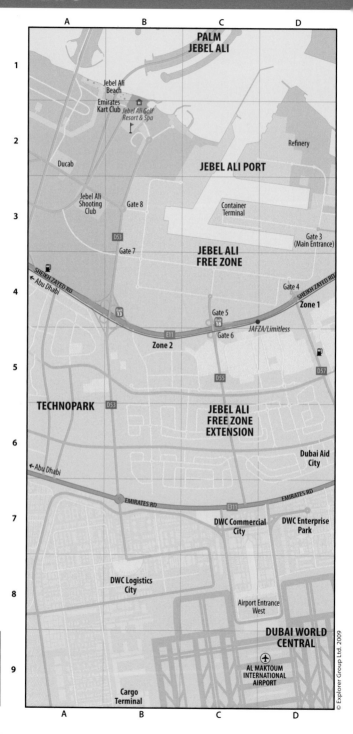

Arabian Gulf

DUGAS

DUBAL

Gate 1

Al Nuwaibi
Police
Post

Gate 2

DUBAL

E11

DUBAL

Sheraton
Jumeirah
Beach

DEWA
Power Station

SHEIKH ZAYED RD

JBR

Ibn Battuta
Ibn Battuta Mall

Nakheel
Harbour
& Tower

Mövenpick
Hotel & Residence

JLT
JLT

E22

JEBEL ALI
VILLAGE

The Gardens

D59   D591

Jumeirah
Heights

Jebel Ali
Industrial

E77

Al Furjan

Discovery
Gardens

Jumeirah
Islands

JEBEL ALI
INDUSTRIAL
AREA

Jumeirah
Park

E311

EMIRATES RD

EMIRATES RD

Premiere Inn

Green
Community

The Market

Courtyard
by Marriott

Intl Media
Production
Zone

DUBAI
INVESTMENT
PARK 1

Green
Community West

Palisades

Jumeirah
Golf Estates

Dubai Lagoon

DUBAI
INVESTMENT
PARK 2

Arabian Canal

1100m

↘ Al Ain

© Explorer Group Ltd. 2009

2

Maps

1

The Fronds

PALM JUMEIRAH

↑ 🏨 Atlantis

Marina Residences

Oceana Apts

Tiara Residence

2

The Trunk

QE2

Burj Al Arab

Mina a' Salam

Le Royal Meridien

Habtoor Grand

Le Meridien Mina Seyahi

One&Only Royal Mirage

Al Qasr

Madinat Jumeirah

Hilton

Grosvenor House

Westin

Radisson SAS

Dubai Pearl

Knowledge Village

AL SUFOUH RD

AL SUFOUH

3

DUBAI MARINA

DMC

DIC

D94

Jumeirah Lake Towers

Emirates Golf Club

Greens Centre

TECOM

Acacia Avenues

Dubai Police Academy

UMM SUQEIM RD

E11

SHEIKH ZAYED RD

D61

The Greens

Sharaf DG

Kempinski

The Meadows

Ramee Guestline 3

AL MAFRAQ RD

Mall of the Emirates

Bur Dubai Traffic Dept

4

Meadows Village

The Montgomerie

The Lakes

Jebel Ali Racecourse

Emirates Identity Authority

AL BARSHA 1

Lulu Hypermarket

UMM SUQEIM RD

EMIRATES LIVING

Emirates Hills

D611

Al Barsha Mall

Town Centre

AL BARSHA 3

5

The Springs

AL KHAIL RD

E44

D63

6

Jumeirah Village

AL BARSHA SOUTH

D611

AL QUDRA RD

7

Dubai Sports City

DuBiotech

D63

Victory Heights

Cricket Stadium

Coral International

Business Park

Arjan

AL QUDRA RD

The Els Club

Dubailand Sales Office

EMIRATES RD

Green Community Motor City

Dubai Autodrome

Motor City

F1 Theme Park

8

Uptown Motor City

Dubai Studio City

Saheel

E311

AL QUDRA RD

Dubai Golf City

Dubai Polo & Equestrian Club

La Coleccion

Arabian Ranches Golf Club

Alma

Alvorada

Hattan

ARABIAN RANCHES

Savannah

Palmera

Al Mahra

Mirador

Terra Nova

9

Al Reem

Remraam

Bab Al Shams

Bawadi

↓ ↓

3

Maps

© Explorer Group Ltd. 2009

THE WORLD

Arabian Gulf

1

2

Jumeirah Beach Hotel
Porto Dubai
Park
Thailand

Dubai Municipality Umm Suqeim Centre

JUMEIRA RD

UMM SUQEIM

D65

D94

Dubai Offshore Sailing Club (DOSC)

Majlis Ghorfat Um Al Sheef

Jumeirah Beach Park

JUMEIRA 2

AL WASL RD

D92

JUMEIRA 3

Public Library

AL MANARA RD

UMM AL SHEIF

AL MANARA

Spinneys

China

AL WASL RD

Park n Shop

AL SAFA

Safa Park

Australia

3

AL THANYA RD

AL HADIYA ST

AL ATTAR ST

UM AMARA RD

SHEIKH ZAYED RD

E11

EXIT 43

Al Quoz

Times Square

AL MANARA RD

Oasis Centre

Metropolitan

Tamani

First Gulf Bank

National Cement Factory

AL QUOZ

5

BUSINESS BAY

4

MEYDAN RD

D69

AL RASAAS RD

AL HADEED RD

AL HAAR RD

318 RD

Grand City Mall

AL QUOZ INDUSTRIAL AREA

Grand Mall

318 RD

Oasis Village

319 RD

318 RD

50

AL KHAIL RD

Al Quoz Pond Park

AL MARQADH

5

Dubai Camel Racecourse

AL RASAAS RD

E44

AL KHAIL RD

D69

Falcon Heritage & Sports Center

MEYDAN RD

EXIT 20

6

Dubai Equestrian Centre

5

MOHAMMED BIN RASHID GARDENS

NAD AL SHEBA 1

7

8

Living Legends

Al Barari

4

E11

EXIT 37

Majan

Maps

EMIRATES RD

Global Village

Aqua Duniya

Mall of Arabia

City of Arabia

Falcon City of Wonders

1100m

9

© Explorer Group Ltd 2009

E   F   G   H

© Explorer Group Ltd. 2009

PALM DEIRA

Deira Market

Hyatt Regency
NAIF RD
AL KHALEEJ RD
D92
Hamriya Port
AL MAMZAR
Al Mamzar Beach Park

Baniyas Square

DEIRA

NBD
D89
DCCI
Marriott Apts
Clock Tower R/A
Detra City Centre
Park Hyatt
Sofitel
Exit 60
Millennium Airport

Reef Mall
D78
D80
HOR AL ANZ
Abu Hail
SAEADIDDIN RD
Exit 61
DUBAI – SHARJAH RD
D62

ABU BACKER AL SOUDIQUE RD
AL RASHEED RD
ABU HAIL RD

ABU HAIL
D91

AL WUHEIDA RD
CAIRO ST
D95
Century Mall
D93

Mamzar Beach

AL ITTIHAD RD
D64
D67
D70
D71
Sharjah →
Sahara Centre

E11
Al Mulla Plaza
Stadium
Lulu
Youth Hostel
AL TA'AWUN RD
AL NAHDA
Al Nahda Pond Park
AMMAN RD

Cargo Village
DUBAI INTL AIRPORT
AL TWAR
Dubai Police HQ
9
10

Al Nahda
DOHA ST
D95
Airport Freezone

DAMASCUS ST
D64

GARHOUD
Airport Terminal 3
Emirates HQ
Emirates
MARRAKECH ST
AL REBAT ST
UMM RAMOOL
D83

AIRPORT RD
NADD AL HAMAR RD
Nadd Shamma Park
D89
Bin Sougat Centre
Rashidiya

RASHIDIYA

AIRPORT TUNNEL
Airport Expo
AL QUDS ST
D93
Dubai Grand
AL QUSAIS
D91
Al Qusais 1
BEIRUT ST
D60
Philippines
AL NAHDA RD
Tasjeel

MUHAISNAH
BAGHDAD ST
Al Qusais Pond Park
Etisalat
AL TWAR RD
Exit 61

AL TWAR
EMIRATES RD
Exit 60
E311
Ras Al Khaimah →

MUHAISNAH
TUNIS RD

Exit 58
Exit 58
Exit 55
EMIRATES RD
Exit 55
D83
D89
D56
ALGERIA ST
D93
TUNIS RD

MIRDIF
AL MIZHAR
Uptown Mirdif
Arabian Plaza
D89
Al Mizhar Mall

TRIPOLI ST
ALGERIA ST
AL KHAWANEEJ RD

AL WARQA
D56
Spinneys
Mushrif Park

1100m

6
Maps

© Explorer Group Ltd. 2009

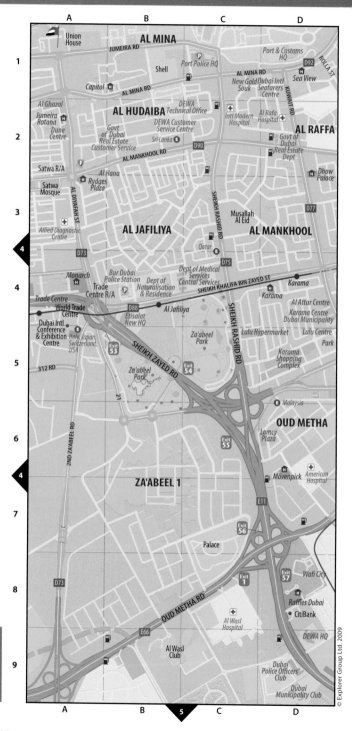

E F G H

1 Highland · AL GHUBAIBA RD · Carrefour · Al Ghubaiba · Ahmadiya School · Al Shindagha Tunnel · Fish, Meat & Veg Market · CORNICHE RD · Bus Station · Central Bank Dubai · Ministry of Finance & Industry · Al Ras · Bus Station · Palm Deira · **AL RAS** · **DEIRA** · Al Raffa Police Station · Norway · Abra · Gold Souk · **BUR DUBAI** · Textile Souk

2 Royal Ascot · ROLLA ST · D79 · Grand Mosque · HH Rulers Court · Souk Area · BANIYAS RD · AL MUSALLAH ST · Dubai Museum · Bastakiya · Abra · Al Khaleej Centre · AL MANKHOOL RD · Saeediya · Musalla Tower · D85 · Carlton Tower · Baniyas Square · Ramada · Al Ain Centre · KHALID BIN AL WALEED RD (BANK ST) · Four Points Sheraton · Netherlands · Twin Towers · Maktoum Hospital

3 Golden Sands Area · Green Metro · AL SEEF RD · D84 · Canada · United Kingdom · Radisson SAS Dubai Creek · Fish R/A · Centrepoint · BurJuman · Dubai Municipality HQ · Union Square · Al Ghurair · Russia · City · Denmark · **9** · Spinneys · SHEIKH KHALIFA BIN ZAYED ST · BurJuman · Egypt · Saudi Arabia · Etisalat HQ · Ministry of · UAE Ministry · Pakistan · Libya · Economic Dept · AL MAKTOUM RD · AL RIGGA RD · Civil Service · of Health · India · Kuwait · Land Dept (RERA) · Jordan · Oman · NBD · **4** · KARAMA · Lebanon · Dubai Chamber of Commerce · ZA'ABEEL RD · Ministry of Foreign Affairs · Hilton Dubai Creek · D89 · KUWAIT RD · D84 · Concorde · Taj Palace · General Post Office · Ramee Royal · TARIQ BIN ZIYAD RD · Dhow Wharfage · **AL RIGGA** · **5** · Dubai Central Laboratory · UMM HURAIR RD · Marriott Apts · UAE Ministry of Environment & Water · Pyramid Centre · Park · Dubai TV & Radio · Port & Custom Ctr · Clock Tower R/A · Al Nasr Club · Dubai Media Incorporated · British Council · Maktoum Bridge · Star Boutique · DNATA · **6** · Al Nasr Leisureland · Oud Metha · Dept of Health & Medical Services (DOHMS) · Dubai Courts · Dubai Jewel (u/c) · Flora Park · Rashid Hospital · Public Prosecution Dubai · Flora Creek · Church · Floating Bridge · **9** · OUD METHA RD · KM Trading · Canadian Specialist · **UMM HURAIR 2** · RIYADH RD · **PORT SAEED** · City Centre · Dubai Shopping · Etisalat · **7** · Creekside Park · Deira City Centre · Rihab Rotana · D81 · Sofitel · Dubai Healthcare City · Public Parks & Horticulture Dept · Dubai Creek Marina · Exit 60 · Garhoud · **8** · Healthcare City · Dubai Dolphinarium · Children's City · Dubai Creek · Park Hyatt · Le Meridien Fairway · Grand Hyatt · Wonderland · Millennium · Welcare Hospital · Airport · **9** · RIYADH RD · Al Boom Tourist Village · Dubai Creek Golf & Yacht Club · Aviation Club · D70 · SHEIKH RASHID RD · Garhoud Bridge · SHEIKH RASHID RD · Exit 59 · 350m · N

© Explorer Group Ltd. 2009

E F **5** G H

PALM DEIRA

Hyatt Regency Galleria

Hyatt Golf Park

CORNICHE DEIRA

AL KHALEEJ RD

D92

AL MURAR

NAIF RD DEWA

D88

Naif Police Station

NAIF

OMAR BIN AL KHATTAB RD

DEWA Customer Service

Musalla Al Eid

AL RASHEED RD

Etisalat Al Baraha Hospital

Dubai Hospital

D78

AL BARAHA ST

AL BARAHA

ABU HAIL

ABU HAIL RD

Marco Polo

MUTEENA

ABU BACKER AL SIDDIQUE RD

Al Hamriya Park

D91

SALAHUDDIN RD

Salahuddin

AL MUTEENA ST

D82

Al Hamriya Shopping Centre

Reef Mall

Renaissance Dubai

Sheraton Deira

Etisalat

Coral Deira

Mövenpick Deira (u/c)

AL MURAQQABAT

Muraqabat Police Station

Abu Baker Al Siddique

HOR AL ANZ

Al Rigga

JW Marriott

Al Shaab Colony

Holiday Inn

Traders

Hamarain Centre

Green Metro

SALAHUDDIN RD

Ministry of Youth & Sports

D80

Abu Hail Centre

D78

AL KHABAISI

Dubai Police Management Security & Est

Abu Hail

Ramada Continental

D74

AL ITHIHAD RD

Exit 61

E11

DUBAI - SHARJAH RD

Ministry of Economy

Exit 62

Dubai Flower Centre

Dept of Civil Aviation

Dubai Police HQ

AL QUDS ST

Dubai Police Dept of Operations

Cargo Village

Traffic Dept

AIRPORT RD

9

Maps

Al Bustan Rotana

Le Meridien Dubai

D89

Terminal 1

✈

DUBAI INTL AIRPORT

Terminal 2

D91

6

Dept of
Naturalisation
& Residency
(Port & Customs)

Al Hamriya Port

AL KHALEEJ RD

Hamriya
Port Office

D92

AL KHALEEJ RD

43

AL MAMZAR

AL WUHEIDA

AL WUHEIDA RD

CAIRO ST

Mamzar
Beach

D93

D95

Al Mamzar Community
Health Centre
(Child Health Section)

AL RASHEED RD

Century
Mall

Al Shabab
Al Arabic Club

Al Mamzar
Lagoon

**HOR AL ANZ
EAST**

The
Square

CAIRO ST

AL MAMZAR

Dubai
Municipality
General
Maintenance
Dept

Deira Main
Post Office

Al Mamzar
Tower

Islamic Affairs
& Charitable
Activities Dept

Al Mamzar
Interchange

AL ITTIHAD RD

E11

Exit
70

All Season

Al Quiadah

Al Mamzar
Centre

Exit
65

AL NAHDA 1

Criminal
Investigation
Dept

Exit
64

Al Mulla Plaza

Exit
67

AMMAN ST

General Dept
of Service & Supplies

Al Ahli Club

Stadium

D97

BAGHDAD ST

NMC
Hospital

Lulu Hyper
Market

AL NAHDA RD

AL NAHDA 2

AL TWAR 1

Youth Hostel

AL QUSAIS 1

Higher College
of Technology
Dubai Women's
College

Al Twar
Health Centre

Ministry of
Culture Youth &
Community
Development

Al Bustan

Park

Al Nahda

Ministry of
Public Works

Emirates
Driving School

D95

Al Nahda
Pond Park

DOHA ST

Ministry of
Social Affairs
Ministry of
Labour

350m

© Explorer Group Ltd. 2009

10

Maps

Index

Index

Index

Index

Index